Descriptive Economics

Descriptive Economics
Seventh Edition

Colin Harbury
Professor of Economics
The City University, London

Pitman

PITMAN PUBLISHING LIMITED
128 Long Acre, London WC2E 9AN

A Longman Group Company

First published in Great Britain 1986

British Library Cataloguing in Publication Data
Harbury, C.D.
    Descriptive economics. —— 7th ed.
    1. Economics
    I. Title
    330   HB 171.5

ISBN 0–273–02483–3

Printed in Great Britain at The Bath Press, Avon

Contents

Preface to the 7th edition

The revised edition of this book differs significantly from its predecessors, and I feel it needs a new preface.

There are two matters to report. The first is that, as usual, the material has been thoroughly updated, so that the content now describes the salient features of the British economy in the mid-1980s.

The second is that the book now starts with two elementary theory chapters. One, on supply and demand, has been expanded, and a totally new chapter has been added, explaining the meaning of the national income and how it is determined, as well as providing a simple version of the modern theory of the determination of the general price level.

I stress that the great mass of the book remains descriptive. The two theory chapters may even be skipped without jeopardy. The main part of the book continues, as stated in the first edition, 'to describe the salient features of the British economy unadorned with the paraphernalia of economic analysis', though 'the nature of economic life in Britain and its institutions are explained in the way that they are because of underlying theoretical justification'.

Nevertheless, there is a notable advantage of reading the two short theory chapters. Those who do so will find more meaning, as well as more interest in many places, especially on matters of economic policy. For example, it must be useful to understand something of the way in which inflation and unemployment are analysed in modern economics, when reading descriptions of fiscal and monetary policy.

The bulk of the book retains the style of its predecessors. The text is virtually devoid of tables of statistics. Instead, liberal use is made of charts, diagrams, maps and graphs, which show, with much greater clarity, the chief orders of magnitude, which are all that it is necessary to grasp. In order to accommodate the new material mentioned earlier, quite a lot of the detailed descriptions of particular industries has been cut (from Chapters 5 and 6 in the 6th edition). Experience suggests that the fine details of individual sectors of textiles, engineering and other industries, were regarded by many as the least useful content of the book for beginning students of economics. I have, of course retained, and relocated, the most important material in those chapters, e.g. agricultural policy, retail co-operatives. Moreover, I have added a substantial amount of new descriptive material of a more generally useful kind, e.g. international comparisons of growth rates, inflation, productivity and taxation; the main national income accounting identities; alternative definitions of the money supply; privatisation; and the world debt problem. A glance at the table of contents should, I hope, satisfy any doubters that the descriptive content is more useful than before.

Each chapter in the main part of the book is, as usual, supplied with exercises. These have four main aims—to foster the intelligent use of data, to encourage the collection of original material of a simple kind, to acquaint the student with some of the more accessible sources of economic statistics, and to provide a means of updating the book between writing and reading on some important matters. Overseas students will be able to substitute data for their own countries for many of the exercises. (To any who would like more exercises, may I immodestly refer them to my *Workbook in Introductory Economics*, Pergamon, 3rd edition, 1982.)

The first edition of this book was written with two types of student in mind. The first was those studying for examinations where the syllabus was mainly descriptive. The second was those studying both theory and institutions, but whose principal theory text was inadequately supplied with descriptive material on the UK economy. Over the years, however, it has become clear that *Descriptive Economics* has been used by students preparing for a notably wider range of examinations than I had anticipated. Probably, the main users have been those doing O-level economics, but there are many who have used the book (presumably in conjunction with other books) for A-level economics and business studies, university/polytechnic, BEC, OND/Certificate in Business Studies, and many professional examinations, such as those of the Royal Society of Arts, the Institute of Bankers, and various bodies in the accountancy profession. Overseas students who find themselves required to know about the British economy for British examinations, have also, I know, found *Descriptive Economics* useful. I hope this new edition will fill the needs of all, better than before.

Acknowledgments

Full acknowledgment of sources is, for obvious reasons, an impossible task without cluttering every page with footnotes, which would detract from the essential simplicity of the treatment. I am, nevertheless, overwhelmingly grateful to the numerous authors of books and articles whose findings have been incorporated, and I hope they will continue to accept this composite acknowledgment of appreciation. Only in the case of two diagrams, which I have more or less directly borrowed, can I make specific acknowledgment: to Professor Z A Silberston for the material in Fig 4.3, and to the Controller of HM Stationery Office for permission to reproduce in Fig 5.16 a diagram from the report of the Monopolies Commission on the Supply of Electric Lamps (HC Paper 287, 1950/51). Finally, I must still single out for thanks Professor

Arthur Beacham, once of the University College of Wales, Aberystwyth, without whose advice and encouragement this book would never have been written. I am also delighted that teachers and students continue to write to me with useful comments and corrections.

Any errors that remain are, of course, mine.

Colin Harbury
The City University
London

Sources for exercises

At the end of each of the Chapters 3–10 are sets of exercises, to which considerable importance is attached. They are designed, among other things, to acquaint the reader with some of the more accessible sources of information on economic matters.

Some of the exercises call for the construction of graphs, usually of a kind to be found in the book itself. Nevertheless, a student who is uncertain how to draw and interpret graphs would be well advised to brush up with an appropriate text.[1]

More exercises are contained in the author's *Workbook in Introductory Economics*, Pergamon Press, 3rd edition, 1982.

Sources are suggested for individual exercises, using the key initial letters in the following list. Note that a slight modification of the details required for an exercise may, in some instances, enable the questions to be answered from a source other than that suggested, if it is not available. This may also help overseas students, who want to relate the exercises to data for their own countries. Finally, it is worth pointing out that the geographical coverage of published statistics varies in some cases. Officially, the United Kingdom consists of the territories of Great Britain and Northern Ireland; while Great Britain refers to the three countries England, Scotland and Wales.

Publications marked with an asterisk are obtainable from Her Majesty's Stationery Office. *EP* is obtainable (free) from the Central Office of Information, Hercules Rd., London SE1 7DU.

Key

T   *The Times*; the Business News section is especially useful for financial data.

FT   *The Financial Times* covers much the same ground as *The Times* but in greater detail.

AS★   *Annual Abstract of Statistics* is of inestimable value. It covers a tremendous amount of subject matter but requires very careful use.

MDS★   *Monthly Digest of Statistics* supplements the *Annual Abstract of Statistics* for the most recent trends.

---

1 There is an appendix on the use of graphs in economics in the author's *Economic Behaviour: An Introduction*, Allen and Unwin, 1980.

FS*   *Financial Statistics* is a monthly publication which should be used for financial information when the *Monthly Digest of Statistics* is not sufficiently detailed.

ET*   *Economic Trends* is another official monthly which has more limited coverage than the *Monthly Digest of Statistics* but more detail on some economic matters. Several of its statistics are presented in the form of charts and graphs.

B*   *Britain, An Official Handbook* is an annual official book of reference which is not confined to economic matters but is most valuable.

EP   *Economic Progress Reports* are broadsheets published monthly by the Treasury. They contain helpful commentaries on economic trends and a few important statistics.

N   *National Institute Economic Review* is a quarterly publication by an independent research organisation (The National Institute of Economic and Social Research). The appendix to each issue is an extensive selection of very valuable economic statistics, some of which are not easily found elsewhere—e.g. data on countries other than the UK.

E   *The Economist* is a weekly newspaper which sometimes carries useful statistical data.

WA   *Whitaker's Almanac* is an annual publication appearing towards the end of the year. It does not contain as much economic information as it used to, but is still valuable.

KS   *The British Economy, Key Statistics 1900–1970* was published by Times Newspapers for the London and Cambridge Economic Service. It is exceptionally useful as a source for historical statistics and long-term trends.

1 The allocation of resources in a mixed economy

You are about to view a panorama of the economic life of Britain in the last quarter of the 20th century. You will see such things as the number of people who live in Britain, how many of them go out to work, what sort of jobs they do, how they are paid, the amounts of different types of goods and services that are produced, and the way in which production is organised and goods made available in the shops. You will discover the number and size of firms in different industries, the economic importance of the major regions of the country, the principal financial institutions and their purposes, the nature of trade unions, the extent of unemployment, the main activities of the government and the chief taxes which it collects, the types of goods that are imported and exported and the countries with which this exchange is carried on.

By the time you have reached the last page you should be in a position to answer most of the important questions about the British economy which begin: what? where? which? how many? how much? in what ways?—in fact, every type of question except perhaps those beginning how? or why? and requiring an understanding of economic theory. If you would like to know more about how the economy works you will have to go further in your study than this book will take you.[1] It is the author's hope that the knowledge you will acquire will stimulate you to do so. However, although we will be concentrating on describing the British economy, it is important to mention a few basic principles of economics.

The working of economic forces

It is not the prime purpose of this book to teach you economic theory, but to describe the economy in which we live. However, it can be very useful to understand a few basic principles of economics. We, therefore, devote this and the next chapter to outlining some of the rudiments of economic theory, which serve the purpose of providing a framework within which you may learn about the British economy.

1 The author's *Economic Behaviour: An Introduction*, Allen and Unwin, 1980, will take you through some more elementary theory.

These two chapters describe the functioning of the main economic forces at work in a country such as ours. The difference between them is based on two distinctive approaches to economics, known as **microeconomics** and **macroeconomics**, common in our subject. The term microeconomics (derived from the Greek word *micro* meaning small), looks at individual parts of the economy in detail and examines the relationship between them. Thus, in microeconomics, we look at particular sectors of the economy, such as agriculture, manufacturing industry, retail distribution, etc, and we study the allocation of resources among all sectors. This is what we shall do in the present chapter. In Chapter 2, we take a macroeconomic view. The term (derived from the Greek word *macro* meaning large) is used when we are looking at the economy as a whole, ignoring what is happening to the individual parts. We shall explain the macroeconomic approach more fully when we come to it in the next chapter.

The allocation of resources

Our present task is to look, briefly, at the main economic forces that explain why the structure of an economy is what it is—why resources are allocated in particular ways, and why certain goods and services are provided rather than others.

Scarcity

First of all, it is necessary to emphasise that labour, machinery, land and the other resources needed for production, usually called **factors of production**, are limited in supply. Moreover, since the resources are limited and they may usually be employed to produce a variety of goods, those goods and services must also be limited. This scarcity of goods in general, does not mean that it would not be possible to produce as much of any individual good that is desired. It does imply, however, that there are not enough resources to give everyone as much of *everything* as he or she would like.

Opportunity cost

Economists have a special way of looking at this problem of scarcity. It is to regard the cost of producing a good as the sacrifice involved in *not* producing others. This cost is known as **opportunity cost**, a term which describes the fact that factors of production are used for a particular purpose rather than for others of which they are capable. The opportunity cost of producing some good or service is the value of the factors in the next best use to which they could be put.

The scarcity of factors of production involves a problem of **choice**—of deciding how much labour, capital and other resources shall be used to produce computers, vinegar, brown paper, haircuts and all the other goods and services that society might consider worth having. The pattern of production prevailing at any time depends on the decisions made about how much of each commodity should be produced.

Types of economic system

Economics concerns itself with questions of choice. In this connection it is useful to distinguish between three ways in which economic decisions can be taken.

The first is of major importance in some primitive societies, where virtually all production is undertaken within self-sufficient families or tribal units. Tradition usually dictates how much hunting, fishing, cooking and other tasks shall be done and by whom. These societies are often referred to as **traditional**, or **subsistence, economies**. They are characterised by the absence of exchange between the individual families or tribes, and are barely relevant to a consideration of advanced economies in the modern world.

The second method of deciding how much of each and every good and service shall be produced is to leave it to the state to plan the allocation of all resources from a central office. Such economies are referred to as being **centrally planned**, or **command, economies**. In a large industrial country there is obviously a limit to the extent to which detailed central planning and allocation of resources can be carried on. The Soviet Union and other communist countries, however, may be said to make a great many economic decisions in this way.

The third method of deciding how resources should be allocated is of particular relevance. In Britain, the majority of decisions about what shall be produced are not made by the central government in peacetime. That does not mean, of course, that it is a matter of pure chance what goods and services result. Indeed, if you consider that when you go shopping you generally find what you want at prices which you expect to pay, it must be obvious that the system is not completely random. When you reflect further that the articles you purchase have been produced by people with whom you have almost certainly had no direct contact, the whole business seems, perhaps, rather remarkable. Broadly speaking we can attribute it to the fact that the greater part of production is by firms which are owned and controlled by private individuals aiming to make profits. It is the existence of this profit motive, together with the preferences of consumers, working through what is known as the **price mechanism**, which largely determines the pattern of production. Systems in which economic decisions are made in this way are usually called **market** or **exchange economies**, and the way in which they function may be explained by the following simple illustration.

The price mechanism

Imagine that all the firms in Britain decided to produce as much clothing as they could manage, and nothing else. Clearly such a situation is inconceivable for two basic reasons: (1) that there would be more clothing than was required; and (2), because there would be no supply of all the other goods needed—food, drink, fuel, household goods and so forth.

The effects of a surplus of clothing and deficiency of everything else are not difficult to imagine. Individuals will not be willing to spend all their money on clothes, and in order to try to sell the clothes the price will have to be lowered. At the same time, large sums of money will be offered for other goods which are not being supplied. Furthermore, since all the clothing cannot be sold, and the price has fallen, firms making clothing will find that their profits have fallen. Some of them may even be making losses. What is more natural than that they should turn to producing those other things which are in great demand, and in which lines they see the possibility of making profits again? In a sense we can say that the new pattern of production reflects the preferences of consumers for clothing and other goods, since the offer of large sums of money for the latter makes their production profitable and induces producers in unprofitable businesses to turn to producing them.

Even when the new pattern of production is established there is no reason why it should remain permanently fixed. Suppose something happens to make one good more profitable to produce than it was before—a change in people's tastes from eating marmalade for breakfast to eating lemon curd, for example. This would cause the demand for marmalade to fall and the demand for lemon curd to rise. Producers will find that they can sell the latter at a higher price, while the price of the former has to be lowered. Provided that nothing happens to alter the costs of producing either good, the production of lemon curd will be more profitable and the production of marmalade less so. Some firms, therefore, may be induced to change from producing marmalade to lemon curd until the extra amount of curd now coming on to the market forces down the price, and profits are about equal in the two industries. No further incentive to change then exists. In the end, consumers' preferences have guided production, through their effect on prices and profits, to a more satisfactory assortment of the goods which people want.

Although the working of the price mechanism appears to solve the problem of choice, and to allocate scarce productive resources in an efficient and satisfactory way, we must be careful not to jump to the conclusion that it is necessarily the best solution. For one thing there are political considerations to be taken into account. Living in a society which is based on the freedom for individuals to make profits, is different in many ways from living in one in which economic decisions are made by the government. While, as private individuals, we may have distinct views about which system we prefer, it is not the job of the economist, in his professional capacity, to pronounce on what is right or wrong in this matter. Moreover, both planning and pricing systems fail in some ways to allocate resources efficiently. Under central planning there is no certainty that planners will select that combination of goods and services which best suits the community as a whole. An economy working under a completely free price mechanism is likewise deficient in some respects. We shall return to consider the reasons for this shortly. Before doing so we shall have to probe a little further into the nature of the forces which appear to drive production in a market economy since, if price movements direct output, we ought to know what lies behind price movements.

The market

The price mechanism works in what is called a **market**. This term has a much wider meaning in economics than in everyday speech. Any commodity which is bought and sold is considered as having a 'market' in which the transaction is completed. It includes not only places like local vegetable and street markets which exist in certain definite places; the market for each good is *any* arrangement by which buyers and sellers come into contact with one another.

Consider the individuals in a market who wish to do business. They naturally group themselves into two categories: potential buyers and potential sellers. We are interested in buyers and sellers from the point of view of price determination. It is at once clear that both the amounts which buyers are prepared to buy or **demand** and the amounts which sellers are prepared to offer for sale or to **supply**, are related to the market price of a commodity. Let us look, then, at the nature of demand and supply as it might exist in a typical market; for instance, the market for tinned peaches.

Demand

From the point of view of potential purchasers the demand for a commodity is particularly related to its price. Demand is not likely to be for a fixed quantity regardless of price; it may be thought of rather as a **schedule** of amounts that would be bought in a given period of time at various prices. Such a demand schedule can be set out in tabular form as in Table 1.1. (Note that hypothetical figures have been used.)

Table 1.1 A demand schedule for tinned peaches

Price £	Number of tins demanded per week
0.40	900
0.60	500
0.80	250
1.00	100
1.20	75

It is important to stress that the schedule of demand at different prices is *not* meant to represent quantities purchased at different times, either in the past or in the future. Nor is it a list of the quantities that people would somehow 'like to have'. It is a statement of *effective* demand (i.e. backed by willingness to pay the price) of the amounts which would actually be bought per unit of time if market price were at certain levels. In the case of the demand for tinned peaches it is convenient to think of the quantities which might be bought *per week*.

We must now make an important observation about the nature of the demand for a commodity. It is true that the amount purchased is liable to be influenced by factors other than the price of an article. However, it is characteristic of the demand for most goods, that people are prepared to buy larger quantities the lower the price. In the hypothetical demand schedule for tinned peaches, this is the case. At prices rising from 40 pence to £1.20 per tin, the quantities which would be bought decline from 900 to 75. Two reasons may be offered for this. The first relates simply to the total number of purchasers entering the market. At a price of, say, £10 a tin only an addict or a very rich person will buy tins of peaches. As the price drops nearer to that of other substitute foods and comes within the range of more and more people with lower incomes, so the quantities purchased may be expected to rise.

The second reason why demand tends to increase as price falls relates, not to the total number of purchasers, but to the quantities bought by each individual purchaser. We can fairly reasonably assume that, if someone buys something it is because it gives some satisfaction. Moreover, it is also reasonable to believe that the amount of satisfaction derived from having *additional* units of a good, tends to fall the more one has. We do not have to be able to measure the abstract quantity of satisfaction to be able to see this. Assuming that I like tinned peaches, for instance, I enjoy them a great deal when I have only a single tin a week. A second tin also gives me much pleasure, but perhaps a little less, the third tin certainly less, the fourth tin less still, and by about the tenth tin per week I am hardly enjoying them at all. Now the extent to which satisfaction falls off as consumption in a given period increases must clearly differ both from one good to another, and for different individuals. A person cannot, in general, be expected to pay more for a commodity than the money value of the satisfaction obtained from consuming it. Hence, if the price is low, people will tend to buy more than if the price is high.

We can summarise the argument of the last two paragraphs in the following way. The larger demand of 825 tins at the price of 40 pence, compared with that of £1.20, is most likely to come partly from more people buying tinned peaches, and partly from existing purchasers buying extra tins when they are cheap.

Supply

A demand schedule represents the quantities of a commodity that would be bought at different prices. A **supply schedule** represents a parallel relationship between price and the quantities which potential sellers are willing to offer for sale. A typical supply schedule, also hypothetical, might be as follows:

Table 1.2   A supply schedule for tinned peaches

Price £	Number of tins supplied per week
0.40	50
0.60	200
0.80	250
1.00	275
1.20	300

This schedule contrasts sharply with that of demand, in that it shows the amount supplied increasing with a rising price, and dropping with a price fall. It is convenient to think of the reasons for this, first, in terms of the changing amounts supplied by an individual producer—for example, a manufacturing firm putting the peaches into tins. We may assume that a firm would generally be prepared to produce a larger output if it was offered a higher price for its product. This would depend, of course, upon the costs of production. However, it is more than likely that if a firm produces a higher output with its existing factory and machinery there will come a point at which it costs more to do so. A producer will increase output only if the price is high enough to warrant it. As a business grows, especially in the short-term, premises may become cramped and bottlenecks may start to interfere with the flow of production, as some equipment reaches maximum capacity. In addition, the price of the resources used in production may be forced up by the increased demand for them. For these and other reasons costs of production will tend to rise, and the supplier will only increase output if the price is high enough to make it worthwhile.

In addition to the tendency for costs to rise as a firm expands, there is another reason why the quantity supplied may increase as price goes up. Extra production can result from the entry into the market of new, less efficient firms whose costs are above those of existing producers. They will commence production when the price is high enough to make it profitable.

Before leaving the subject of supply, we must point out that not all businesses are characterised by conditions of rising costs. In some industries costs per unit of output do not change as production rises but may, indeed, even fall—at any rate up to a point. Motor vehicles are a good example. Average costs tend to fall as production grows. It is, on average, cheaper to produce 100 000 cars than a mere 1000 per annum. In industries where mass production techniques are used there are usually heavy capital costs incurred initially in order to set up factories with high productivity machinery. These are known as **fixed** or **overhead costs** and do not vary with output. They should be distinguished from **variable costs** which, as their name implies, do vary with the level of production—for example, the cost of raw materials used. As output expands, fixed costs are spread over larger and larger quantities, and average costs fall, especially in the short run. However, there may well come a point at which average costs stop falling. They may then be constant, or even rise, with increasing output.

Price determination

The supply and demand for tinned peaches are both related to price. This being the case, it is apparent that price can act in such a way as to balance supply and demand. Indeed, the purpose of this discussion is to demonstrate that the activities of buyers and sellers tend to drive price to a level at which supply and demand are balanced. In our example it can be seen that the price at which such a balance exists is 80p. At this price consumers are prepared to buy 250 tins, which is exactly the same amount as suppliers are prepared to offer for sale. If the market price is 80p there will be no disappointed buyers or sellers.

Compare the situation with any other price. At £1.20 a tin, for instance, suppliers would be offering 300 tins, while only 75 would be bought. There would be an *excess of supply* over demand. What would happen to this excess supply? In conditions of free competition the disappointed producers with unsold stocks would be forced to cut their price in order to dispose of them. It would only be when the price had fallen to 80p that supply and demand would be balanced.

Conversely, suppose the price were only 40p per tin. It would now be among consumers that we should find disappointment, since they would be prepared to buy 900 tins at that price, but producers would be prepared to supply only 50. The latter would soon find that they could get much more than 40p a tin if consumers were free to bid for them. In other words, there would now be *excess demand* forcing price up. Again, it would only be if the price rose to 80p that supply and demand would be balanced.

Market equilibrium

Economists use a term to describe the state of a market where the quantities buyers wish to purchase is exactly equal to the quantities that sellers wish to offer for sale. The term is *equilibrium*, and implies a balance between the forces of supply and demand. When a market is in equilibrium, price is such that there are no economic forces working on either the demand or the supply side to change the quantities bought and sold, which are also said, therefore, to be in equilibrium.

The allocation of resources by means of the price mechanism may be explained by means of a diagram as well as with demand and supply schedules.

Such a diagram is Fig 1.1, which uses the information contained in Tables 1.1 and 1.2.

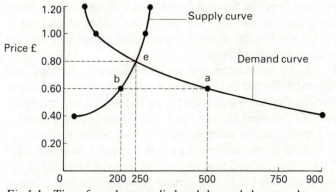

Fig 1.1   Tins of peaches supplied and demanded per week

The diagram is of the form of a graph, where the price of tinned peaches is measured along the vertical axis; while quantities of peaches are measured along the horizontal axis. The data contained in Table 1.1 is used to plot what is called a *demand curve*, which shows the quantities demanded at different prices. To find the quantity demanded at the price of £0.60, for example, we draw a vertical line from the point on the price axis representing £0.60 to meet the demand curve, at point *a*. If we, then, drop a perpendicular from *a* to the quantity axis we read there the quantity demanded of 500.

Fig 1.1 contains a *supply curve* as well as a demand curve. The supply curve is plotted from the data in Table 1.2 and shows the quantities that would be supplied at different prices. To find the quantity supplied at the price of £0.60, for example, we use the same vertical line that we drew to find the quantity demanded, i.e. the line passing through £0.60 on the price axis. The point of intersection of this line with the supply curve is marked *b* on the graph. Dropping a perpendicular from *b* to the quantity axis, we read the quantity supplied as 200.

Market equilibrium is obtained at the point of intersection of the supply and demand curves; point *e*. At *e*, market price is £0.80, which leads sellers to offer 250 tins of peaches per week—the same number as buyers wish to purchase. This is the only price at which the quantities supplied and demanded are equal, and where there are no economic forces causing market price to change. At prices *below* the equilibrium price, the quantities demanded exceed those that producers are prepared to supply, and price is pushed upwards as buyers compete for a limited supply. At prices *above* the equilibrium price, the amount that producers offer for sale exceeds that which buyers wish to purchase, and price tends to fall as sellers compete to unload the excess production. Only at the equilibrium price, of £0.80, are supply and demand in balance, with no economic forces causing it to change.

Changes in supply and demand

So far, we have shown how the forces of supply and demand bring about market equilibrium. But we can also use supply and demand analysis to demonstrate the price mechanism at work, reallocating resources whenever there are changes in market conditions.

In order to do this we must recognise that the quantities supplied and demanded are liable to be affected by changes of many kinds, as well as those of the price of the commodity, on which we have up to now focused attention. We cannot consider all the other factors which affect supply and demand in detail here, but we shall mention some of the most important of them.

Let us start by looking at the determinants of the quantity supplied other than the price of the commodity. These include the costs of production, the prices of *other* goods, and acts of the government. Consider the first of these. Suppose that we have constructed a supply curve for tinned peaches on the assumption that the price of tinned pears is 50 pence per pound, and that, for some reason or other, that price rises to 60 pence. What would happen to the supply of tinned peaches? The answer is that it would be likely to fall, because peach canning factories would switch at least part of their production to tinning pears instead.

We may now show how to represent the fall in supply on the kind of diagram we have used to demonstrate supply and demand analysis. Fig 1.2 reproduces the supply curve from Fig 1.1, and the two diagrams are basically identical, except that we have dropped the numerical scales in favour of letters to indicate price and quantity. The way to represent the fall in supply is to shift the entire supply curve to the left. Thus, if S is the original supply curve, the new supply curve is S'. This new curve shows that smaller quantities are offered for sale at each and every price. For example, at price p_0, the quantity supplied falls from q_0 to q_1.

Leftward shifts of the supply curve would follow a change in any of the 'other' determinants of supply (i.e. other than the price of the good itself)

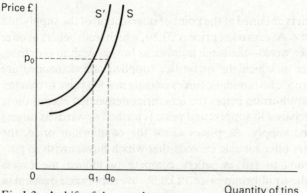

Fig 1.2   A shift of the supply curve

mentioned earlier, which cause supply to fall. For example, if costs of production of tinned peaches were to rise, say, because the price of labour used in the manufacturing process rises, the supply curve would shift as in the diagram, from S to S^1. The supply curve would also shift in the same direction if, for instance, the government were to impose a tax on the sale of tinned peaches, thereby reducing sellers' receipts. Rightward shifts of the supply curve would follow any change in the determinants of supply, other than the price of the commodity, which caused the quantities offered for sale to rise rather than to fall; e.g. a fall in the price of tinned pears; a reduction in production costs due to an increase in productivity; or the granting by the government of a subsidy on sales of tinned peaches.

Having explained the consequences for the supply curve of changes in the determinants of supply other than the price of the commodity, we may be briefer in our explanation of the demand side. The quantities demanded of a commodity depend on many factors including the level of consumers' income, the prices of other goods, and consumer tastes. When any change occurs in one of these, the demand curve will shift, to the right in the case of increased quantities being demanded, and to the left in the case of reduced quantities. Thus in Fig 1.3, which reproduces the demand curve, labelled D, from Fig 1.1, a shift to D' could be the result of a fall in consumers' income, a fall in the price of tinned pears (which are substitutes for peaches) or a change in consumer tastes in favour of peaches and away from pears.

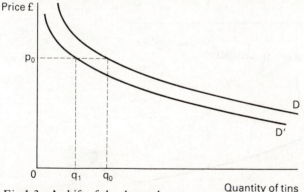

Fig 1.3   A shift of the demand curve

This section has been concerned with explaining how to handle changes in supply and demand, when a change occurs which shifts one or both of them. It is important to realise that supply and demand curves are drawn on the assumption that there are no changes taking place of any factor which affects demand or supply other than the price of the commodity. It is common to describe such an assumption by the Latin expression *ceteris paribus* (which means other things being equal). When there is a change in the ceteris paribus assumption, there is a shift in either the supply or demand curve (or possibly both), and we are now ready to examine the effects of such shifts on the market situation.

Consider Fig 1.4, which shows the effect of a rise in demand due, say, to a rise in the price of tinned pears—a substitute for tinned peaches. The original equilibrium (as in Fig 1.1) is found at the point of intersection of the supply and demand curves, point e. Equilibrium price is p_0, with q_0 as the equilibrium quantity bought and sold. When the demand curve shifts rightwards to D', price rises to p_1 and the quantity rises to q_1 in the new equilibrium, at e'. Now consider Fig 1.5, which shows the effect of a rise in supply due, say, to an increase in productivity in tinned peach production. The original equilibrium is again found at point e, with price p_0 and quantity q_0. When the supply curve shifts rightwards, to S', price falls to p_1, and quantity rises to q_1 in the new equilibrium, at e'.

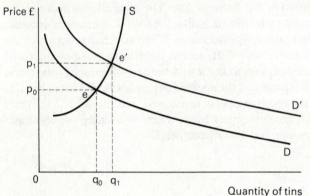

Fig 1.4 The effects of a rise in demand

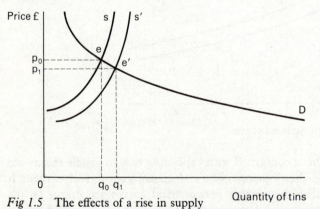

Fig 1.5 The effects of a rise in supply

The responsiveness of demand and supply to price

The analysis of price cannot be taken much further here. It should, however, be made clear that demand-price and supply-price relationships differ from one commodity to another. This means, of course, that demand and supply schedules and curves differ also. It does not affect the conclusions reached in the previous section concerning the effects of changes in supply and demand, but it implies that such changes may have quantitively different effects on price and on quantity bought and sold. When analysing any particular case, one needs to know how responsive demand and supply are to price changes, and a few remarks on the main determinants of such responsiveness may be helpful.

From the demand side one can say that, in general, a given change in price tends to have a greater effect on the quantity demanded the more substitutes there are for a good. For example, one might well expect larger variations in demand for tinned peaches, toffees or daffodils than for toothbrushes, sugar, or vacuum cleaners. Moreover, the demand for a particular make or brand of commodity, such as a vacuum cleaner, tends to respond rather more to price changes than demand for the whole class of commodities, for the same reason of the availability of substitutes. It should be noted, too, that the demand for most goods is inclined to respond more to changes in price the longer the time it is given to do so, as the news spreads and habits are broken. As cod has become relatively expensive in recent years people have started switching to substitute foods such as trout and chicken, as these have fallen in price *relative* to cod.

Economists have devised a special measure of the responsiveness of demand to price changes. It is called the **elasticity of demand** and is defined as the percentage change in quantity demanded divided by the percentage change in price. If demand changes by the same percentage as price, the elasticity of demand is said to be equal to unity (numerically = 1). Total expenditure by consumers is the same regardless of price. If the quantity demanded rises proportionately more than price falls, the demand is said to be elastic (i.e. responsive to price). If the quantity demanded rises proportionately less than price falls, then demand is said to be inelastic.

On the supply side, responsiveness to price changes is closely related to costs of production. If, for instance, costs do not rise much as output expands, one can expect a greater increase in supply with a given price increase than if they do. Again, responsiveness will tend to be greater the longer the time one allows for a firm to adjust to changing circumstances and for new producers to enter or leave the industry. If we look for a moment behind the bare costs, to the factors determining them, we might observe that this is very much a question of the techniques of production used in a particular industry, and of how easily extra resources can be attracted to increase output.

It should be noted that there is a measure of responsiveness of supply to price changes, called the **elasticity of supply**, parallel to the elasticity of demand. Supply is elastic if quantity supplied changes proportionately more than price changes. It is inelastic if quantity responds less than proportionately to price. It is neither elastic nor inelastic (equal to unity) if price and quantity change by exactly the same percentage.

The responsiveness of supply and demand to price changes for different commodities can be said to determine the extent to which market price will be affected if anything happens to change either of them. It means, for instance, that a material drop in the supply of petrol tends to lead to significant increases in price (especially in the short-term because of the difficulty of running vehicles on other fuels) even though it may cause some decline in demand as people economise in using their cars. A similar drop in the supply of pears, on the other hand, would probably have a smaller effect on price, as people switched to buying more apples and other fruit instead. Conversely, a sudden increase in demand for a good, the supply of which can be readily increased without a substantial rise in costs, would not push up price as much as if the extra supply was only obtainable at much greater expense.

Factor markets

The discussion of the working of the price mechanism in this chapter has run in terms of markets for goods and services. It must be added that, in a market economy, prices act also to allocate factors of production, e.g. land, labour and capital. This takes place in factor markets, which function in a manner broadly similar to goods markets, i.e. there are demand and supply curves for each factor of production, representing the quantities of that factor which are demanded and supplied at a range of prices. The demand for the services of a factor, such as labour, comes from businesses which seek to employ workers, and is derived from the demand for the product that labour helps to produce. The supply of factor services, such as hours of work offered on the market, comes from those persons wanting employment.

Equilibrium in factor markets, as in goods markets, occurs where supply and demand are balanced and there are, therefore, no economic forces tending to cause price or quantities to change. Two implications of the operation of factor markets must be mentioned. They follow from the fact that factor prices can be regarded in two ways—as business costs, and as factor earnings. Factor prices perform, therefore, two distinct functions. The first is related to the view of those prices as business costs, whereby they can guide business firms on the cheapest methods of production to employ. For example, firms can compare the prices of, say, labour and capital, with the productivity of those factors, to decide whether to adopt labour-intensive or capital-intensive methods in their factories. The second way of looking at factor prices, as the earnings of factors of production, reminds us that factor markets play a part in the determination of the distribution of income. For example, the price of labour can be viewed as the wage rate that a worker receives, say, per hour. Given the number of hours worked, therefore, we can deduce the worker's income.

The price mechanism and economic efficiency

The price mechanism has been shown to involve a system for allocating scarce resources among competing uses, in which the relative values placed by consumers on different commodities and their relative costs of production play a part. As it is sometimes put, the price mechanism helps to answer the question of *what* shall be produced. Moreover, since factor prices affect the distribution of income, they help to answer the question of *for whom* goods and services are produced. Finally, since factor prices guide business decisions on the cheapest production methods to employ, they also help solve the question of *how* production is best organised.

We end this chapter by returning to consider how well the price mechanism does its job. From what we have said so far, it must be clear that there are considerable merits in allowing resources to be allocated in a market economy. Such a system is cheap, in the sense that no bureaucratic costs are incurred in running it, such as are involved in central planning. Moreover, the system does result in the production of goods and services that people actually want to buy. And it seems legitimate to observe that if people are prepared to pay for a good, the price they part with to buy it must bear some sort of relationship to its value to them. In addition, we have seen that a market system is flexible, and whenever there are changes, in costs of production or in consumer tastes, for example, prices act as signals to alter production. With regard, for instance, to the sort of change in tastes mentioned earlier in the chapter— from marmalade to curd—it would seem that, if the price mechanism brings about a shift of resources from marmalade to lemon curd production, there is at least something to be said for it.

Despite the merits of a pricing system mentioned in the previous paragraph, we must not conclude that the pattern of resource allocation it brings about is always ideal, or even better than would occur under any other system. For there are certain well-recognised deficiencies associated with market economies.

In the first place, in order for the price mechanism to be regarded as working well, it is essential that, when relative prices change, as for instance with a change in tastes, there should not be any artificial barriers which prevent production changes following suit. In terms of the demand and supply analysis which we have been using, if there is an excess of demand over supply at the ruling market price, then firms in the industry should be able and willing to expand output or, if not, then other firms should be free to enter the industry and do so instead. This, indeed, is the function of **competition**.

If certain conditions obtain in the market then competition is said to be perfect and these results should follow. (Perfect competition is not a term which is meant to imply excellence. It merely refers to the fact that there is an extremely *high* degree of competition.) The conditions are:

- that all firms should be 'price takers', in the sense that no single firm should be able to influence market price by changing its own output. This will follow if:
  (a) all firms are small
  (b) the products of all firms are identical (homogeneous)
- that buyers and sellers should be fully aware of demand and supply conditions throughout the market
- that there is freedom for firms to enter the industry

If the market for a product is, in some way, restricted, competition is said to be imperfect. In fact, it is well known that in some industries there are only a few firms which, because of their size, possess a degree of monopoly power. They are able to sell at a relatively high price by restricting production, and at the same time entry barriers, like the existence of patent rights, restrict the ability of other firms to compete with existing producers. Moreover, when a firm is protected from competition by other producers, it is not under the same pressure to seek the most efficient techniques of production.

Secondly, the pattern of prices ruling in the market depends partly upon the amounts of various goods which people are prepared to buy at different prices. However, we cannot assume that everybody necessarily knows enough about all the goods and services available to be able to plan expenditure wisely. Disappointments follow some purchases, simply because we do not fully appreciate all the characteristics of articles—how well some household appliance will work, or how suitable a fabric is for a particular purpose, for example. This may be due to sheer ignorance, misleading advertising, or any other cause. In the provision of some goods and services it is even deemed right for the state to interfere with the freedom of the individual in order to ensure at least minimum provision, for example, of education and health. There are others, such as habit-forming drugs, which for similar but opposite reasons are subject to control on sales.

Next, there are some goods and services which benefit not only the people who buy them but spill over to others as well. For example, a man who buys a car which has efficient brakes is likely to save the lives of pedestrians and other road users as well as his own. Taken to an extreme, there are even some goods and services, such as the police force, which can be said to benefit society collectively rather than as individuals. These kinds of goods would hardly be provided on an adequate scale, if at all, if they were dependent on being sold to individual consumers. One should mention in this class, too, some goods which may have what are called negative spill-over effects and cause harm or loss of satisfaction to other people. An example might be the annoyance to a non-smoker of being in a confined space with someone smoking a pipe or cigarette. Pollution associated with the waste by-products of some industries comes into this category too.

Another important matter to take into account when considering a market economy and how efficiently it operates is that the pattern of prices in the market depends on the goods which consumers decide that they need. Needs alone are not enough, however; it is amounts actually spent which are critical. Insofar as the influence which each individual exerts upon prices is related to the amount which he personally has available to spend, the resulting pattern of prices depends, also, upon the distribution of income and wealth among individuals.

It is true that the income a man or woman receives is itself influenced by demand and supply considerations. One reason why an architect earns more than a bus conductor, for instance, is because the former's scarce special skill is more highly valued by society than the latter's. However, unless we are prepared to say that the distribution of income is satisfactory we cannot conclude that the pattern of prices ruling in the market reflects best the wishes of the community as a whole.

Finally, it is necessary to take account of the speed at which the market system operates, and, in particular, of how quickly production changes in response to changes in price. In many cases, this is very satisfactory, but there are some markets which may be described as sluggish, where response is tardy. For example, certain agricultural markets fall into this category, as you will find out if you take your study of economics beyond this book.

The mixed economy

We have now seen some of the advantages and disadvantages of the market system from the viewpoint of the allocation of resources. We shall have more to say on this subject from the viewpoint of the working of the economy as a whole, at the end of the next chapter. We are not, however, in a position at this stage to make a firm assessment of the balance of pros and cons. To do so would involve not only economic issues, but political ones on which we, as economists, have no special rights to speak. Moreover, a market system can be judged only in comparison to alternative methods of arranging the allocation of resources, e.g. by central planning, which has advantages and disadvantages of its own.

It would be, to say the least, interesting to compare the respective merits of prices and planning. Fortunately we do not have to make a clear choice. It is hardly surprising, perhaps, to be told that Britain is really best regarded as a **mixed economy** and contains elements of both pricing and planning. The price mechanism operates quite strongly in major private sectors of the economy, while, in peacetime, relatively little detailed central planning of production takes place. However, the government certainly does interfere with the flow of activity in many ways. It engages in production itself in such areas as education, health and defence. Action is taken to improve the way in which the market works, e.g. through the control of monopoly and promotion of competition. The state raises taxes and spends the proceeds in ways designed to affect the distribution of income and the output of many goods and services. These are but a few of the diverse ways in which the government intervenes in the running of the British economy. We shall encounter others in the next chapter, and, indeed, throughout the rest of this book.

2 **The economy as a whole**[1]

This is the second chapter devoted to explaining how economic forces work in a country such as the United Kingdom. In Chapter 1, we concentrated on how they influence the allocation of resources (in what we called a microeconomic approach). In this chapter, we take a macroeconomic view, and concentrate on the working of the economy as a whole. Our new approach allows us to ignore the detailed structure of individual industries, and to observe the broad magnitudes of the economy. These broad magnitudes, often known as aggregates, include the level of total output and employment, and the general level of prices.

The difference between the macroeconomic view and the microeconomic view, is basically one of perspective. They are complementary, in much the same way as photographs taken with a camera using different lenses are complementary. A telephoto lens gives us a close-up picture where we can observe fine details of a subject, in a micro fashion. A wide-angle lens gives us a picture where we miss the fine detail but can see the broad outlines of our subject in macro style. For example, if we are photographing a wood or copse, our telephoto lens allows us to study a particular tree; while the wide-angle lens lets us see the wood as a whole.

We are now adopting a macroeconomic approach. Hence, we are no longer concerned with price and output in individual markets. Our focus is on the total output and employment in the economy as a whole, with the average general level of prices, and how these are influenced by economic forces.

Our approach will not be so very different from that of output and price determination in individual markets. Supply and demand will, as we shall see, still be relevant. But the market we shall study now is the entire national market for all goods and services. We shall examine first the determination of the level of total output and second, that of the general price level.

---

1 At several places in this chapter the reader may feel the need for fuller explanations of the theory than it is possible to give here. There are many textbooks which provide this, including Lipsey R G and Harbury C, *An Introduction to Economic Principles* (forthcoming).

The national income

Before we can throw light on the forces which influence the level of total output, we must explain exactly what we are dealing with. The total output of a nation is known as its national income, or national product.

The national income is a measure of the sum of all goods and services which are produced in an economy over a given period of time, such as a year. Note, first, that this sum is expressed in money terms, because the most convenient way of adding up the assortment of all the different goods and services that are produced is to express them in value terms. Thus, the quantities of each good are for the most part[1] multiplied by their prices to give their total market values; the sum of the market values of all goods and services is the value of the national income or output.

The second point to note about the national income is that it is measured *over a period of time* as the flow of goods and services produced during that period. It is *not* the stock of goods existing at any moment of time. This distinction between a flow and a stock is important to appreciate in economics. An analogy may be helpful. The passage of water along a river is a *flow*, the amount of water in a lake fed by the river is a *stock*. The national income is like the river. We measure its flow over a period of time, in terms of the value of goods and services produced. The economic parallel to the stock of water in a lake is the accumulated value of goods produced in the past and still in existence at any moment of time. It is called the stock of national capital, but we are not at present concerned with it.

The circular flow of national income, output and expenditure

At the start of the previous section we stated that the total output of a nation was called either its national income or its national output. We must now explain the reason for this statement which might, at first glance, seem somewhat surprising.

The identity of national income, national output, and another macroeconomic aggregate—national expenditure, can be seen with the aid of Fig 2.1. This diagram has been drawn to represent an extremely simple economy—one in which there are only two sectors, which we call 'households' and 'businesses'. We assume that businesses do all the producing of goods, and that households consume them. Moreover, to avoid complications we assume that the economy engages in no transactions with other countries in the world;

---

1 Market prices are used to value all goods and services which are bought and sold in markets. For some goods provided by the government, such as defence and health services, the values used are costs of production.

and that there is no government. These simplifying assumptions will be dropped shortly, and we shall see the implications of introducing these two sectors.

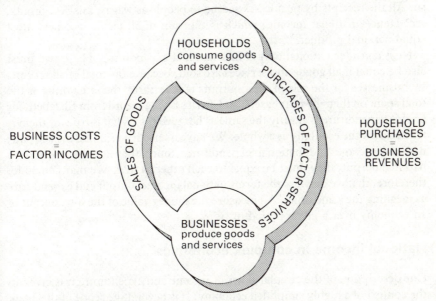

Fig 2.1   The circular flow of income and expenditure

In such a simple economy, production takes place as a result of businesses employing factors of production (*see* page 2) which are provided by households. Businesses incur costs of production by purchasing the services of factors of production, for which they pay wages, salaries, profits, etc. in return. Businesses are able to cover these costs of production by the sale of goods to households. Thus, money flows from businesses to households, as payments for factor services; and money flows from households to businesses, as payments for goods and services.

These money flows are depicted in Fig 2.1. The left hand side of the diagram shows a channel through which money is flowing, from businesses to households. This flow may be seen as the costs of production of businesses, and also as the incomes received by households for factor services. The right hand side of the diagram shows a channel through which money is flowing back from households to businesses. This flow may be seen as the sales of goods and services to households, and also as the revenues (or incomes) of businesses.

The equality of national income, output and expenditure

The diagram helps to make clear why the aggregate money flows discussed above all give the same total value, which may be viewed as either national income, national expenditure or as national output, all of which are equal to each other. Let us take these three concepts in pairs. First national output and national income. Their equality follows from the fact that the factors of production engaged in producing all the goods and services, are paid for doing so. All the receipts by businesses accrue to people as wages, salaries, profits, etc. Hence, national income, which is the sum of all factor incomes, must equal national product.

Next consider national output and national expenditure. These two must also be equal if all goods and services are sold, because the total of all receipts by businesses for the sale of their outputs is necessarily the same thing as the total spent on them by purchasers.[2] If Charles buys a record from Elizabeth for £5, his expenditure is exactly the same as her receipts. What is true for them is true also for the economy as a whole. We have no need to examine the last pair, national income and national expenditure. Since they are both equal to national output, they must be equal to each other as well. We may conclude, therefore, that we may use the terms national income, output and expenditure as meaning the same thing. All measure the money value of the total output of an economy over a given period of time.

National income in complex economics

Our description of the circular flows of income and expenditure was given in the context of a highly simplified economy. It is beyond the scope of this book to describe those flows in more complex economies. We should, however, mention some of the main additional channels through which money flows in such cases. Two illustrations are government, and the rest of the world.

In the first place, in an economy such as the UK money flows to and from the government. Inward flows result largely from taxes paid by households and by businesses.

Outward flows result from government expenditures on goods and from subsidies paid to households and to businesses. In the second place, money flows between nations. If a country engages in trade with other countries in the world, money flows into and out of the country. Outward flows include payments for imported goods, while inward flows include receipts for exports.

All flows of income and expenditure can be incorporated into an explanation of the mechanism of economies with both government and overseas sectors. We could indeed, construct a diagram along the lines of Fig 2.1 to show the direction of money flows in a more complex economy. It would be complicated, but there could be no departure from our conclusion that the total income, output and expenditure in the system would be equal to each other.

2 There is one relatively small problem that ought to be mentioned. The careful reader will have noticed the conditional phrase 'if all goods and services are sold'. If this is not the case then stocks of goods somewhere will have changed. If some goods remain unsold, for example, it is necessary to make an adjustment to national expenditure, by adding the change in stocks to achieve our equality.

National income determination

Now that we have a workable understanding of the national income, we may proceed to explaining the nature of economic forces which determine its level and cause it to change. Our explanation will parallel, in one important respect that given in the previous chapter, of the determination of price in individual markets. You may recall that we introduced the idea of equilibrium in a market as being that state of affairs obtaining when supply and demand are in balance, and when there are no economic forces at work which would cause price to change. The same idea of equilibrium can be applied to the economy as a whole. We say that national income is at equilibrium level when there are no economic forces at work causing it to rise or fall.

Our search for the equilibrium level of national income must start by identifying the economic forces that determine it. This will not prove very hard, because we know from our study of circular flows, in the previous section, that incomes are created by expenditure. Households' expenditure on goods produced by businesses, provides businesses with their income. Similarly, business expenditure on the purchase of the services of factors of production, provides households with their income. Therefore, in order to find the determinants of national income, we must look at the determinants of total expenditure. When national expenditure is rising, we shall find that national income is also rising; and when national expenditure is falling national income will also be falling.

The determinants of total expenditure

The amount that households and businesses wish to spend on goods and services of all kinds depends on many factors. We may, however, begin by concentrating on a single one of them—the level of national income itself.

The aggregate expenditure curve

The relationship between national income and aggregate expenditure is a well-established one. The total amount that people wish to spend on goods and services tends to be greater, the larger their incomes. In Table 2.1 we set out some hypothetical figures that illustrate the relationship between total income and the total expenditure that the community desires to make.

The table tells us that people wish to spend £600 million when their income is £400 million, and so forth. Notice, that desired expenditure is greater at high incomes than at low incomes. This should appear quite plausible, and is evidenced by fact. (You may notice too that expenditure at low incomes is greater than income. There is no need to worry about this. Such behaviour is understandable. At very low income levels, people may naturally spend more

Table 2.1 Schedule of expenditure at different income levels

Income (£m)	Expenditure (£m)
200	500
400	600
600	700
800	800
1000	900
1200	1000
1400	1100

than their incomes, financing such expenditure, in part, by using up past savings, or by borrowing.)

Let us look, now, at what happens to national income when people plan to spend different amounts. Consider first, the results of national income being at 1200 (note that we shall, for convenience, omit the £ million for the remainder of this section).

At an income level of 1200, we see from the Table that people wish to spend only 1000, which is less than national income. What happens? Well, if people spend only 1000, while businesses produce 1200 of goods and services, it follows that the level of stocks of unsold goods must rise—by 200, in fact.

In the face of such an increase in the size of their stocks, it is to be expected that businesses will cut back on production, with the immediate effect that national output (or national income) will fall. In other words economic forces are causing income to change and it is *not* at an equilibrium level.

Look, next, at what happens to national income when its level is 200. At that income we see from Table 2.1 that people plan to spend 500, which is greater than national income. What happens? Well, if people succeed in spending 500 (by using some of their capital, or by borrowing), then since businesses have only produced 200 worth of goods and services, there will be a running down of the stocks of goods held by businesses. In the face of such a reduction in their stocks, it will be expected that businesses will increase production, with the immediate result that national output (or national income will rise).[3] In other words, economic forces are causing national income to change and it is, again, *not* at an equilibrium level.

Finally, consider the results of national income being 800. At that income level, we see from the Table that people wish to spend 800—exactly the same amount as their income. Here, in contrast to the two previous cases, businesses find that they sell what they have produced without any rise or fall in their stocks. There is no reason to expect that they will wish to increase, or to cut back, on production. Total expenditure that people wish to make, out of a given national income, is equal to that income. Expenditure exactly matches

---

3 If there are not enough stocks to be sold to satisfy demand, the analysis is slightly different. Shortages of goods appear, and *they* may be the incentive for business to increase production.

output, and there are no economic forces causing national income to change. In other words, national income is at an equilibrium level.

Equilibrium national income

In Chapter 1, we described the working of economic forces using schedules, and repeated the argument using graphs. We do the same here, partly because it is often helpful to have alternative presentations of a theory, and partly because graphs are extensively used in economic analysis.

In Fig 2.2, we show the Aggregate Expenditure curve, which corresponds to the schedule of figures in Table 2.1. The diagram contains, however, another line, which is labelled the 45° line, because it bisects the right angle made by the axes of the graph where they intersect, at 0.

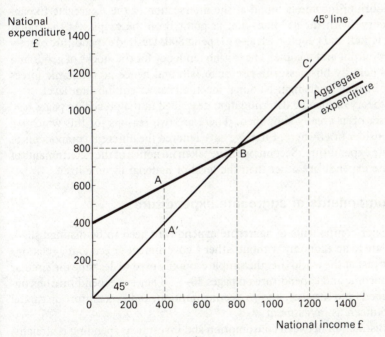

Fig 2.2   National income determination

The 45° line has a very special property. Every point on the line shows a relationship between income and expenditure such that the two are equal to each other. If you inspect the diagram, you will see that the vertical distance between any point on the line and the income axis, is equal to the horizontal distance between the same point and the expenditure axis. Thus, at point A on the graph, income and expenditure are both 400; at point B they are both 800, and at point C they are both 1200.

We make use of the relationship between the Aggregate Expenditure curve and the 45° line, to identify equilibrium income. Suppose income is 400, then expenditure, read off the Aggregate Expenditure curve, is 600 (point A). The expenditure that people wish to make is greater than income, by AA′, which is a measure of the falling stocks of goods held by businesses. The desire by businesses to replenish these stocks, is the force that pushes national income upwards. Suppose, however, income is 1200. Then expenditure that people wish to make is 1000 (point C′), which is less than income by CC′, which is a measure of rising stocks of goods held by businesses, and which, as explained earlier tend to push national income downwards. In other words, if income is at a level where the aggregate expenditure curve lies above the 45° line, economic forces tend to cause national income to rise; while if income is such that the aggregate expenditure curve lies below the 45° line, national income tends to fall.

Equilibrium income is found at the intersection of the Aggregate Expenditure curve with the 45° line—i.e. at point B on the graph. At that point income is 800, and people wish also to spend 800. Desired expenditure exactly matches output and income. There is no tendency for the stocks of goods and services held by businesses to rise or to fall, and hence no economic forces causing income to change. National income is at an equilibrium level.

The theory of income determination described in the preceding pages has, of course, been greatly simplified. There are two reasons for this which we must consider briefly here. First, we have ignored the different components of aggregate expenditure. Second, we have taken no notice of the determinants of aggregate expenditure other than the level of national income itself.

The components of aggregate expenditure

Four major components of aggregate expenditure need to be distinguished. Two relate to an economy without either a government or economic relations with the rest of the world (i.e. the simple economy used to describe the circular flow of income and expenditure on pages 20–1). They are expenditure on consumer goods and services, known as **consumption,** and expenditure on capital goods, known as **investment.**

The distinction between consumption and investment spending is straightforward. The former comprises expenditure on goods and services wanted by consumers for their own sake—e.g. on food, drink and tobacco, clothing, household goods, etc. Investment comprises expenditure on capital goods which are not wanted for present consumption, e.g. on factories, machinery, plant and equipment.

The distinction between consumption and investment expenditure is of importance in the determination of national income, because the decisions on how much to spend on each are made, on the whole, by separate groups of people. Consumption decisions are made by households, while investment decisions are made by businesses. We can take the implications of this distinction no further here, than to advise you that a key to understanding the theory of income determination in greater depth than we have described it, lies in identifying the different determinants of consumption and investment expenditures (see next section), and in analysing the relationship between them. In economies which trade with the rest of the world, and where there is also a government, total money flows are affected by activities involving two sectors, in addition to households and businesses. We cannot discuss these in detail here. But it should be clear that total expenditure is affected by both of them.

The government sector influences money flows as a result of the state's power to levy taxes and to spend the proceeds. The difference between government income and expenditure is a measure of the net addition to (or subtraction from) expenditure flows arising from state activities.[4] The overseas sector influences expenditure flows, because some part of a nation's income may be used to import goods and services from other countries; while a nation's exports also result in money flows. In so far as imports siphon off income—creating expenditure from other countries—we may observe that the difference between exports and imports plays an important role in national income determination. Net exports (i.e. the value of exports minus the value of imports) are a measure of the addition to total national income—creating expenditures that result from money transactions with the rest of the world.

Determinants of aggregate expenditure other than income

The second simplification of our theory of income determination, which must receive attention, relates to the determinants of the various categories of expenditure which we have identified. The theory we outlined relates expenditure only to the level of national income. However, there are other determinants of expenditure which need to be taken into account, since changes in expenditure, whatever the cause, influence the level of income. We have space here only to mention briefly some of the more important of these other determinants. We do so separately for each of the major components of expenditure which we have distinguished.

1 *Consumption expenditure* is made by households and depends not only on current income, but also on past income, expectations of future income, and the distribution of income among the population. It may also, at times, be affected by such matters as the terms and conditions of credit (e.g. the rate of

---

4 This difference (which may be positive or negative) is sometimes called the Public Sector Borrowing Requirement (PSBR). Changes in the PSBR form part of the government's stabilisation policy (*see* pages 36–7).

interest), the stock of wealth owned by consumers, the size and age distribution of the population, and psychological factors, such as the desire to bequeath a fortune to one's heirs.

2 *Investment expenditure* is made by businesses—not by households—and is, therefore, influenced by some rather different factors. Though the level of national income may be a determinant of investment expenditure, there are others which often assume greater significance, by influencing profit expectations, either from the side of costs or sales prospects. On the cost side, it is necessary to appreciate that businesses often need to rely on borrowing in order to finance investments, which yield returns only after some time has passed. Hence, the rate of interest that must be paid for borrowing may be a key determinant of whether or not a decision to invest is made. On the sales side, the state of business confidence must be mentioned, though it is difficult to generalise on the reasons why this may be high or low. Optimism and pessimism about trading conditions tend to spread among the business community, regardless of their underlying origins, which may often be political rather than strictly economic—e.g. the prospects of a change in government.

3 *Expenditure on imports and exports* is the third category of expenditure we must consider. In so far as imports comprise consumption or investment goods, their determinants include those already mentioned—e.g. national income in the importing country, profit expectations, etc.

The determinants of a nation's exports, however, are likely to be quite different. There is reason to expect that conditions inside a nation will affect its level of exports less than will conditions in the rest of the world. If you reflect on the fact that country A's exports are country B's imports, you will appreciate that their determinants will include the level of national income in country B. Thus, expenditure on exports is affected by national income levels in the rest of the world.

One new determinant of expenditure flows between one country and another, needs to be introduced here. This is the rate of exchange between domestic and foreign currencies. This will exert an influence on both the import and export sides. Imports come from other countries, and their price is set in terms of foreign currency. When the rate of exchange between currencies changes, then the price paid by importers *in their own domestic currency* changes accordingly (without any change occurring in the prices received by foreign exporters). The same is true of exports, which are set in terms of domestic currency. When the rate of exchange changes, the price paid by foreign importers *in terms of their own domestic currency*, changes also (without any change occurring in the prices received by exporters in their domestic currency).

An example may help to make this clear. Consider trade between the UK and the USA, where the British are buying American computers priced at

$10 000, while the Americans are buying British cars priced at £5000. Suppose the exchange rate between pounds and dollars is £1 = $1.50. The sterling price paid by an importer in the UK for an American computer is £6666.67; while the dollar price paid by an importer in the USA for a car is $7500.

Now, suppose the exchange rate alters to £1 = $1. Dollars have become dearer for UK importers, who only get $1 for every pound, whereas they previously got $1.50. At the same time, pounds have become cheaper for American importers, who have now to give only one dollar for every pound, whereas they previously had to give up $1.50.

The price of computers in terms of pounds paid for them by UK importers rises from £6666.67 to £10 000 when the exchange rate changes from £1 = $1.50 to £1 = $1. We would therefore expect the number of computers imported into the UK to fall as a result of the alteration in the exchange rate. At the same time, the price of British cars to American importers falls from $7500 to $5000 as a result of the alteration in the exchange rate from £1 = $1.50 to £1 = $1. We would therefore expect the number of cars exported to the USA to rise as a result of the change in the exchange rate.

We cannot go into the question of how exchange rates between domestic and international currencies are determined since this is beyond the scope of this book. But it is important to appreciate that the volume of imports and exports are affected by the rate of exchange, which therefore influences the volume of expenditure flows and national incomes in trading nations.

4 *Government net expenditure* is the final expenditure category to be considered. There is, however, little to be said about its determinants. The level of taxation and of government spending is largely determined by political matters, though both taxes and expenditure may be varied when the state wishes to influence the level of total national expenditure in what is called fiscal policy (*see* page 37).

Output and employment

The theory of income determination outlined above may be summarised by saying that national income will tend towards the level at which aggregate expenditure desired by the community exactly matches national output. It is necessary to add that aggregate expenditure affects the level of employment (and unemployment) as well as that of national income.

Although output and employment are not identical, there is a clear relationship between them, in that rising national output of goods and services is usually accompanied by rising levels of employment of factors of production, and vice versa. The fact that unemployment tends to be relatively high when national output is low (and vice versa) is of great relevance to those who are concerned with national economic policy. Indeed, the great English economist, the late John Maynard (later Lord) Keynes, built his reputation on the advocation of policies to increase government expenditure in the 1930s when unemployment was unprecedentedly high, in order to reduce that unemployment level. Keynes's policies still enjoy a considerable following, but they have to be reviewed in the light of the different economic conditions of the world in which we live today. Prime among such differences is the fact that the present age, unlike that of the 1930s, is one where inflation is present. Our next task must, therefore, be to turn our attention to the second macroeconomic variable that we have so far ignored. This is the general level of prices.

The general price level

Before discussing the way in which economic forces determine the general price level, it is perhaps worth reminding you that we are not concerned here with price determination in the market for individual goods and services. That subject was considered in the previous chapter. The price level on which we now focus attention is the *average* level of prices of all goods and services. When this changes in an upward direction, as it has of course been doing for very many years, we describe the movement of the price level as inflation. Our macroeconomic theory of the behaviour of the general price level includes, therefore, that of the determination of the rate of inflation.

The equilibrium price level

In spite of the warning in the previous paragraph that we are not now concerned with price determination in individual markets, we shall make use of the concept introduced in Chapter 1: that of market equilibrium. You may remember that we described the equilibrium price in the market for a commodity, as the price which balanced the supply and demand for that commodity. In a similar way we can identify the equilibrium general level of prices as that price level at which aggregate demand and aggregate supply, in the economy as a whole, are balanced.

In order to determine the equilibrium level of prices we shall need to make use of an aggregate supply and an aggregate demand curve, such as are shown in Fig 2.3. The aggregate supply curve AS shows the total output that businesses are prepared to offer for sale at different prices, i.e. at price level p_0, aggregate supply is q_0 output; at the price level p_1 aggregate supply is q_1. The aggregate demand curve AD shows the total output that people are prepared to buy at different price levels, i.e. at the price level p_0 aggregate demand is for q_0 output; at the price level p_2, aggregate demand is for q_2 output.

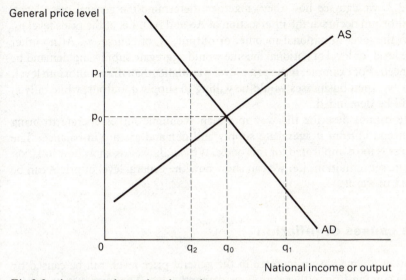

General price level

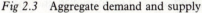

Fig 2.3 Aggregate demand and supply

The aggregate supply curve AS slopes upwards, indicating that businesses will offer larger outputs for sale when the price level is high than when it is low. The reason for this parallels that given for the upward slope of the supply curve for an individual commodity in the previous chapter—that costs of production rise as output increases. Indeed, it is as true for the economy as a whole as it is for individual suppliers, that rising production costs necessitate rising prices if output is to increase. We deal with an important exception to this assumption of rising costs, and an upward sloping aggregate supply curve (*see* page 34), but we start with this general case in order to explain the meaning of equilibrium of the general price level.

The aggregate demand curve AD slopes downwards, indicating that people are prepared to buy more goods when the price level is low than when it is high. The reasons for this are complex and cannot be fully explained here. However, you may not find it too hard to accept if we give you one reason, which is that the purchasing power of national income falls as the price level rises.[5] Just as you, as an individual will tend to buy less commodities out of your income of, say, £50, when inflation forces prices up—so the same is true for the community as a whole.

If we put the aggregate supply and aggregate demand curves together, as in

5 A second reason why aggregate demand tends to be less at high than at low prices, is that rising prices are associated with a shortage of money. When money is scarce, interest rates charged by borrowers (and received by lenders) tend to be high. As pointed out (*see* page 28) business expenditure on investment is affected by the rate of interest. When it costs more for businesses to borrow money, they tend to spend less on investment—i.e. aggregate demand is lower at high price levels than at low ones.

Fig 2.3, we can see how they, together, determine the general price level. Equilibrium occurs at the intersection of AS and AD, i.e. at the price level p_0, when the level of national income, or output, is, of course, q_0. At no other price level, or level of national income would aggregate supply and demand be balanced. For example, if the price level was higher than the equilibrium level, say at p_1, then businesses would be willing to supply q_1 output, while only q_2 would be demanded.

We cannot describe the way in which economic forces operate to bring about equilibrium if aggregate supply and demand are not in balance. The process is too complicated for this book. We can, however, show how inflation may be set in motion, i.e. we can show how the general level of prices can be forced upwards.

The causes of inflation

Inflation, defined as an increase in the general price level, can be caused by forces coming from either supply or demand sides. The former is known as **cost push** inflation; the latter as **demand pull**.

Cost push inflation results from a shift in the aggregate supply curve. As explained earlier, the AS curve shows the quantity of goods and services that businesses offer for sale at different price levels. But, other things can cause businesses to alter their outputs than changes in the general level of prices. In particular, if costs of production rise, businesses will be likely to reduce the quantities of commodities they offer for sale at the existing, and at every other,

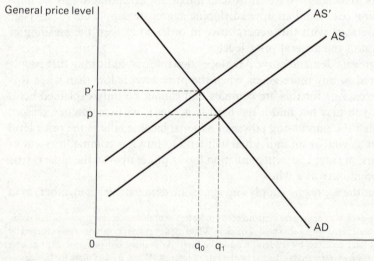

Fig 2.4 Cost push inflation

price level. This would cause the aggregate supply curve to shift to the left, i.e. from AS to AS′ as in Fig 2.4, with the effect that the price level rises towards p'.

Demand pull inflation results from a shift in the aggregate demand curve. Again, as previously explained, the AD curve shows the quantity of goods and services that the community wants to buy at different price levels. But different factors can cause aggregate demand to change other than changes in the general level of prices. For example, businesses may decide that they wish to spend more on investment in capital goods (perhaps because they have greater confidence in the prospects of future profits); or consumers may decide to spend a larger proportion of their income (perhaps because there has been a redistribution of income towards the poorer groups in the population who spend more).

If there is an increase either in investment or in consumption expenditure, then aggregate demand increases at the existing, and at every other, price level. This would cause the aggregate demand curve to shift to the right, i.e. from AD to AD′, in Fig 2.5, with the effect that the price level rises towards p'.

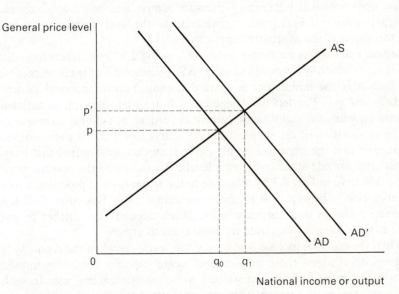

Fig 2.5 Demand pull inflation

Stagflation

It is important to notice that the two distinctive causes of inflation, termed cost-push and demand-pull, may have different effects on the level of total output. As can be seen by comparing Figs 2.4 and 2.5, although the price level is forced upwards in both cases, the leftward shift in the AS curve, in Fig 2.4, is accompanied by a *lowering* of national income, while the rightward shift of the AD curve in Fig 2.5, causes a *raising* of national income.

When inflation resulting from cost push (and a shift of the aggregate supply curve to the left), is accompanied by falling output and rising prices, it is called **stagflation**. This phenomenon has characterised much of the period since 1974. In that year, the price of oil rose fourfold following the action by the so-called OPEC group of oil exporters. Inflation shot up to 25 per cent in Britain in the following year, and remained at the double digit level (i.e. 10 per cent or more) for the rest of the decade, while the unemployment rate also rose dramatically from 2.6 per cent in 1974 to 6.4 per cent in 1980.

Demand-pull inflation

As previously explained, demand-pull inflation, caused by an increase in aggregate demand, should be contrasted with cost-push inflation, caused by a fall in aggregate supply. When aggregate demand rises, however, it does not follow that sustained inflationary pressure always and necessarily ensues. Whether or not it does depends on two factors—the level of national output, and the shape of the aggregate supply curve.

Consider the aggregate supply curve AS″, in Fig 2.6. This differs from AS in Fig. 2.3, which was upward sloping. AS″ is composed of three segments, of which only the middle one is upward sloping (between national income levels q_0 and q_1). The left hand segment is horizontal (flat), up to national income q_0; while the right hand segment is vertical, at national income q_1.

The explanation of the shape of the AS″ curve in Fig 2.6 is quite simple. Remember that the aggregate supply curve shows the total output that businesses offer for sale at different price levels. We explained the upward slope of the AS curve in Fig. 2.3 by reference to the rising costs of production that might normally be expected to obtain as output rises. But costs need not necessarily rise in such circumstances. Much depends on whether or not there is spare capacity available for businesses to expand.

When the national income is at a very low level—as when the economy is in deep depression—there is plenty of spare capacity available: unused factories, plant and equipment waiting to be taken back into use. In such circumstances, output may be increased without any rise in costs. Hence the aggregate supply curve need not slope upwards but may be horizontal, as the left hand segment of AS″ in Fig 2.6 up to the level of national output q_0.

Beyond output q_0, the economy is approaching full employment of its resources. Spare capacity still exists in some sectors, but bottlenecks start to appear and, in consequence, costs of production tend to rise. These conditions produce the upward sloping segment of AS″, between national income levels q_0 and q_1, because rising costs require rising prices for output to be increased.

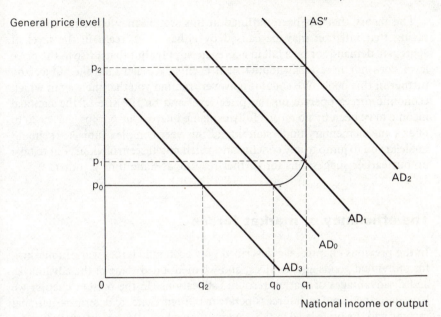

General price level

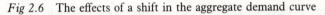

Fig 2.6   The effects of a shift in the aggregate demand curve

Eventually, output reaches its maximum potential level, at q_1. All resources are fully employed and no increase in production is possible. Even a rise in the price level cannot cause national output to rise, hence the AS″ curve becomes vertical.

Consider, now, the effects of a rise in the level of aggregate demand, which shifts the AD curve to the right. They will differ in the three different sets of circumstances represented by the three segments of AS″. Let us start with the already familiar middle section, where AS is upward sloping, and suppose that the aggregate demand curve shifts from AD_0 to AD_1. The results, as we pointed out earlier, will be that *some* inflation ensues, as the price level is pushed up from p_0 to p_1, but there is also *some* increase in output, which rises from q_0 to q_1.

The second case to be considered, is where the AS curve is vertical: at national income level q_1. If there is an increase in aggregate demand now, no increase in output is possible. The economy is at its maximum potential output, and the only effect must, therefore, be on the price level. Thus, in Fig 2.6, if the AD curve shifts from AD_1 to AD_2, the price level rises, from p_1 to p_2, causing considerably more inflation than in the previous case, and there is no change in the national output.

The third case to take account of, is where the AS curve is horizontal—below national income level q_2. The economy has plenty of spare capacity at such output levels, so that a shift of the AD curve from AD_3 to AD_0 causes a rise in the level of output, and no inflation.

The theory that has been outlined in this section may be summarised by saying that inflation may be caused by either an increase in the level of aggregate demand, or by a fall in aggregate supply, but that a rise in the price level does not necessarily follow such events. We can take the subject no further in this book. We should, however, remind you that the way in which economic forces operate on the price level and on the size of the national income have been by no means fully explained here. Our purpose has been to offer some elementary understanding of this very complex subject. It should not lead you to jump to any conclusions which might seem obvious, but to take up our earlier suggestions for further reading at some time or other.

The efficiency of market forces

In the previous chapter, we described how economic forces work in markets for individual goods and services, and we mentioned some of the advantages and disadvantages of market resource allocations. In the present chapter we have described how such forces operate in the aggregate, to determine national income and the price level in the economy as a whole. We would, therefore, be consistent if we were to offer some further comments on the efficiency of the market system and the case for state intervention. Unfortunately, it is harder to do so in this chapter than in the last. This is partly because of the complexity of the way in which market forces work on the economy as a whole, and partly because there is controversy among economists as to how far they may be made to work more efficiently by government actions.

The crucial question to be asked is whether a freely functioning market system can bring about satisfactory levels of national income and prices. Such levels would be those which ensured full employment of factors of production and stable prices. The evidence from the world about us is that inflation has been accompanied by high levels of unemployment, for many of the most recent years. Moreover, the theory we outlined suggests that the equilibrium price and output level towards which an economy tends need not necessarily be where there is full employment and price stability.

Stabilisation policy

The conclusion to be drawn from theory and evidence is, therefore, that a fair case exists for state intervention to prod the economy in the right directions. Stabilisation policy is the name given to government actions designed to do just this. There are several instruments of stabilisation policy, targeted at full employment, growth of national output and the avoidance of inflation. Some have been hinted at in the foregoing pages—e.g. the control of taxation and government expenditure, so that the level of aggregate expenditure of all kinds is neither too high nor too low. Such acts are collectively known as **fiscal policy**, which may be either expansionary when aggregate expenditure is increased, or contractionary, when it is reduced. There are two other major policy instruments: **monetary policy** and **prices** and **incomes policies.** The former aims to influence expenditure through changing the rate of interest which, in turn, can affect investment expenditure by businesses, in particular. Prices and income policies set out to control the level of inflation by limiting price and income increases by mutual agreement (though they can, in principle, be made legally enforceable, too).

Stabilisation policies have been adopted by most countries in the western world for at least half a century. Their record was one of considerable success in the early years, especially in the 1930s, when unemployment was high and there was virtually no inflation problem. More recently, the record has been less successful—witness the appearance since the early 1970s, of the new phenomenon of stagflation. One of the reasons for this recent poor record is to be found in the realisation that the twin aims of full employment and price stability are independent, and may even be conflicting. For example, it is one thing to raise the level of national output and employment by government expansionary fiscal policy when national income is at a very low level (e.g. at q_2 in Fig 2.6), and quite another to try the same policy nearer full employment (e.g. at q_0 in Fig 2.6). In the former case, output can be expanded without any inflationary effects, but not in the latter.

Clearly, we cannot engage in a lengthy discussion of the problems of stabilisation policy in the modern world. That is a large and complex subject. Moreover, it is a controversial one. Economists are not all agreed on the best policy instruments to employ, nor how precisely to employ them. We can only warn you that it can be no easy task to achieve full employment and price stability at the same time. Later in your studies of economics, you will be better placed to learn about the alternative ways to try and achieve them.

Our brief excursion, in this and the preceding chapter, into the theories behind the ways in which the price mechanism allocates resources, and behind the operation of market forces in the economy as a whole, as made in order to give you some notions about why the pattern and level of economic activity in Britain happens to be that which is described in the rest of this book.

The order of treatment adopted is not the only possible one. It seems to suit the material satisfactorily enough, and is best followed by the reader, since some chapters assume background knowledge acquired earlier.

3 Population

The economic world in which we live is more than a little influenced by the number of people who are in it. The more people there are, the more mouths there are to feed, but at the same time the more hands there are to do work. It is sensible, therefore, to commence our survey of the economic life of Britain by taking stock of its population. We are fortunate in that every 10 years since 1801 (with the exception of 1941 when the war prevented it) the population has been counted in a full national census, the last being taken in 1981. The census is carried out by distributing to every dwelling in Britain a form containing a number of questions addressed to the head of the household. These questions have varied considerably in the past, but today include details of the age, sex, marital status, education and occupation of the individuals who are living there. The amassing and arranging of all this material, of course, takes a long time, and it is usually several years before all the information is published in a number of large volumes. Population details, therefore, are often a little out of date, but the speed at which any changes take place is normally so slow that this does not matter greatly. The information available, however, is very valuable. It helps to ascertain not only how many men and women there are in the country, but also how many there are of different ages, where they live and how they earn their living.

Growth

In 1801 when the first census was taken the total population of Britain was roughly 12 million. Thereafter it grew at an astonishing rate. As Fig 3.1 shows, it had doubled itself in 60 years, and by 1861 there were over 24 million people. It had more than doubled itself again by 1951, when the population was over 50 million. It had mounted still further 20 years later to about 56 million, at which figure it has, at least temporarily, more or less stabilised.

It may seem puzzling at first that the number of people living in Britain should have multiplied so slowly as to reach only 10 million after many thousands of years, and yet should have risen to over 50 million in a mere century and a half. A moment's reflection, however, reveals one simple reason —the more people there are the easier it is for the population to increase by a large amount. When there was only a small number of people a doubling of

38

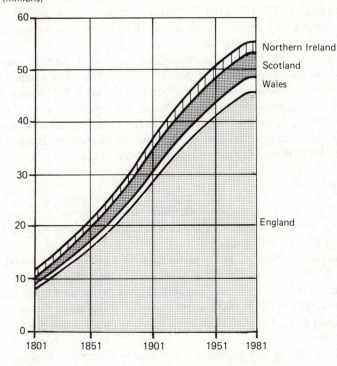

Population
(millions)

them made only a small number more, while a doubling of 10 million, as we have seen, raised the population by 10 million.

Whilst this piece of elementary mathematics helps to account for the population increases in the 19th and 20th centuries, it is not a sufficient explanation. A population of 10 000 which doubles itself every second generation will reach 10 million in 5–600 years, whereas we know that it took very much longer to reach this figure. Clearly we must seek some further reason which will explain why the population did not double itself in such a short period, and at the same time why the rate of increase was stepped up so rapidly about 200 years ago.

One key to the problem is found in the decrease in the **death rate** (that is, the number of people who die each year per 1000 of the population)—particularly the infant mortality rate. This decrease accompanied the great advances in industrial and agricultural techniques beginning about the middle of the 18th century. Before then approximately 7 out of every 10 children died before reaching the age of 5, while today only one baby in 100 fails to live through those crucial years. Now, migration apart, the population will increase in any year if the number of births exceeds the number of deaths. The fall in the infant mortality rate, of course, meant more than simply an immediate rise in numbers; as more babies survived, so more of them grew up to have children of their own. The population in consequence continued to rise, and the rate of increase was stepped up. The fall in the death rate is probably traceable first to more food and better living conditions, reinforced later by medical advances, new hospitals and improved sanitation.

It is also thought by some scholars that the earliest population increases were due more to a rise in births than to a decline in mortality. The available evidence is not strong enough to settle the controversy entirely, though it seems certain that birth rates did start rising in the 18th century as a result of social changes such as a fall in the marriage age. In any event, the increase was responsible for the concern expressed by Malthus in his famous *Essay on Population* in 1798, that the population might become too large.

The sex ratio

Statistics of the size of the total population are very useful, but for many purposes they are insufficient, and we need also to know something about the relative numbers of men and women.

Taking Britain as a whole we are confronted with a considerable female predominance; there are about $1\frac{1}{2}$ million more women than men, so that the former outnumber the latter by about 5 per cent. This is not the case for all age groups, however, and it is all the more surprising when it is realised that more boys are born than girls. For almost all ages, however, male death rates are higher than female.

Why women are able to survive better is not easy to determine. Biological factors are clearly of major importance and seem to make women less susceptible to many fatal diseases. There are probably also social and economic reasons. The most obvious case of men fighting wars and getting killed for their womenfolk was doubtless important in earlier times, although it is hardly very applicable today. Some remaining part of the explanation may lie in the nature of the work done by some men, exposing them to greater danger and stress than women. In any event these factors combine to ensure that the male predominance in early life is reversed. Women begin to outnumber men around 50, but the difference only becomes substantial after the age of 70, when for every 100 men there are over 170 women (*see* Fig 3.2).

Marriage

Another matter affecting population size is marriage. The earlier men and women get married and the more of them that do so, the greater the probable number of babies that will be born. In Britain as a whole, roughly 40 per cent of the population is single, although most of the unmarried people are children and many of the rest have been widowed or divorced. The majority of marriages, in fact, take place between people in their 20s, although it is perhaps remarkable that over a quarter of all brides get married before their 21st birthday. A great many people also marry later, of course, and the proportion

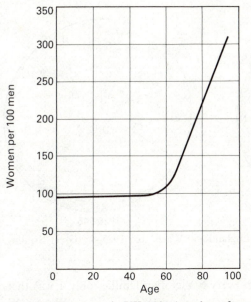

Fig 3.2 The sex ratio UK 1981 (number of women per 100 men)

of married couples in the total population rises with age; in the 35–44 age group nearly 9 people in every 10 are married. These facts remain true today, despite the five-fold rise in the divorce rate over the past twenty years. (In England and Wales, the rate rose from 2.4 per thousand of the married population in 1962, to 12.2 per thousand in 1983.) One marriage is dissolved for every $2\frac{1}{2}$ new marriages in Britain at the present time, though, of course, many divorcees remarry.

Family size

Consideration of the frequency and age at marriage, leads conveniently to a most important feature of the population—the average size of the family. We cannot assume that children will adopt the same traditions of family size as those followed by their fathers and mothers. In fact, one of the most important changes in the structure of the population between the 19th and 20th centuries was in the size of the average family.

A family census was taken shortly after the end of the Second World War. It examined the size of families of couples who married in 1925, assuming that after 20 years of married life they would have no more children. Fig 3.3 compares these figures with those for couples who married over a century ago in the 1860s and 70s, in the middle of the Victorian era of large families. The contrast is startling. Whereas every fourth Victorian family had at least 9 children, only 1 in every 40 in the generation of families of 1925–45 was as large as that. Moreover, while 2 out of every 3 of the latter group of families

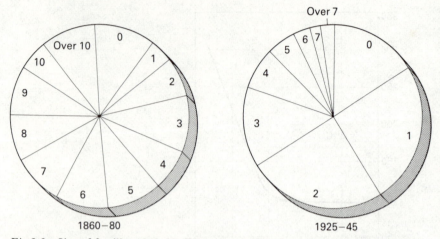

Fig 3.3 Size of families 1860–80 (England and Wales) and 1925–45 (Great Britain) (number of children per family)

had no more than 2 children, in every 5 Victorian families only 1 was that small.

The reasons for this tremendous fall in the size of families are extremely interesting, even if they are not all understood. They are clearly associated with increasing knowledge and use of contraceptive techniques, themselves reflecting other changes—the growth of the middle classes who tend to have fewer children, the emancipation of women, and changing attitudes towards family life and parental responsibility.

These arguments should not be carried too far. The period since 1945 has had a different history. Immediately after the war there was a natural increase in the number of births, as servicemen returned to raise families deferred during the war. The birth rate—defined as the number of babies born per 1000 of the population—then declined once more. It picked up again in the 1960s but dropped sharply in the following decade to a figure of less than 12 per 1000 of the population compared with 18 in the 1960s (and 28 around the turn of the century). In 1978 the decline in the birth rate was apparently arrested, but it will be some years before one can confirm that there is a real new trend. A relatively new feature is that the illegitimacy rate has risen steadily over the period since World War II. During the first half of the present century, 5 per cent or less of births were illegitimate; in 1983 the figure was 15 per cent.

It is worthwhile pausing at this point to add a word to distinguish families, with which we have been concerned, from households. Households are the units in which people live and which therefore include all persons living together, such as grandparents and friends. There are about 18 million private households in Britain. During the century, their number has risen more rapidly than the population itself, as a result of the decline in family size and other social forces. Changes in the number of households are of great relevance when certain economic matters, such as the availability of dwellings, are under consideration.

Age structure and population trends

We have examined, in this chapter, both historical and recent trends in the size of the population. What can be said about the future? At this point it has to be admitted that long-distance forecasting of population trends is not an entirely reliable business, and past predictions have often turned out to be wrong. The first time a decline in the population seemed to be reasonably close at hand was in the 1930s. This prompted the government to appoint a Royal Commission in 1944 to report on the situation. By the mid 1950s estimates of the future UK population had put the prospect of any decline beyond 1980. By the early 1960s forecasts of the population in the year 2001 were put at over 70 million, but the most recent projections are for a much slighter increase, to about 58 million.

Despite past variations in official and other forecasts, which only emphasise the complexity of the process, it is useful to look a little more closely at the three main factors on which the size of the population depends. They are the birth rate, the death rate and the balance of migration movements. We shall consider them in reverse order.

Migration

Emigration and immigration naturally have an affect on the size of the population. Throughout the 19th century migration was an important factor restraining the growth of Britain's population; the range of opportunities, particularly in America, ensured that emigrants greatly outnumbered immigrants. Towards the end of the century immigration into Britain had also assumed sizable proportions, but in the 60 years after 1871 there was a *net* loss from migration of the order of 4 million. In the 1920s most foreign countries put up barriers to immigrants and the balance of movements between the censuses of 1931 and 1961 was reversed, to become one of a net gain of some half a million people. This figure, however, conceals the fact that, after the Second World War, Britain reassumed her traditional role as a country of emigration, chiefly to the Commonwealth (especially Australia and Canada), and that this movement was offset in the late 1950s by increasing numbers of immigrants, again mainly from the Commonwealth (especially the West Indies, India and Pakistan). Net immigration around 1960 approached 150 000 per annum. This prompted the government to pass the Commonwealth Immigration Acts, the first of which came in 1962, and which gave it power to restrict immigration from the Commonwealth. A sharp fall in the number of immigrants followed, and in the 15 years since 1969 Britain experienced a net loss of over half a million people, some of whom were returning to their native lands.

The death rate

The fall in the death rate, particularly the infant mortality rate, has already been referred to as being partly responsible for the earlier great increase in population. In the present century, war years apart, death rates have continued to decline for all age groups as a result of medical advances and higher living standards, including better nutrition. Death rates have been less than 1 per cent for all age groups under 55 for over a quarter of a century, so that any further substantial influence on total population size from this direction might be expected to come from improvements for the higher age groups. The current situation may be summarised by the fact that a baby born today could expect to live to be almost 70 if he is a boy, or over 76 if she is a girl. By comparison, average life expectancies at the beginning of the century were 49 and 52 respectively.

The birth rate

The third determinant of population changes after migration and the death rate is the birth rate. About 85 per cent of the total number of births nowadays are legitimate, so the number of babies born depends principally on 3 factors: the number of women of child-bearing age in the population, the proportion of them that marry and the number of children each of them has.

The number of women of child-bearing age is fairly easy to predict for periods of up to 15 to 20 years, since it is largely determined by the number of girls under that age alive at the time. We can see that during the period of rapid population expansion in Victorian times the rise in the birth rate itself produced increasing numbers of potential mothers of the future. When the birth rate started to fall off the effect was the reverse, after a time lag, with a continuing decline in the numbers of women in the fertile age groups. Compare the age structure of the female population in 1871 and 1981 in Fig 3.4.

If we want to forecast population changes we must, of course, also incorporate predictions about family size into the calculations. These predictions are particularly difficult to make because there can be more than one interpretation of a change in the birth rate in any one year. A fall in the birth rate, for example, can mean a decline in family size, but it can also merely reflect a change in habits relating to the time in their married lives when couples want to raise families. When it is remembered that decisions about how many children to have, and when to have them, depend on a whole range of economic and social circumstances, it is not surprising that population projections are not always as accurate as one might like them to be.

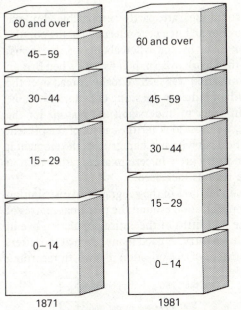

1871   1981

Fig 3.4 Age distribution of female population in Great Britain 1871 and 1981

Before leaving the subject of the age structure of the population, we may observe that while rising birth rates tend to increase the proportion of the population in lower age groups, falling death rates tend to raise the proportion of older people. Referring again to Fig 3.4 the contrast between 1871 and 1981 can be seen. At the earlier date only 1 woman in 12 was 60 years old or over, while in 1981 there were over twice as many in that age group. This kind of consideration is most relevant to several important economic questions, such as providing pensions to people on retirement.

Geographical distribution of the population

The population of Britain is by no means evenly spread over the whole country. Turning back to Fig 3.1 it is clear that England, Wales, Scotland and Northern Ireland have very unequal shares of the total population. If the population of each of these countries is related to its size, however, the inequality is even greater, since England has over four fifths of the people and only just over half the land, whilst Scotland has a third of the land, but only about a tenth of the people. Wales has a tenth of the land but only a twentieth of the people and Northern Ireland has a twentieth of the land but a mere 3 per cent of the population. We can express these facts in another way by saying that in England there are about 900 people per square mile, in Wales about 350, in Northern Ireland less than 300 and in Scotland only about 175.

The reasons for these very unequal densities of population are to be found in history. Differences in climatic conditions are partly responsible, but the overwhelming causes are economic. For all but a very select few of the population, where to live is decided for them by the whereabouts of the farms, factories, shops or offices at which they work to earn their living. When Britain was an agricultural country the population was fairly equally spread over the good farming land. With the growth of industry the siting of factories became the predominant influence, and in order to understand the reasons for the present distribution of population, we must look for the causes of the present distribution of industry. This will be dealt with in Chapter 5. At the moment it is sufficient to recognise that, as industry grew in certain areas rather than in others, so the population of those regions increased.

The map (Fig 3.5) reveals the main features of the geographical distribution of the population and shows the concentration around the principal centres of city life. At present something like four fifths of the entire population live in urban areas, and only one fifth in the country. A good many, even of the latter, work in towns. To emphasise the extent of urbanisation it is worth recording

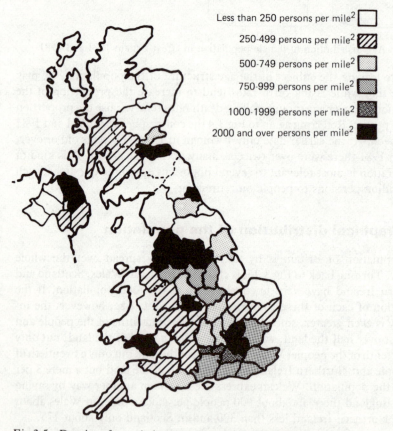

Less than 250 persons per mile²

250-499 persons per mile²

500-749 persons per mile²

750-999 persons per mile²

1000-1999 persons per mile²

2000 and over persons per mile²

Fig 3.5 Density of population per square mile Great Britain 1981

that in 1984 there were nearly 20 cities in Britain with more than a quarter of a million inhabitants.

Counting city dwellers, however, hides one important fact. Since the 1920s many of the largest cities extended suburbs outwards so as to cover areas considerably larger than the actual city limits. In many of them one can go for 20 or 30 miles in the same direction without leaving the built-up area, and with no more sight of the country than an occasional park. These sprawling 20th century urban tracts are known as conurbations. The census distinguishes six of them in England (around Manchester, Birmingham, Leeds, Liverpool, Newcastle and London) and one, Clydeside, in Scotland. Together they occupy about 3 per cent of the land space in the country, yet they house a third of our people. Even more significant, perhaps, is that every seventh Englishman lives in Greater London, every third Scot in the Clydeside area around Glasgow, while a quarter of the inhabitants of Northern Ireland live in Belfast. The Welsh also congregate in the South East of the country and half of them live in the counties of Mid, South and West Glamorgan.

The background to this picture of an essentially urban society that modern Britain presents today is, of course, one of a prolonged rural exodus from the English villages, Scottish Highlands and Welsh hills into cities in the Midlands, the London region, the Clyde Valley in Scotland, and elsewhere. As rural depopulation has continued the countryside has largely dried up and the towns have grown mainly by natural increase. Furthermore, behind the general trend there have also been important shifts in population between different urban areas themselves. In the main, such movements have been relative rather than absolute. This means that, since the total population has been expanding, there have not been many periods when major regions have suffered absolute declines in numbers, although the years between the two world wars were exceptional in this respect in the case of Wales, Northumberland and Durham.

Fig 3.6 brings out the main changes in regional distribution of population which have taken place since 1911. It shows that the greatest increase in population occurred in the Midlands, South West, East Anglia and South East England, while Scotland, Wales, Northern and North West England experienced *relative* declines. These changes are the result of internal migration of workers and their families attracted by employment opportunities in the areas involved, and natural increases of the populations themselves.

One feature of recent trends, not observable from the chart, is that there has been a tendency in recent years for people to live in outlying suburbs rather than in the centres of large cities, which have suffered something of a decline. The population of Greater London, for example, fell from 8 to 7 million in the 20 years up to 1980. After the Second World War it was the medium-sized towns and the districts surrounding large cities that tended to grow most rapidly. These trends were both helped and hindered by a so-called 'green belt' policy restricting urban spread.

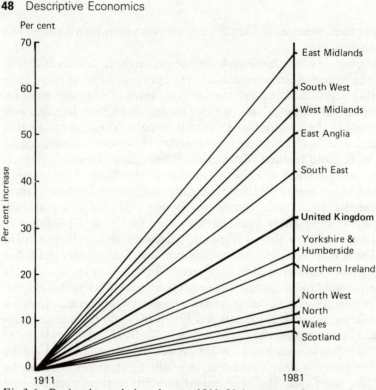

Per cent

Per cent increase

70 — East Midlands

60 — South West

West Midlands

50 — East Anglia

40 — South East

30 — **United Kingdom**

Yorkshire & Humberside

Northern Ireland

20 — North West

North

10 — Wales

Scotland

0 —

1911   1981

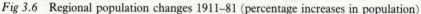

Fig 3.6   Regional population changes 1911–81 (percentage increases in population)

In an attempt to encourage some dispersal from the centres of heaviest concentration and in an atmosphere coloured by projections of continued substantial increases in population, the government in 1946 embarked on a policy of the creation of new towns. These were designed to be new independent communities, catering for industry as well as residential accommodation. By 1980 there were over 30 new towns in the country. The policy has become rather less urgent recently with revised downward population forecasts (*see* page 43) and the appearance of decaying inner city areas.

The working population

We have investigated the size and geographical distribution of the population. One last important question remains. In what ways do the people earn their living? Before answering, a distinction must be drawn between those who are 'working' in the sense of being employed; working for themselves or employing others; and the rest of the community. The size of this labour force is clearly of the greatest importance for the production of goods and services which everyone wants. Ideally, it might seem best if there was no one who did not contribute to the common pool by working, and the occupied population thus included every person in the country. This is far from being the case; only something like half of the total community can be regarded as being available for work in the ordinary sense of the term.

How then do the remainder spend their time? Fig 3.7 helps to provide the answer. First, about half are busy growing up; the school-leaving age ensures that the 13 million boys and girls under 16 shall not undertake full-time work and they must therefore be excluded from the labour force. At the other end of the scale there is a similar, though smaller, group of women over 60 and men over 65 (the ages of entitlement to retirement pensions). The remainder consists mainly of housewives and others who are busy keeping homes going. Most of these are not counted as part of the working population, not because they do not work, but because they are not paid a wage for doing so. True, they may be given a housekeeping allowance by their spouses, but by no stretch of the imagination can they be thought of as being employed by them! Keeping house is an essential job, of course, and is often a full-time one, especially when there are young children in the family. However, a substantial increase in the number of married women in the labour force has taken place during the second half of the present century. In the generation after 1950, the proportion of married women going out to work approximately doubled, from 22 to 50 per cent. These percentages are known as the **activity rate** (or the **participation rate**). Since 1980, because of a fall in the general level of economic activity, the participation rates have declined to about 75 per cent for men and 47 per cent for women.

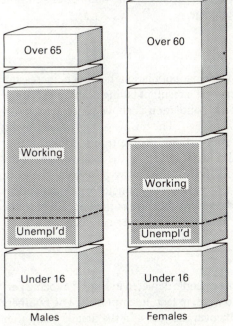

Fig 3.7 The working population UK 1983

The longer-term effect of rising female and falling male participation rates on the sex distribution of the labour force has been substantial. Whereas women comprised less than a third of the total working population in 1950, they made up about two-fifths in 1984. This is the long-term trend. Cyclically, however, the female participation rate fluctuates a good deal more than the male counterpart, rising and falling more with upturns and downturns in economic activity.

As far as the remainder of the non-working population are concerned, they are a mixed bunch, and numerically, not particularly important. Some of these men and women of working age are idle rich, or even merely idle, and a few thousand more are in prison. The majority fall into one of two groups: those who stay on at school or are engaged in full-time education at universities or other institutions of further education, and those who are crippled or chronically sick.

The working population of Britain, then, on whom the young and the old depend, comprises some 27 million persons. Nearly three fifths of them are men, and they are almost all between 16 and 65 years old. Over 90 per cent are employees, the remainder being employers and the self-employed.

Two important observations remain to be made. The first concerns the relative size of the working and dependent populations. This changes, of course, with changes in birth and death rates, which determine the number of young and old in the population, although some effects take years to materialise. For example, a rise in the birth rate pushes up the number of youthful dependents, until they reach working age.

Dependent population

The ratio of dependents to the working population has been increasing throughout the present century, largely as a result of falling death rates. At the present time about 17 per cent of the population is above retirement age— roughly double the proportion 100 years ago. The raising of the school leaving age in 1972 and the tendency for more young people to undertake further education after the age of 16, has also had its effect on the relative sizes of the dependent and working populations. Against this, as we have seen, the birth rate fell during the 1970s reducing the young component of the dependent population. The expectation nowadays is for the ratio of the dependent to the working population to rise a little as we approach the year 2025.

Unemployment

The second observation concerns those people depicted in Fig 3.7 as being part of the 'working' population but who were, in fact, unemployed. The numbers out of work have varied substantially over the years. In the first 25 years after the end of the Second World War something between a quarter and half a million men and women were jobless, representing about $1\frac{1}{2}$ to $2\frac{1}{2}$ per cent of the labour force. In the 1970s the numbers unemployed started to creep up and by mid 1985 were well in excess of 3 million—about $13\frac{1}{2}$ per cent of the work force. Before the war, however, unemployment was even higher, and at one stage in 1932 reached a figure of about 20 per cent of the entire working population. The proportions in some industries and certain districts were even greater.

Most of the higher levels of unemployment are involuntary in the sense that there are more men and women in the economy seeking jobs at current rates of pay than there are vacancies for them to fill. No one knows what will happen to unemployment rates in the future. Some current estimates are for continued rises before they eventually come down. No sensible consideration of the size of the working population can ignore the numbers out of work. We shall return to consider the subject of unemployment in Chapter 6.

Problems of classification

To find out how many people are employed in different jobs is a considerable problem. If we were to count all the engine drivers, bricklayers, mechanics, clerks, dress designers, lawyers, coppersmiths, plumbers, market gardeners, computer programmers and all the thousands of other specialists, we should soon fill this book. In fact, the census report itself includes such a book, and it makes very dull reading. What we need is some method of grouping occupations into a small number of categories which are easy to handle, and which bring out the most important details.

There are two principal methods of classification:

Occupational grouping which is grouping according to the type of job which individuals perform
Industrial grouping which is grouping according to the industry in which individuals work

Each of these classifications has its uses, and the one adopted can affect the classification of some workers. For example, a bus driver would be both occupationally and industrially grouped as a driver in the transport industry, but a lorry driver employed by a firm of chemical manufacturers would only be classified occupationally as a driver; under an industrial grouping he would be placed in the chemical industry.

Occupational grouping

Let us start by examining the occupational grouping since that is probably the category which is most important to the individual. Fig 3.8 distinguishes the principal types of occupations.

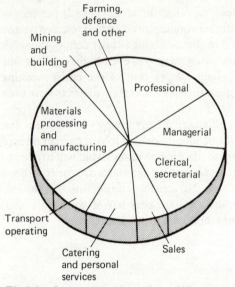

Fig 3.8 Occupational grouping of the working population Great Britain 1981

Napoleon once called the English a nation of shopkeepers. Today, only about one person in twenty in the working population is involved directly in the business of selling. The largest groups work in materials processing and manufacturing, mainly in factories.

However, the most rapidly growing occupational group in recent years, has been that of professional workers. In the single decade between the censuses of population of 1971 and 1981 the numbers of professional workers rose by more than 20 per cent, while those in materials processing and manufacturing fell by about 20 per cent. This was the result of technological advance and the replacement of men and women by machines, as well as of the decline of manufacturing industry itself, known as deindustrialisation (*see* page 53).

Other major groups worthy of mention are managers, who increased in numbers by more than 10 per cent over the same intercensal period, and now account for about 1 in 10 of the working population; clerks and secretaries, who maintained their position at around 15 per cent of the total; catering and personal service workers, and transport operators. The remainder, including farming, mining, building workers and the armed forces, are all relatively small, accounting together for fewer than 10 per cent of the working population.

Industrial grouping

The grouping of workers by the industry in which they are employed rather than by the jobs they do is shown for the main industries in Fig 3.9. The new classification emphasises the importance of the manufacturing industry, which accounts for the employment of about a quarter of the working population. However, it must be pointed out that the relative importance of manufacturing as an employer of labour has been declining for the last twenty years, while the share of service and other sectors has been growing. This trend of so-called 'de-industrialisation' has not been confined to the UK, but has been experienced to varying extents in several other industrialised countries, including the United States. The causes of this trend are not fully understood, but it is certainly partly a result of the rapid advance of technology in manufacturing. Whether it is a natural stage in economic development or a matter of grave concern remains controversial.

The relative importance of the non-manufacturing sectors is shown in Fig 3.9. Finance and the professions employ about 5 million people, about a

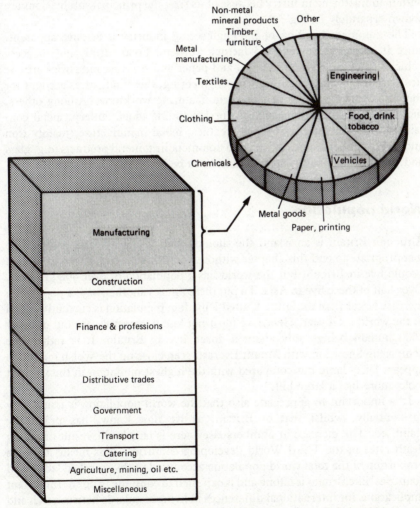

Fig 3.9 Industrial grouping of the working population Great Britain 1984

quarter of the total. About 1 person in 6 works in distribution and 1 in 12 in government. This last figure relates only to those directly employed by central and local government. It excludes others who work for the state, for example in schools, nationalised industries and the health service. The relative importance of the state in the economy as a whole is a different matter which is discussed in Chapter 9.

A disadvantage of the broad industrial grouping used for the main block in Fig 3.9 is that it fails to identify a number of medium-sized but clearly defined industries. It is important to know, for example, not only how many workers are employed in manufacturing generally, but also how many are in the engineering industry, the textile industry, and so on. This is particularly the case with manufacturing industry because of its size; the principal subdivisions are shown separately in Fig 3.9.

The dominant position of the engineering industry is at once apparent, since it employs 1 in every 4 factory workers. Food, drink and tobacco, vehicles (including shipbuilding), and paper and printing industries are the next largest groups. Together with engineering, these industries account for the employment of over half the manufacturing workforce. Among others, metal goods (a miscellaneous category including tools, cutlery, metal containers, etc), chemicals, clothing, textiles, metal manufacture (mainly iron and steel), timber and furniture, and non-metallic mineral products (e.g. glass and ceramics) are sufficiently important to be separately distinguished.

World population

Although Britain is an island she should avoid insularity, and it would be inappropriate to end this chapter without venturing abroad. Over 50 million people live in Britain, but the world has a population of over 4000 million. Over half of these live in Asia. To put these figures another way, a population increase larger than the entire United Kingdom population is currently added to the world each year. Hence we must not lose perspective, for out of every 1000 human beings only about a dozen live in Britain. It is rather like comparing Snowdon with Mount Everest; seen close up the Welsh mountain appears fairly large but compared with the highest mountain in the world it looks more like a large hill.

It is important to appreciate also that the world population is rising very substantially, whilst that of Britain, as we now know, has practically stabilised. The increase in numbers elsewhere is largely the result of falling death rates in the Third World developing countries. This means that the proportion of the total world population accounted for by so-called 'advanced countries' like Britain is falling and is expected to continue to do so. Important implications for international differences in living standards between rich and poor countries follow from this fact. They are discussed in Chapter 9.

Exercises

For key to symbols indicating sources *see* pages xi to xii.

1 Draw a chart showing the number of men and women in the total population of Britain in 1931 and at the last census. Has the ratio of men to women changed in these years? (*WA, AS, B, F*)

2 Find out how many children there were in your grandparents' family and in your parents' family and estimate how many you would like to have yourself. Assemble the information for the whole class, and calculate the average family size for all 3 generations.

3 On a rough skeleton map of Great Britain underline all towns with a population of over 200 000. What proportion of the total population lives in these cities? (*F, WA*, or the handbook of one of the national motoring organisations)

4 What is the population of your home town? What was it 20 years ago and 100 years ago? Has it increased more or less than the total population? Can you explain why?

5 Find the number of people engaged in manufacturing and the total in civil employment for the following years: 1937, 1965, 1985 and the latest year available. Express the former as percentages of the latter. (*KS, AS*)

6 Prepare a simple form to be used in a small population census for the households in which all the members of the class live. Request information concerning age, sex, occupation and industry in which employed, for each member of the household. Tabulate your results and, wherever possible, compare them with the national averages. (*AS, WA*)

7 Find out the number of women in the labour force in the most recent year available and express this number as a percentage of the total female population of working age. Make the same calculations for the previous year and compare your results. Has the trend in the female participation rate changed? (*AS, F*)

8 Prepare a chart similar to that of Fig 3.4 showing the age distribution of the population for the year 2025, as estimated by the Registrar General. How do the relative sizes of the working and dependent populations compare with those for 1981 and for the last year for which statistics are available? (*AS*)

9 Find out the total number of unemployed in the UK in a recent month and in the same month 2, 5 and 10 years ago. Express the figures as percentages of the total labour force and examine your results. How large is the difference between the highest and lowest percentage? (*EP, F, AS*)

4 Industrial organisation

The standard of living in a country depends to a large extent on the amount and variety of goods produced, and on the efficiency with which this production is carried on. We shall shortly examine the structure of British industry, looking especially at such details as the size of firms, the location of industry and the characteristics of a few of the most important industries.

In order to properly understand this structure we devote this chapter to examining the legal and institutional framework within which economic activity takes place. For there is little doubt that the character of production in Britain has been much influenced by the background of institutions which have grown up with it and, in particular, by the forms of business organisation. Briefly, we may distinguish two principal groups of business organisation:

Private enterprise by which is meant all business organisations which are owned and controlled by private individuals who take the responsibility for decisions

Public enterprise by which is meant all organisations within industry which are owned or controlled by the state, which endeavours to operate them in the general public interest.

Private enterprise

Privately owned businesses are usually known as firms and they generally try to make profits. Indeed, economists often assume that they try to make as large profits as possible—to maximise them. In industries where business is highly competitive this is probably not far from the truth, although the measurement of profits is not entirely straightforward and one cannot, therefore, be certain about it. However, in some cases firms may seek objectives other than profit maximisation, for example the growth of sales or the stability and security of the firm, even if this means some sacrifice of profits. Moreover, a firm may be content to make small profits, or even losses, in the short run if it can thereby increase its profits over a longer period.

There are four main forms of business organisation in Britain:

- one man businesses
- partnerships
- co-operatives
- joint stock companies

One man businesses

The oldest and simplest form of business organisation is the one man concern. The distinguishing feature of this type of enterprise is not that all the work is necessarily done by one man, though this may be the case, but that the business is owned by one individual. Such businesses are flexible in that the sole trader is independent and need consult no one before making decisions relating to the operation of the firm. However, the one man firm is no longer of great importance in British industry, although this form of organisation still flourishes in some sectors, such as farming and shopkeeping.

Partnerships

More common than the one man concern, though still of relative insignificance in the whole of industry, is the partnership. Whenever a sole operator feels that the burden of his business is too great, the alternative of going into partnership with one or more other people may be an attractive solution. Partners may have complementary contributions to make. For example, an inventor may go into partnership with an accountant. However, a major reason for seeking a business partner is often that the capital needed for operations is more than a single owner can provide. In such circumstances a partnership with others who contribute shares of the capital and take out proportionate shares of any profits may be a suitable form of business organisation. Each of the partners has the right to take a share in the running of the business and each, acting independently, may bind all his partners to abide by any agreements he has made with outside people. The risk of being in partnership with people who prove to be unreliable, unscrupulous or even merely inefficient is consequently great, since the partners are all legally liable for the debts of the partnership, even if they have been incurred by the activities of another partner.

There is no limit to this liability, which extends to the whole of a firm's debts, regardless of the amount of capital which the individual partners have originally contributed. Thus, for example, in a two man partnership where one partner supplies £20 000 of the original capital and the other only £1000, if the partnership incurs net debts to the extent of £5000 and the first partner becomes bankrupt and unable to meet any of the debt, the partner who put down only £1000 in the first place may have to meet the whole of the £5000, even if it means selling his house and any other property in order to do so. The great risk involved in this kind of enterprise has quite naturally led to its dwindling in importance in Britain.

Today, partnerships exist only in relatively small numbers, generally where 2 or 3 members of a family are in business together and mutual confidence is strong. The local butcher's shop, run by father and son, is typical of this compact family partnership arrangement. It is also common among members of certain professions, such as doctors, accountants and solictors.

Mention should also be made of one exception to the rule that all partners are liable to the full extent of the partnership debts. There are a few so-called limited partnerships, where any partners who do not take part in the running of the business are only liable to the extent of the capital they have put into it. Limited partnerships, however, are not a common form of business organisation in Britain, since the advantage of limited liability is available to a far more attractive institution—the joint stock company (*see* page 59).

Co-operatives

The third form of organisation, co-operatives, applies to businesses which are controlled either by their workers, or by the consumers of their products. The former, *producer* co-operatives, involve the sharing of profits among workers. These organisations were flourishing 100 or more years ago, but went into decline in the present century. In recent years they have enjoyed some revival, when workers have refused to accept management decisions to shut down businesses, and have taken them over and continued operations, e.g. in shipbuilding.

Consumer co-operatives operate mainly in the retail trade. The origins of consumer co-operation are found in the political movement associated with the name of Robert Owen. The first successful experiment was in Rochdale in 1844, co-operation in retailing expanding greatly after that. Today there are under 200 retail societies, although their number is gradually being reduced by amalgamations.

The distinctive feature of co-operative societies lies in their ownership. While other shops belong to individuals or are joint-stock companies, co-operatives are, in a sense, 'owned' by those of their customers who pay a minimum deposit on a share in the business. The co-operatives sell to the general public but part, at least, of the capital comes from members, most of whom contribute only small sums, and there is an upper limit on the amount of share capital which may be held by any individual. Many districts have their own local 'co-op'; the members elect a committee of management from among themselves who decide upon the general policy of the store and appoint a manager and full-time staff to do the work. The principle on which co-operative societies grew was one whereby goods were sold at normal retail prices. At the end of each half year the profits, in the form of a 'dividend' of so many pence per pound of purchases, were distributed to members in proportion to their purchases during the period.

Consumer co-operatives have suffered from intense competition from other types of organisation and, like producer co-operatives, have been on the decline during the present century. Many retail outlets have closed and small societies merged. Modernisation has taken place, with the help of the Co-operative Wholesale Society (CWS), owned by the retail societies. The CWS is a large manufacturer and importer and also operates its own banking and insurance business. Outside the single sector of retail milk distribution, however, the retail co-operatives have, so far failed to restore their former importance in retail trading.

Joint-stock companies

The fourth and last type of business organisation, the joint stock company, is so important that we shall discuss it at much greater length.

Public prejudice against the joint stock form of organisation in the 18th and 19th centuries was strongly influenced by the abuses of company promoters at the time of the South Sea Bubble, and it was not until 1855 that the great privilege of **limited liability** was made generally available. Limited liability arises from the fact that companies are regarded in law as entities separate from the individuals who own them. A company can enter into contracts, it can sue and be sued, it can own property, it can contract debts, and its obligations are not those of its owners. Companies have a continuity of life unaffected, therefore, by changes in ownership, and they have become the most important form of business enterprise in Britain.

Such companies must include the word 'Limited' (or 'Ltd') in their name so that outsiders may know that the liability to meet the debts of the company is limited for every individual owner of the business (known as a **shareholder**) to the extent of the amount of capital that he or she has contributed or promised to contribute. The advantages of this privilege are very substantial. Two, in particular, are of outstanding importance:

Large amounts of capital become much easier to raise This follows from the reduced risk to the individual investor, who knows from the outset the maximum amount of money he can lose, should the worst come to the worst. He will no longer be so afraid of venturing into business with other people whose names he may not even know. In fact, in many large companies there are thousands and even hundreds of thousands of shareholders, the vast majority of whom contribute only a minute proportion of the total capital of the business. Were it not for the privilege of limited liability it would be impossible to raise anything like so much money for one concern. The widow with a small inheritance and little business acumen, for instance, rarely dares to risk going into partnership with another person. She may, however, be quite prepared to acquire a small shareholding in one or more joint-stock companies without having to take any part in the management, secure in the knowledge that, even if the firm should go bankrupt, she would be liable only to the extent of her participation in the ownership of the capital.

Transfer of ownership can take place with a minimum of formality Since reduced risk calls for a less urgent need for each shareholder to know the others intimately, it is a matter of comparative indifference who actually owns the capital of the firm. It consequently becomes possible for any shareholder to sell his share in the business to anyone else. This gives the additional security, which is absent in a partnership, that if one needs cash in a hurry one can always sell out immediately. The great importance of this transferability of shares has given rise to the appearance of a specialised market place where shares in joint stock companies may be bought and sold. It is called the **Stock Exchange** (*see* pages 182–5).

The advantages which limited liability bestows on an individual company are, as we have seen, considerable. They are matched to some extent, however, by an increased risk to others, especially companies and individuals who do business with it and minority shareholders whose interests might be lost sight of in very large companies. There is also a risk that unscrupulous company promoters may fraudulently try to raise funds from the public for their own ends. In attempting to safeguard the community from these risks, the state has introduced a number of regulations concerning the management and publication of information about joint-stock companies in a succession of Companies Acts. The rules have changed over the years, and they also vary according to the type of company.

There are two principal types of company, **public** and **private**. The latter are not permitted to offer their shares for sale to the general public. For this reason private companies are not obliged to publish as much information about their affairs as are public companies, which, by EEC law, must describe themselves as public limited companies (plcs). They are greatly outnumbered by private companies but tend to be much larger.

There are over half a million companies in existence, but only about 3 per cent are public companies. On the other hand, the great majority of large businesses in Britain are organised as public companies. Some indication of the importance of giant companies is given by the fact that the 100 largest groups of joint stock companies in manufacturing produce over 40 per cent of total output. (*See* pages 103–14 for a discussion of business concentration.)

Public companies

The chief legal requirements for the formation of a company are:
1 The promoters of the company must draw up what might be called its 'constitution'. This takes the form of two documents which must be submitted to the Registrar of Companies for approval:

The Memorandum of Association which must set out the name of the proposed company, where the registered office will be situated, and the amount of authorised capital. It must also give some details of the objects of the company. This latter provision, originally intended to restrict the scope of the company's future activities, is now largely a nominal one, as present day Memoranda give such very broad and general limits to the objects of companies that they are rarely precluded from entering into any kind of business at all.

The Articles of Association relate to the internal constitution of the company. It gives such details as the rights of shareholders, the frequency of company meetings, the methods of appointing company officers, and so on.

When these two documents have been submitted and certain other relatively minor requirements have been met, the Registrar may issue a **Certificate of Incorporation** which grants the company the right of limited liability and, if it is a private company, authorises it to commence business.

2 If shares are to be offered for sale to the public, the company must also file with the Registrar of Companies a **Prospectus** giving all the financial details of the company, including its assets and liabilities and its expectations of earning power. If a public company can raise its capital without appealing to the public, a **Statement in lieu of Prospectus** is filed. In the case of a public company, the Registrar of Companies requires to be assured of the success of the issue of shares before he grants a trading certificate.

3 As soon as a company has complied with the two previous conditions it can commence business. After incorporation, the most important provision concerning public companies relates to the **publication of accounts**. At the end of each financial year every public company is under an obligation to publish, and to file with the Registrar of Companies, copies of certain of its accounts and related documents. These, taken together, give members of the public an idea of the financial operations of the company over the period. This provision is a vital one both for shareholders and prospective shareholders. It is also vital for other firms who may wish to do business, perhaps on a large scale, with the company in question; by virtue of the limitation of liability which the company enjoys they might not otherwise be prepared to take the risk.

Business accounts

The two main accounts which are prepared by companies are the balance sheet and the profit and loss account.

The balance sheet A business operates by virtue of the fact that it has various resources, or assets, at its disposal. The balance sheet consists of a statement of the value of these assets on a particular day when the account is drawn up, together with all the **liabilities**, or financial claims on these assets.

It is usual to distinguish between two kinds of assets. In the first place, there are **fixed assets** like land, buildings, machinery and equipment belonging to the company, which are essential to the operation of the business.

Secondly there are **current assets** which are, so to speak, the results of business operations, and which are frequently being changed into and out of cash. They include stocks of raw materials and finished products, debts due to the company from traders who have purchased its products, and cash itself. There is usually also a special kind of asset called 'goodwill', which is classed as a fixed asset. Whilst often difficult to value, **goodwill** is a financial estimate of the benefit deriving from a firm's reputation.

The liabilities of a business are financial claims on its assets. Since all the assets must be owned by someone total liabilities must equal total assets. Among liabilities a twofold classification is common; between liabilities to the owners of the business and to other creditors. The former are the shareholders, who will be considered shortly (*see* pages 64–6). The latter include for instance, unpaid raw material suppliers and other trade creditors as well as a bank which has loaned money to the company. The balance sheet of a hypothetical company is shown below.

The Arealcon Co Ltd

Balance sheet as at 31 December 19-0

Capital and liabilities	£	Assets	£
Issued capital		Fixed assets	
Ordinary shares	x	Land, buildings	x
Preference shares	x	Machinery, equipment	x
Loan from XYZ Bank Ltd	x	Goodwill	x
Current liabilities		Current assets	
Sundry creditors	x	Stocks of raw materials	x
		Stocks of finished products	x
		Current debtors	x
		Cash at bank	x
	x		x

A single balance sheet gives a picture of the financial state of a business at the time it is drawn up. To appreciate a company's prospects, however, it is necessary to compare a run of balance sheets over at least two years and to observe the progress that has occurred in the growth or depletion of its assets. Furthermore, a company's financial state may most usefully be studied with the help of the second important account of its activities—the profit and loss account.

The profit and loss account Whereas a balance sheet relates to the financial position of a company at a particular *point of time*, the profit and loss account is a record of a company's operations over a stated *period of time*, such as a year. As its name implies, it is a statement of the residual profit or loss achieved by a company in the period. It is derived by taking all the revenue earned by a firm and subtracting all costs incurred in earning it.

The extent of detail about costs shown in the published profit and loss account is naturally limited. Behind the summary figures given we may distinguish between manufacturing costs, selling costs (including advertising and distribution, etc.), the costs of administration, and financial costs (e.g. interest on bank loans). An example of a simple profit and loss account is given below. It is useful, especially from the viewpoint of managerial control of a business, to consider separately the **prime** or **variable costs** (sometimes called **direct costs**), which tend to vary directly, as production varies—and **overhead** or **fixed costs** (sometimes called **indirect costs**), which are not closely related to the volume of output. Examples of variable cost items are wages of operatives, raw materials used and fuel consumed. Overheads include managers' remuneration, office expenses, rent and the cost of research and development.

Profit and loss account for the year ending 31 December 19-0			
	£		£
Expenditure		*Income*	
Manufacturing costs (prime and overhead)	x	Revenue from sales	x
Selling costs (distribution, etc.)	x		
Administrative costs (salaries, office, etc.)	x		
Financial costs (interest)	x		
Depreciation	x		
Taxation	x		
Net profit after tax for year	x		
	x		x

An important and special kind of deduction from the *gross* profit of a business is usually made to allow for the **depreciation** of its assets, which are subject to physical wear and tear and may also become obsolete. Depreciation allowances are provided for in the account and must be subtracted from the revenue to arrive at the total *net* profit. It is sometimes convenient to think of these depreciation provisions as building up sums which could replace assets at the end of their lives. This does not imply, of course, that all assets either will or should be replaced. In periods of generally rising prices, and in the face of uncertainty about the eventual life of an asset, it should not be expected that exactly appropriate sums are always provided. Depreciation allowances are only estimates and there are a number of alternative conventional formulae for allocating depreciation. A final deduction must then be made in respect of tax due to the government, and the remainder represents profit available for distribution.

As with a single balance sheet, the profit and loss account for one year's operations may not afford a very good guide to a company's financial state. This is particularly likely if a company has, for instance, been expanding its factory space or installing a lot of expensive equipment. Expenditure of this nature can pull down the profit for a particular year, but with new long lasting assets it can lead to higher profits in the future. Taken together, a series of balance sheets and profit and loss accounts afford a much more useful picture. However, even these may be misleading. The valuation of balance sheet assets and liabilities, for instance, may not be adequate. Not all assets are continually offered for sale on the market, and balance sheet assessments inevitably involve some rather arbitrary judgments about their value. This can be of great importance if comparisons between companies in different lines of business are attempted by calculating their respective profits as a percentage of capital employed. Moreover, one should beware of assuming that conditions which gave rise to the satisfactory performance of a company in the past will continue unchanged in the future. Finally, published accounts may not contain as much detail as one would like for some purposes, although changes in company law have generally increased the amount of information available to the public.

Private companies

As we have seen, the great majority of companies are not public but private, and are relatively small in size. A private company is required to file its Memorandum and Articles, but in order to qualify for certain privileges, such as freedom from the obligation to issue a Prospectus, the number of share-holders must not exceed 50 and shares cannot be offered for sale to the general public. Until 1967 some private companies were excused from publishing accounts, although certain small companies still need not disclose information on sales turnover, employment and certain other matters.

Types of shareholders

A joint stock company is a form of business organisation in which a number of people invest their money with the object of making a profit. The way in which profits are distributed among them, in the form of **dividends** on shares, and the extent to which shareholders can exercise control of the firm's operations, depend principally on the type of shares which they hold. There are two main groups; preference and ordinary.

Preference shares

Preference shares, as their name implies, entitle their holders to shares in the firm's profits before other shareholders. The money they receive is known as a *dividend* and is usually fixed as a percentage of the capital invested. Courtaulds plc, for example, issued a $7\frac{1}{2}$ per cent preference share which yields £7.50 for every £100 of shares held. So long as the company makes sufficient profit to meet the dividends of the preference shareholders, they all receive their dividends in full. Of course, if the company makes no profit at all no dividends are paid (the dividend is then said to be 'passed'), but even if the company has a phenomenally profitable year, preference shareholders get no more than their fixed rate of dividend.

It is usually presumed, unless stated to the contrary, that preference shares are *cumulative*, i.e. when a dividend is passed shareholders have the deficiency made good in a later year if profits recover. Often the right is evidenced by the word 'cumulative' being included in the name of the shares, e.g. those of Courtaulds plc. There may also be more than one class of preference share and, occasionally, *participating* preference shares are issued which allow the holders a share in profits over and above the stipulated figure.

Preference shareholders may or may not be allowed a vote at company meetings, but they rarely have much power.

Ordinary shares

Holders of ordinary shares (known also as **equities**) are distinguished from preference shareholders by the fact that their rate of dividend is neither fixed nor stipulated in advance, but depends on the amount of profit made from year to year. If a business consistently makes a loss, no shareholders receive dividends, but if only a small profit is made ordinary shareholders are not entitled to anything until preference dividends have been paid in full.

The rates of dividend declared on ordinary shares are stated as percentages of the *nominal* value of the shares. They do not represent the rates of profit which all shareholders receive on their capital. They may be the profit rates received by an original shareholder who bought the shares when they were first issued. It depends upon the price which the person who became a shareholder actually paid for them. Tate & Lyle Ltd, for example, paid a dividend in 1984 of £31.40 on every £100 nominal value of its shares. It is, however, unlikely that many shareholders paid exactly £100 for the shares. For them the rate of profit is not 31.4 per cent but something else. In 1984 the market price of these shares was in the neighbourhood of £550, so a person buying shares then would have paid not £100 but £550 for them. The dividend thus represents the relationship between the £31.40 received and the £550 invested, which is not 31.4 per cent but more like 5.7 per cent. It is usual to call this relationship between the dividend and the market value of the share the **yield** of 5.7 per cent, to distinguish it from the dividend of 31.4 per cent.

Debentures

Some part of a company's trading capital may be issued as **debentures**, sometimes called **bonds**, or **loan stock**. Unlike ordinary and preference shareholders, who are in effect owners of the company, debenture holders are creditors of the firm. A debenture is, essentially different from a share though it resembles a preference share in one respect – it carries a fixed rate of interest.

It may most properly be regarded as a kind of IOU which the company gives to a person in return for a loan. The rate of interest on debentures is fixed in advance, such as the United Biscuit Company's 8 per cent debentures, holders of which have the prior right to receive this interest before any dividends are paid on preference or ordinary shares.

In the event of the company going into liquidation (i.e. being wound up) debenture holders, as creditors of the company, have the first claim (together with any other trade creditors) to return of their capital. For this purpose their holdings may be additionally secured by a guarantee on any specific asset belonging to the company. Thus, when issuing the debentures the company may pledge that a building or any other piece of equipment shall be attached to them so that, on winding up, that asset may be sold and the proceeds used exclusively for the repayment of the debt to the debenture holders.

Gearing

The riskiness of any shares obviously varies with the riskiness of the business in which a company is engaged. But that of ordinary shares depends also on the ratio of equities to total capital. This is known as the **gearing ratio**, which is said to be high when the proportion of fixed interest bearing capital (e.g. preference shares and debentures) to equities is high (and vice versa).

Consider the businesses HIG Co Ltd and LOW Co Ltd in the example below. Both have the same profits available for distribution in each of 2 years and the same total of issued capital, but they have different gearing ratios. HIG Ltd is highly geared with 80 per cent of its capital in the form of 5 per cent debentures. When profits double in a good year from £5000 to £10 000 it

HIG Co Ltd			LOW Co Ltd	
		£		£
Share capital 100 000	Debentures	80 000	Debentures	20 000
	Ordinary shares	20 000	Ordinary shares	80 000

Interest and Dividends

	Allocation of profits		Dividend rate per cent		Allocation of profits		Dividend rate per cent	
	Year 1 £	Year 2 £	Year 1 %	Year 2 %	Year 1 £	Year 2 £	Year 1 %	Year 2 %
Debenture	4 000	4 000	5	5	1 000	1 000	5	5
Ordinary shares	1 000	6 000	5	30	4 000	9 000	5	11¼
Total	5 000	10 000			5 000	10 000		

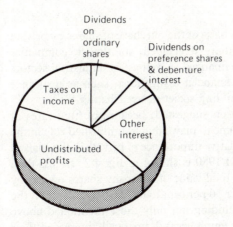

Fig 4.1   Company profits UK 1983

would be possible to raise the dividend on ordinary shares 6-fold from 5 to 30 per cent, after meeting the obligations to debenture holders. LOW Ltd, on the other hand, is low-geared with only 20 per cent of its capital in 5 per cent debentures. The same doubling of profits would only permit a rise from 5 to 11¼ per cent for the ordinary shareholders.

It should not be assumed that the rates of dividend on ordinary shares necessarily fluctuate as much as this example suggests. For purposes of illustration extremely different gearing ratios have been used. It also does not follow that merely because large profits are available for distribution they will always be distributed. There are good reasons why a portion should often be retained in the business to provide a reserve in case profits should fall in the future, to replace machinery and other capital equipment, and to enable the company to expand its activities—for example by installing new or bigger premises. Fig 4.1 shows how company profits were allocated in 1983. It can be seen that undistributed profits far exceed those distributed to shareholders and debenture holders, and provided, therefore, a major source of finance for expansion. (For other ways of raising capital, *see* pages 184–5.)

The control of joint stock companies

Companies, as we have seen, are owned by their shareholders. Therefore, in theory, ultimate control lies with them. However, this is somewhat of an oversimplification, and in order to discover where effective control lies in the real world it is necessary to take note of three important considerations:

a   the decline of the private investor
b   the role of company managers
c   the distribution of share ownership among large and small shareholders

The decline of the private investor

The capitalist system grew up on the basis of the purchase of shares by private individuals. However, as the economy developed, joint-stock companies began to assume a major role in the financial as well as the industrial sectors with the appearance of large-scale financial institutions, such as insurance companies, merchant banks and building societies (*see* Chapter 8).

In recent years—partly, it has been suggested, because of high rates of taxation—the private investor has come to play a much diminished role in the finance of British companies. The relative importance of private individuals in the ownership of shares in 1963 and 1980 is shown in Fig 4.2. In less than twenty years, the proportion of the total value of company shares owned by private individuals fell from well over 50 per cent to under 40 per cent. At the same time financial institutions (including not only those mentioned above but also pension funds operated for employees) dramatically increased their stake in company ownership by more than 50 per cent.

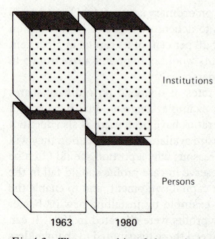

Institutions

Persons

1963   1980

Fig 4.2 The ownership of shares in companies 1963 and 1975

The new dominant position of financial institutions in the ownership of capital does not mean, of course, that private individuals do not benefit from the profitability of British companies. They benefit indirectly rather than directly. More important as far as the question of the control of companies is concerned is the fact that institutional shareholders are often large, giving the managers of such institutions important voices in the companies in which they have bought shares. Institutions such as the Prudential Assurance Company may only own, say, 5 per cent of the voting shares in some large businesses. But, as we shall shortly see, that holding may give them a disproportionate degree of control over such companies. First, however, we must take account of the way in which decisions are taken about the day-to-day business of joint-stock companies.

The board of directors

Shareholders of large companies are generally remote from the company business. They rarely know enough about the affairs of the company to be involved in day to day decision-taking, which is the concern of the board of directors. **Directors** are officials of a company, nominally appointed by shareholders at the annual general meeting, although they may often be (and for public companies are required by law to be) shareholders as well.

The power that shareholders are able to exercise over directors depends very much on the particular circumstances of a company. Often the power may be slight. This is especially the case where the distribution of shares is very wide and there are no really large shareholders. It is also the result of small attendances at company meetings. Absentee shareholders have the right to appoint 'proxies', or agents, to vote for them at the meeting, but as directors are in by far the best position to secure proxies, they themselves may be armed with an overwhelming number of votes and be able to control the decisions of the meeting.

The directors elect one of their number to be chairman and titular head of the company, and another (sometimes the same person) to be managing director, who is personally responsible to the board of directors for the running of the company. The managing director is nearly always a full-time appointment, and it is usually he or she who appoints the staff—works manager, sales manager and the other heads of department, each of whom is responsible to the board. Some of the other directors meet only infrequently, and many of them may be directors of several other companies at the same time.

Share ownership and control

Effective control of a joint stock company lies in the ownership of the voting shares. Industrial democracy is based on the principle of one vote for every voting share held. Whoever can raise a majority of votes at company meetings can, therefore, control the meetings.

There is no general rule concerning the minimum percentage of total voting shares which qualify for a controlling interest. It is probably rare, except in small companies, that as much as 51 per cent is necessary. If ownership is widely diffused and because of the absence of the majority of small shareholders from company meetings, the proportion of votes needed for effective control could be as little as 10 per cent. It would be an oversimplification to associate control of a company with a single individual. Groups of shareholders may act collectively, whether related by family or by common interests, as in the case of institutional shareholders.

It is thought, not unreasonably, that companies whose boards of directors collectively control a large number of voting shares may to some extent ignore the wishes of outside shareholders. They may, for example, be less concerned with trying to maximise profits for shareholders than with aiming for expansion of the firm which will protect their jobs and raise their own remuneration.

Some interest attaches, therefore, to identifying director-controlled and owner-controlled (i.e. shareholder-controlled) companies. Such a distinction is not easily established, partly because full information on share ownership is not available.

Some shares are held by 'nominees', concealing the true beneficial ownership. Fig 4.3 has, however, been drawn up with the use of data collected in the course of independent research. It shows the percentage of voting shares in the hands of the board of directors (or their families) for a number of companies in 1976. All the companies are large ones—in the 'top 250' in Britain ranked by the value of their net assets or sales in the year in question.

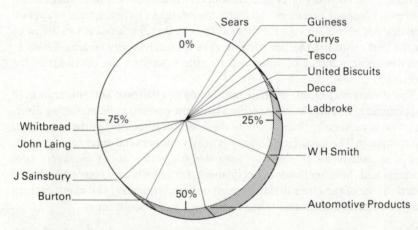

Fig 4.3 Director shareholdings in selected British companies 1976; percentage of voting shares owned by directors or their families (the percentage for each company is measured separately from the 12 o'clock origin)

The diagram shows a wide variation in the shareholdings of directors in this group of a dozen companies. It must be emphasised, however, that they are not intended to be representative of British industry as a whole. In particular, they exclude large companies such as ICI and Shell, where directors' holdings are too small to be represented. The point of the diagram is to indicate that there are a number of large companies where directors appear to exercise control. It is no easy matter to identify exactly which they are. Much depends on how diffused non-directors' shareholding are, how many proxy votes the board acquires, the precise identity of the chairman and managing director (including his relationship to the founder of the firm and his family), and other matters. Moreover, it must not be thought that, even where the directors are able to assemble enough votes to control meetings, they can necessarily completely ignore the views of other shareholders, particularly with regard to the level of profits. This may be true for companies where a single firm or institution holds more than 50 per cent of the voting shares, but it is rare with large public companies. Boardroom battles can take place indicating that even the directors are not all of the same mind regarding policy. Ultimately, if the directors fail to operate a company efficiently they have to face the risk that some outside interests (individuals, institutions or other companies) may try to move in by acquiring sufficient shares to give them a controlling interest and enable them to unseat all or some of the existing directors. Such **take-over bids** for the control of a company are dealt with in the next chapter.

Other types of private business

A number of other relatively minor forms of business enterprise are to be found in Britain. Some of these are variants of the joint stock company and include companies incorporated by Royal Charter, such as the Hudson Bay Company, clubs, and even charities (e.g. their business in Christmas cards).

Public enterprise

So far in this chapter we have concentrated on the organisation of production in the private sector of the economy. Readers may, however, recall that in Chapter 1 we described Britain as a 'mixed economy' with the state taking an active role in certain aspects of economic life.

State activity takes several forms. In the first place there are services that are run directly by government departments, both central and local. They include the social services, the administration of taxes, the staffing of embassies and so on. Secondly, there are major areas, of which health, education and defence are among the most important, where the government decides on the size and form of provision of the service and employs doctors, nurses, teachers, soldiers, etc. for the purpose. Thirdly, there are the nationalised industries, such as coal, rail transport and electricity supply, which possess certain of the characteristics of commercial enterprises and which are run for the state by special public corporations set up for the purpose. Finally, there is a host of other activities of the government which do not fit into any of the first three categories. They include measures to control private businesses, measures to redistribute income and wealth, measures designed to influence the general level of economic activity, etc.

Our concern in this chapter is with the organisation of the nationalised industries, although we shall conclude with an account of some of the general activities included in the fourth category. The direct provision of services by central and local government is a subject to which we shall return in Chapter 10. It is, however, necessary to emphasise one characteristic of the activities of the first two categories here. It is that although they may involve some of the work being done by firms in the private sector (e.g. in the building of roads and houses and in the supply of armaments) they are financed largely out of general taxation. In consequence they are subject to fairly close control by the

Treasury, Ministers of the Crown and Parliament. In contrast, the major nationalised industries, as previously stated, resemble commercial enterprises. They generally charge for their services and, although they may from time to time receive subsidies from public funds, they are expected to operate commercially to an extent and they are given a degree of independence to do so.

The public sector in its widest sense employs about a quarter of the labour force in Britain, while the nationalised industries proper account for less than a third of this total. Nationalisation is, of course, a political as well as an economic matter. The major period of extension of public ownership occurred in the period 1945–51, when the Labour Party first held a majority of seats in the House of Commons. Recent trends have been in the opposite direction. The Conservative governments of 1979 and 1983 set about the task of selling some of the nationalised industries to the private sector in part of its so-called 'privatisation' programme. Privatisation, however, has come to be regarded as involving more than merely the sale of state-owned assets to private individuals (*see* page 117).

The various nationalised industries, and the size of their labour forces are shown in Fig 4.4, which includes previously nationalised but currently privatised industries as well. By the time this book is published, there is likely to be a need to transfer from the top to the lower section of the diagram. Present plans to privatise British Gas, for example, have been announced recently, and British Airways may well follow. Meanwhile, we can see from the diagram that coal, rail and postal services are the largest employers of labour, accounting for over half the total.

Organisation and control of nationalised industries

The structure and organisation of the various nationalised industries have not been identical in all details. Before examining some of the more important industries that are, or have been until recently, in the public sector, we should note certain features that are common to most.

The public corporation

Nationalised industries in Britain are run by what are known as public corporations. The form and functions of these bodies differ somewhat from case to case, but in all there is a close resemblance to the boards of directors of joint stock companies. The chairmen and members of the corporations are appointed by the appropriate Minister (e.g. Secretary of State for Energy, Secretary of State for Industry) but the corporations are otherwise free from day to day interference in the management of their affairs. Many members of the boards of nationalised industries come from private industry and, since 1978, have included civil servants and employee representatives. The major appointments are generally made for a fixed period of years, and matters of

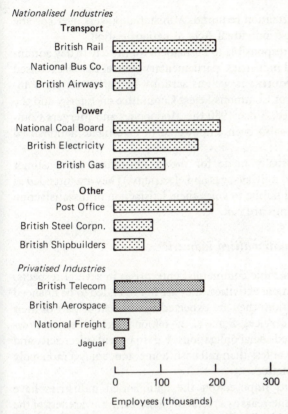

Nationalised Industries
Transport
British Rail
National Bus Co.
British Airways

Power
National Coal Board
British Electricity
British Gas

Other
Post Office
British Steel Corpn.
British Shipbuilders

Privatised Industries
British Telecom
British Aerospace
National Freight
Jaguar

0   100   200   300

Employees (thousands)

Fig 4.4   Employment in the major and nationalised industries 1983

wages and conditions of service for the staff are generally determined independently from those in the Civil Service.

For many years the Post Office was in a rather special category, being run as a government department, but the essentially commercial character of most of its operations was recognised in 1969 when it was made a public corporation, similar to the other nationalised industries.

The control of nationalised industries

Since public corporations are to a certain extent independent bodies which do not have to face a shareholders' meeting every year, it is clearly important that they should have to submit to some control from outside. This they do in three main ways.

In the first place, each nationalised industry is subject to a considerable measure of control from the appropriate Minister. As already mentioned, he appoints the members of the boards of the corporations. He can also dismiss them. The Minister has general powers of direction and can call for statistical, financial or any other information required. Ministerial powers over specific matters are written into the individual Acts of nationalisation.

While Ministers are not responsible to Parliament for the day to day administration of the nationalised industries, parliamentary control can be exercised through the normal procedures, as well as scrutiny by parliamentary committees such as the House of Commons Select Committee on Energy and the Public Accounts Committee. Since 1980 the Monopolies and Mergers Commission (*see* page 114) has also been empowered to investigate nationalised industries.

Finally, provision is usually made for the establishment of consumer councils for the Post Office, railways, gas and electricity. They are intended as vehicles for the consuming public to voice their satisfaction or dissatisfaction with the way in which things are run.

Financial obligations of nationalised industries

Nationalised industries resemble commercial enterprises in several respects. Unlike many other government activities, they are not intended to be financed mainly, if at all, from taxation; they are expected to cover all or part of their costs by charging for their services. Some of the nationalised industries, however, have certain recognised social obligations, e.g. to provide electricity and rail transport to rural areas at less than full cost. Some, too, enjoy a monopoly position which can be exploited.

The financial obligations imposed on the nationalised industries have changed significantly over the years as a result of an increasing awareness of the commercial side of their operations and of a desire to compare their performance with that of companies in the private sector of the economy. Capital for development, over and above the capital generated internally, is borrowed from the National Loans Fund operated by the central government, which, in turn, borrows from the market in order to obtain the best terms.

The original requirements in the Acts setting up the early corporations called for each industry to break even over an average of good and bad years. A substantial change in policy, however, followed the publication of two White Papers in 1961 and 1967. The second of these was the more important from the viewpoint of the conduct of the internal affairs of the nationalised industries. Whilst recognising the existence of certain social obligations, it emphasised the commercial side of their operations and recommended that prices should be set to reflect costs at the margin of production.

As far as investment policy is concerned the earlier of the White Papers led to the setting of target rates of return on capital for each nationalised industry. The targets were arrived at after consideration of the social obligations of the different industries and their financial histories. They varied from $12\frac{1}{2}$ per cent for electricity to a break-even formula for coal.

The 1967 White Paper was more concerned with *new* investment than with the average rate of return on capital employed. The main innovation at this time was the introduction of a so-called 'test discount rate', intended as a measure of the real cost of using capital in the public sector of the economy. It could be changed from time to time, reflecting changes in the cost of raising capital. It was set at 8 per cent, but later was raised to 10 per cent.

More recent developments in investment policy followed the publication of a new White Paper in 1978 which endorsed the general commercial approach of its predecessors. The policy recommendations of the 1978 White Paper were for the setting of financial targets for 3 to 5 years ahead and the adoption of a 'required rate of return' (RRR) of 5 per cent. The RRR, allowing for inflation, would reflect the real cost of capital in the economy and form the basis for targets for individual industries. A further measure of control introduced was the so-called **external financing limit (EFL)**, which can be used to limit the amount a nationalised industry can raise from external sources in a particular year.

The profitability of nationalised industries

Economists often try to use the yardstick of profit to measure an industry's efficiency. However, this approach is not very helpful for some of the nationalised industries for two basic reasons. In the first place nationalised industries may be asked to fulfil certain social obligations which may not be profitable. For example, they may be expected to prevent unemployment in an area (e.g. on Clydeside); they may have to provide transport for people living in isolated parts of the country; they may need to maintain national prestige (e.g. airways); they may be told to keep the prices of their products low as part of an anti-inflation policy.

In the second place some nationalised industries possess a degree of monopoly power which, if used to the full, could allow them to make large profits without necessarily reflecting great efficiency. One should, therefore, be cautious about judging the efficiency of nationalised industries according to whether they make profits or losses. Separation of some of the 'social' from the commercial activities since the White Paper of 1967 has helped assessment of the performance of certain of the major public corporations. However, one should bear in mind the reasons why an industry was nationalised in the first place before passing judgment on its profit record.

The major nationalised and privatised industries

The scope of the nationalised sector of British industry has been in the throes of change during the 1980s as a result of the privatisation policy of the governments of 1979 and 1983, already mentioned. It is likely to continue to change, either as the process continues, or as a result of any renationalisation measures that the next government might introduce. We shall, therefore, describe the main characteristics of the chief industries which are, or have until recently been, nationalised.

Power

The coal, electricity, gas and nuclear power industries have all been nationalised. So has a portion of the oil industry, until its privatisation in 1982. Gas is the next industry due to be sold to the private sector.

Coal

The first important industry to be taken into public ownership in the wave of nationalisation that followed the Second World War was coal. Indeed, the transfer in 1947 of the 750 undertakings employing about three quarters of a million workers can be viewed as a major step in the nationalisation of industry.

By the 1980s the structure of the coal industry had not materially changed, although its labour force had fallen to less than a quarter of a million. The National Coal Board has charge of the whole of the coalfields of Britain and has the right to work certain other minerals as well. The distribution of coal, however, is largely in private hands. The members of the Board are appointed by the Secretary of State for Energy, who retains a general power of direction. The Board maintains a centralised form of organisation, but exercises control over its separate collieries in a divisional (area) structure.

Electricity

The key position which the supply of electricity holds in the economy of the country led to some state control as far back as the 19th century. The first major Act of nationalisation, however, dates from 1926. This was when the Central Electricity Board was established, not to take over the generation of electricity, which was left in the hands of private owners and local authorities, but to construct and operate a national system of electricity transmission over the whole country. The national grid was set up to link the most important generating and distributing stations and ensure that, within limits, any area is adequately supplied with electricity even if its local generating plant is out of action or unable to fill its requirements.

Public ownership was carried a stage further 20 years later when, by an Act of 1947, electricity generation as well as the national grid was taken over by a new body—the British Electricity Authority (subsequently renamed the Central Electricity Authority). At the same time 14 separate area electricity boards were set up to organise the distribution of electricity in the different regions of the country. Apart from certain rearrangements in Scotland, where electricity supply is controlled by 2 bodies—the North of Scotland Hydro-Electric Board and the South of Scotland Electricity Board—the industry continued to operate in this manner for a decade.

The organisation of the industry was criticised, however, by a committee appointed by the government (the Herbert Committee) in 1956, mainly on the grounds that too much power lay in the hands of the Central Authority. In order to meet some of these objections, certain measures for decentralisation were introduced by an Electricity Act in the following year. The area boards were given greater independence and the Central Electricity Authority was dissolved and its place taken by 2 new bodies. Bulk generation and the responsibility for the grid were given to a Central Electricity Generating Board, while an Electricity Council, which included in its members the chairmen of the 12 area boards in England and Wales, was given the task of promoting efficiency and coordination within the industry. The Council is also charged with making financial arrangements for capital needed for development, and acts in an advisory capacity to the Secretary of State for Energy. The electricity undertakings in Britain employ nearly 200 000 people.

Gas

The supply of gas for domestic and industrial purposes before nationalisation was in the hands of some 1000 private companies and local authorities. The distinguishing feature of the Gas Act of 1948, which brought about the transfer to public ownership, was that, at its inception, the structure laid down for the industry was in essence one of decentralisation. It is true that a central body, the Gas Council, was set up as with the other public corporations, but the main responsibility for the supply of gas was entrusted to 12 almost autonomous area gas boards from the outset. This situation continued until 1973 when a new Gas Act was passed to increase the amount of central control called for by the changeover from manufactured to natural gas from the North Sea, accounting for about 90 per cent of total production. The Act created the British Gas Corporation which took over the responsibilities of the Gas Council and of the 12 area boards. It employs about 100 000 people, and plans for the sale of British Gas to the private sector were announced in 1985.

Oil

The discovery of oil under British waters in the North Sea in 1969 transformed the country's energy supplies as they became productive in the late 1970s. Together with the natural gas referred to in the previous section and other energy sources they made the country virtually self-sufficient in the 1980s. It is uncertain how long this state of affairs will last, however.

Oil production has always remained largely in the hands of private companies, such as Shell and BP (though the government used to hold a substantial share in the latter company). The British National Oil Corporation (BNOC) was set up in 1976 to give the state a direct interest in North Sea oil. BNOC remains a large trader in oil, but its exploration and production activities were transferred to a new company Britoil, and sold to the private sector in 1982.

Nuclear power

The nuclear power programme in Britain can be traced back to 1956 and the construction of the first nuclear power station at Calder Hall. By 1966 nuclear energy supplied less than 5 per cent of the country's energy consumption.

Britain has 15 nuclear power stations, the majority of which are operated by the electricity authorities. The remainder are run by the research oriented UK Atomic Energy Authority (1954) or its more commercial subsidiary, British Nuclear Fuels Ltd, which also provides nuclear fuel services including some to overseas countries.

Transport

Most forms of inland transport, the second important industry to be nationalised after 1945, had already been subject to public control for a long time. The railways had always had to comply with a variety of state regulations and had even been run by the government for the duration of both the First and Second World Wars. The traffic problems of London also led, as early as 1933, to the creation of the largest public corporation established before 1939—the London Passenger Transport Board—in order to provide a 'properly coordinated' system of transport in the capital.

The transport industry that was nationalised by the Act of 1947, however, was by far the most complicated that had ever been transferred to a public corporation. It also employed close on 900 000 workers. Disagreement between the principal political parties at the time was, moreover, strong and both the organisation of the industry and the sections of it remaining in the public field have since been subject to more than one radical change.

The Act of 1947 made provision for a central body, the British Transport Commission, and 6 executives responsible for the management of the railways, road haulage, docks and inland waterways, road passenger transport, hotels, and London Transport. All of these, with the exception of the London Transport Executive, were subsequently abolished by the Transport Act of 1953. At the same time the road haulage industry was largely denationalised, the plans for gradual acquisition of road passenger transport undertakings were abandoned, and the railways and remaining activities of the industry were taken directly under the control of an enlarged British Transport Commission, with specific requirements for the decentralisation of railway management.

These arrangements continued until 1960 when the government, prompted by the serious financial plight of the railways, appointed a special advisory group to report on the organisation of the Transport Commission. The main conclusion reached by the government after receiving the group's report was that the activities of the Commission were so large and diverse that it was virtually impossible to run them as a single undertaking. A new structure was therefore introduced by the Transport Act of 1962. It abolished the British Transport Commission and provided for decentralisation and the replacement of the Commission by separate authorities: the British Railways Board, the London Transport Board, the British Docks Board, the Inland Waterways Authority, and individual boards to run British Road Services and each of the other subsidiary activities of the nationalised transport industry.

The policy of distributing the functions of the British Transport Commission among independent bodies was continued by the 1968 Transport Act. The British Railways Board was reduced in size, and concentrated its activities on main line inter-city transport. At the same time it was decided to award grants to British Rail for socially desirable unremunerative operations, so that it could cease making losses and pay its way.

The 1968 Act set up certain new bodies, among them a National Freight Corporation (NFC), the largest operator in a predominantly privately owned transport sector. The NFC was one of the first of the nationalised industries to be sold off (in 1981–2). The same, 1968, Act also set up the National Bus Company to take over nationalised bus services in England and Wales, except for those operated by London and other municipal authorities. The 1980 Transport Act removed many restrictions on private bus and coach operation, and encouraged the return of competing private businesses. The National Bus Company itself is on the list of industries due to be privatised.

Civil airlines

The British Overseas Airways Corporation (BOAC) and British European Airways (BEA) were the last pre-war and the first post-war public corporations. Since 1971 they have been embodied in a single new corporation, British Airways. The government originally entered the field of civil aviation in order to establish and develop a national service in circumstances which inevitably involve important political issues and impinge on international relations. BEA was given a statutory monopoly position in Britain until 1961, after which it had to face increasing competition from independent airlines, such as British Caledonian and Laker Airways, on many domestic routes and in other services including package holidays abroad. The government also set up the Civil Aviation Authority, an independent body, responsible for the regulation of the industry. It oversees charges, routes, safety, etc. and issues licences to approved operators, both private and public. Plans for the privatisation of British Airways and of the British Airports Authority have been announced.

Other nationalised industries

In addition to public enterprise in the fields of power and transport, the state has, or does, operate some other nationalised industries.

Steel

The last of the industries transferred to public ownership by the first post-war Labour government was steel; without doubt it was the most controversial of its nationalisation measures. Delays were caused by the Conservative majority in the House of Lords, and the Iron and Steel Corporation of Britain did not come into being until 1951. The new corporation was, however, to have a short life. By 1953 the succeeding Conservative government had brought in a second Steel Act to denationalise the industry, and by the time a new Labour government committed to renationalisation had been elected in 1964 all but one company had been sold back to private owners. The 1967 Iron and Steel Act then transferred the assets of 13 major steel companies to a new British Steel Corporation (BSC).

At the time of second nationalisation BSC employed around a quarter of a million workers and produced about 90 per cent of steel output. This share has dropped since then to nearer 80 per cent. The industry has also been trying to reduce capacity in the light of falling world demand and intensified international competition. Employment has fallen accordingly to less than 100 000 by the mid-1980s.

Postal and telecommunications

As previously mentioned, the Post Office was run directly by a government department until 1969, when it was turned into a public corporation, responsible for both postal and telecommunication services. The sale of British Telecom in 1984 was the largest of any of the privatisation measures involving transfer of ownership from the public to the private sector. The Post Office remains, however, one of the largest nationalised industries, though its statutory monopoly in the delivery of mail has been somewhat relaxed to encourage competition from private businesses.

Shipbuilding

Towards the end of the 19th century Britain led the world in shipbuilding, four fifths of world tonnage being built in British yards. However, the industry has been in long-term decline for a great many years. State aid for unprofitable private companies has often been sought, not least because of the heavy dependence of certain regions, especially Clydeside, on the industry for employment. In 1977, a new public corporation, British Shipbuilders, was set up to save major sections of the industry by the acquisition of a couple of dozen essentially weak private firms, then employing nearly 100 000 workers, but now nearer to half that number.

Aerospace

The final industry to be described here is one that has already been denationalised. The advent of the state into the industry occurred in 1971; the shares in the aero-engine division of Rolls Royce Ltd were transferred to public ownership at a time when the company faced serious financial circumstances. A public corporation was later set up, in 1977, when British Aerospace (BAe) acquired the assets of Hawker Siddeley and certain other aircraft manufacturers. BAe employed about 70 000 workers when it was sold to private buyers in 1981.

Other forms of state involvement in industry

The previous pages have described the major nationalised industries run by public corporations. Government involvement in British industry, however, takes other forms as well as straightforward nationalisation. There are three main ways in which this occurs: *a* direct ownership of shares in private industry, *b* general planning machinery, and *c* intervention in specific sectors of the economy.

State ownership

The government has from time to time held a stake in some private companies. It owned a major shareholding in BP (British Petroleum Ltd) for many years, for example. The Industry Act of 1975 established a National Enterprise Board (NEB) with responsibility for improving industrial efficiency, especially in areas of high technology, in regions of heavy unemployment and for small firms. The NEB was also given the power to buy shares in private firms. Since it was a Labour government which set up the NEB it was feared by some people that it might be used for large-scale extension of public ownership by the back door, as it were. However, the amount of funds at its disposal did not make this a real possibility in practice.

The government's acquired shares in Rolls Royce (*see* above) were transferred to the NEB. So were those of British Leyland, when that company found itself in comparable parlous circumstances a little later. The state found itself, in consequence, with something of a reputation for rescuing 'lame ducks'. It must be emphasised, however, that this was not the prime purpose laid down for the NEB, which was intended to buy shares in profitable companies. The terms of reference of the Board were flexible, though the NEB was abolished in 1981, when yet another new body was formed, British Technology Group (BTG). BTG was created by merging the National Research Development Corporation (NRDC) with portions of the NEB. Among BTG's functions are the promotion of and provision of finance for the development of advanced technology in British industry.

General planning machinery

Britain is not a country where detailed central planning of the allocation of resources plays a major role as it does elsewhere. As we have seen, major sectors of the economy are in the hands of private enterprise and even the public sector is decentralised to an extent. However, the complexity of the economy and the degree of interdependence between its various parts has led governments since the Second World War to introduce some machinery which, by coordinating the plans for several industries, might assist individual firms to formulate their own production programmes with more confidence. Government forecasting is also important in connection with policies designed to control the rate of inflation and the level of unemployment and to stimulate economic growth.

In 1962 the government set up the National Economic Development Council (NEDC, but popularly known as 'Neddy') comprising representatives of public and private enterprise and of organised labour. It is served by a National Economic Development Office (NEDO). The Council was given the task of examining the economic performance of the economy and considering ways of increasing its rate of growth. A number of more specialised economic development committees (known as 'little neddies') were also established for individual industries, to assist in considering problems and obstacles to growth on a smaller scale.

The change in government after the election in 1964 was followed by a movement to strengthen the economic planning machinery, and a new government department was created to formulate a long-term economic plan for Britain with the help of a reconstituted NEDC. In 1965 the Department of Economic Affairs published a 'national plan' aimed at an increase in total production of about 25 per cent between 1964 and 1970 (an annual average growth rate of about 4 per cent). The plan was regarded as a failure and was not repeated. In 1970 the Department of Economic Affairs was disbanded and its activities reverted to the Treasury. The Treasury then became the government department responsible for forecasting economic trends and for formulating policies designed to achieve the main economic objectives at which the nation was aiming.

In the 1980s, few traces of state institutions involved in general planning remain, other than at the discussion level of 'Neddy'. However, in keeping with its professed aim of stimulating competition, the Conservative government of Margaret Thatcher introduced measures designed to help small, and especially new, businesses. For example, the Business Expansion Scheme (BES) was set up in 1981, and allows relief from income tax up to £40 000 a year for new investment in unquoted UK trading companies outside agriculture and finance.

Intervention in specific sectors of the economy

The last category relating to state involvement in the economy is an omnibus one covering many kinds of intervention designed to deal with specific sectors or problem areas. There is an extremely wide range of activities of government departments and state sponsored organisations to be considered. For example, there are measures to influence the location of industry, to encourage industrial investment, to regulate monopolies and restrictive practices, to improve the marketing of agricultural products, to control the rents of dwellings, to restrict imports, to redistribute income, to assist in the settlement of strikes and other industrial disputes, to control prices and incomes in order to control the rate of inflation, and so on. We shall deal with such policies at the appropriate places later in this book.

Exercises

For key to symbols indicating sources *see* pages xii–xiii.

1 Go through the company reports which appear in the back pages of the past 2 issues of *The Financial Times* or *The Economist* and make 3 lists:

a those firms which made more profit than last year
b those firms which made less profit than last year
c those firms which made losses

Now do the same thing for exactly 1 year ago. Were there relatively more firms making more or less profit or loss this year than last?
2 From *The Times* or *The Financial Times*, find out the current price of the shares in the following privatised companies:

British Telecom
Britoil
British Aerospace
Jaguar

Compare the current price with that a year ago and with the price at which the shares were offered to the public on privatisation. Would you have done well to buy them at either date?
3 Rank the public corporations in electricity, coal and railways according to the

surplus or deficit each made last year. Then re-rank according to the percentage increase in surplus (or reduction of deficit) over the previous year. (*WA*).

4 Draw a diagram on the lines of Fig 4.1 showing the allocation of gross company income into the following categories for the last year for which statistics are available:

a dividends and interest
b UK taxes on income and profits due abroad
c undistributed income after taxation (*AS*)

Compare your diagram with that in the book.

5 Find out the names of the chairmen and their salaries, of the following public corporations. What were their previous occupations? (*WA, Who's Who*)

British Airways
Electricity Council
British Railways Board
Post Office
National Coal Board
British Steel Corporation

6 From the yellow pages of your local telephone directory, find the proportion of the total number of businesses which appear to be joint stock companies in the following trades:

Coal merchants
Furniture manufacturers
Plumbers
Shirt manufacturers
Shoe shops
Paint manufacturers

Would your results have been very different if you had been able to calculate the proportions on the basis of the value of total sales?

7 From the list of London share prices in *The Financial Times* select any 6 companies which have issued preference shares and list them in order of the fixed rate of interest which they pay. Now make a note of the price of the shares (i.e. the price you would have to pay to buy now), and calculate the yield you would receive if you bought £100 worth of them. (*Hint* Divide £100 by the price of the shares. This gives you the number of shares which you will be able to buy. Now, using the guaranteed rate of dividend, work out how much you would earn each year on your investment. This is the yield of the share.) List them again in order of yield. Can you suggest any reasons why the order may not be the same?

8 Find out:

a the gross trading profits of 'listed companies' for the last 5 years
b the total net assets of the companies for the same years

Express *a* as a percentage of *b* and set the results of your calculations alongside each other. Does there seem to be any relationship between them? (*AS*) (*NB* 'Listed companies' are large public companies whose shares are quoted on the Stock Exchange. *See* pages 182–5.)

5 The structure of British industry

Economic prosperity depends, in the last resort, upon the quantity and quality of goods and services produced. The institutional framework within which production is carried on is, as we have seen, a complicated one. There is a further aspect of complexity that we must face which results from specialisation.

Specialisation

There are two principal types of specialisation. First, there is specialisation between individuals. Discussion of the occupational distribution of the population has already told us something of this. We know that some people are clerks, others plumbers, electrical engineers, unskilled labourers and so on, with the result that it is rare to find that a single commodity is produced entirely by one individual. Production today is a complex process because it is the result of co-operation between large numbers of individuals each doing a very small part of the job. Consider, for example, the production of a simple article like a reel of thread. Who has 'produced' it? Clearly, so many people have had a hand in it that it would be difficult to mention them all. In the factory where it is made there is the person who operates the machine which spins the thread, but there is also the supervisor who watches that the machine operator works properly, the buyer who orders the raw material, the mechanic who keeps the machine working efficiently and the cleaner who keeps the place fit to work in, to mention a few.

It is this specialisation, or **division of labour** as it is sometimes called, which accounts for our relatively high standard of living. For it is not difficult to appreciate that as every person concentrates on a single task, not only does he save time by not having to change from job to job, but he also develops greater efficiency in the job he stays in. Our society is far removed from the days of cavemen when it was really possible to say that one man made a primitive hatchet. He simply looked for a pointed stone, which he sharpened by rubbing it against a hard rock, and fastened it to a stout stick with a length of strong grass. He alone made the hatchet. Specialisation among individuals was almost non-existent.

The second type of specialisation in our industrialised society today is between firms. This is slightly less complex, largely by virtue of the fact that there are, of necessity, fewer firms than individuals in the country. It is none the less as important as specialisation between individuals in maintaining the efficiency of production. The sewing thread factory is dependent upon many other firms in different industries: on producers of raw materials, machines, office equipment and everything else that the factory uses and, of course, on farmers who grow food without which workers would starve. The degree of dependence on other firms naturally increases the smaller the firm in question, but even in highly integrated large industries it is still very great. The finished product of one firm is often the raw material of another. (It is then referred to as an **intermediate** product.)

A useful way of keeping the importance of specialisation in mind is to classify productive activity under one of three basic headings: primary, secondary and tertiary production.

Primary production

This consists of all economic activity which is a first step in the productive process; that is, the harvesting of the natural resources of the world, especially agricultural crops and minerals, which provide the foodstuffs and basic raw materials upon which other production depends. By and large, the producers who come under this heading are in agriculture and mining. Cotton growers are primary producers; so, too, are coal miners and wheat farmers, fishermen and oil prospectors. For cotton, coal, wheat, fish and oil are raw materials secured from nature rather than by a form of manufacture.

Secondary production

This is concerned with later stages in the production of finished goods. An industry which does not produce a raw material, but which processes material to manufacture its product is an example of secondary production. Thus, a flour mill which uses wheat to make flour, a shoe factory which transforms leather, a fish cannery which processes fish, and an oil refinery which makes petrol from mineral oil, are secondary producers. They process raw materials or foodstuffs in order to *manufacture* products, but they do not actually make the raw materials themselves.

Tertiary production

Tertiary production, which becomes particularly important in advanced industrial countries, concerns not so much the production of goods but the provision of *services*. They make it easier for other producers to get on with their jobs and they also satisfy consumers' demands for such things as entertainment and hairdressing, without providing any material goods. The transport industry provides a tertiary service; so do shopkeepers, bank clerks and doctors. None is directly concerned with the production of a physical good either at the primary or secondary level, but their activities contribute to the country's economy.

The placing of individual workers into any one of the 3 categories is not a straightforward matter, and arbitrary decisions often have to be taken, but Fig 5.1 has been drawn up to show the general pattern of production in Britain.

As can be seen, secondary production, which comprises all manufacturing business, accounts for only about 30 per cent of total output, while primary production, comprising in Britain mainly agriculture and mining, is much less important, and is responsible for about 5 per cent. Tertiary services, on the other hand, are even more important than secondary production; they include workers in transport, distribution, commerce, government and the professions, and cover the remainder of economic activity.

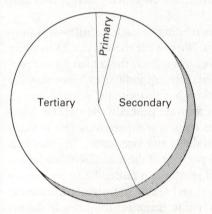

Fig 5.1 Types of industrial activity UK, 1984 (percentage of total labour force engaged in primary, secondary and tertiary production)

This fact—that secondary and tertiary employment account for such a high proportion of the total—is one indication of the advanced state of industrial organisation in Britain. This is clearly illustrated if we compare the situation today with that in the past. The proportion of the labour force engaged in primary production 100 years ago was about 25 per cent. Were reliable figures available for, say, 300 years ago the contrast would be even more striking. At that time agriculture was almost the only important industry, and the proportion of the labour force engaged in primary production was correspondingly high. As agriculture declined relatively over the centuries, mining, especially of coal grew in importance, only to decline in the last 30 or 40 years as well.

Most recently of all, oil mining has been the primary industry that has expanded since the developments in the North Sea.

Employment in secondary production was the first to grow with the industrial revolution. Then, as technical advance raised productivity in industrial production, resources could be released for the tertiary sector while maintaining and even raising the output of manufactured goods available for consumption. The relative importance of the services sector increased and it gained ground from secondary production. It is against this background of long-term trends that one should observe the recent 'de-industrialisation' of the UK and other industrialised countries, i.e. as an acceleration of the decline in the relative importance of manufacturing industry since the mid 1960s.

The structure of British industry

Our knowledge of the distribution of the labour force (*see* Chapter 3, Fig 3.9 and accompanying text) has already given us some idea of the importance of different industries in the economy of Britain. This general picture may now be expanded and clarified.

The government collects information relating to each industry and publishes it in a regular census of production. We can use these statistics to verify our knowledge of the industrial groupings. Moreover, the census figures provide a guide to the relative significance of different industries, since they are concerned not only with numbers of workers but also with the value of output. Although the results measured in either way are generally similar, the latter method is safer because some industries employ comparatively few workers and yet produce a relatively valuable product; and vice versa. The chemical industry is one such. It employs about 5 per cent of the manufacturing labour force, while the value of the chemicals it produces is more like 10 per cent of total manufacturing output. The clothing and textile industries, in contrast, employ over 10 per cent of the labour force in manufacturing, while the net value of their output is nearer to 6 per cent of the total.

Fig 5.2 is based on the census of production and shows the relative importance of major industries according to the value of their outputs. Again, engineering is in the leading position, with an output about 20 per cent of the total. It is followed by energy, construction (i.e. building), food, drink and tobacco, vehicles, chemicals, paper and printing, textiles and clothing, and metal goods and manufacture, as shown.

Industrial change

It is difficult to over-emphasise the fact that the structure of industry is continually changing. It is especially important to stress this fact here because we are often looking at the economy at a particular time, taking a snapshot of it, as

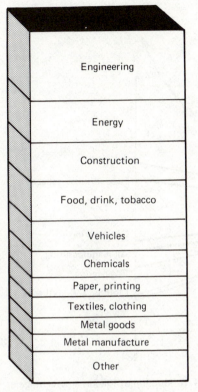

Fig 5.2 UK industry (1981) (relative importance of different industries by value of output)

it were, using an instantaneous exposure to arrest movement. Some idea of the changes which have been taking place can be obtained by comparing the situation at different times. Fig 5.3 does this for the years 1974 and 1984 though it must be noted that because of the length of time between the two dates only broad orders of magnitude should be distinguished. The diagram is drawn up on the basis of the level of output in each industry, after making allowance for changes in the value of money.

The period in question was one in which the volume of manufacturing output fell, due mainly to the persistence of the world trade recession, which affected the UK as much as any other country. There were certainly some years when output rose (1976–8 and 1982–4), but over the whole period manufacturing production in 1984 was about 10 per cent lower than a decade earlier. We can take this average performance of all industries as a benchmark and compare the performance of each sector with it. We may distinguish between industries which are expanding and those which are contracting.

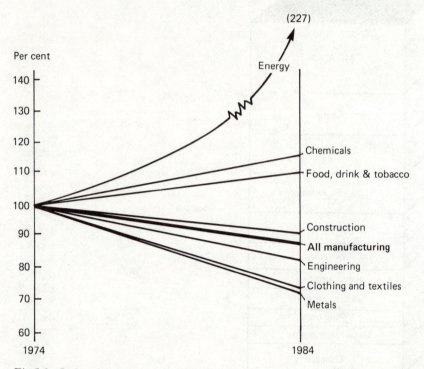

Fig 5.3 Industrial change in the UK 1974–84 (production in 1984 as a percentage of 1974)

Expanding industries

Three major industries stand out in this group. The first is energy. Its expansion has been so enormous that it shoots right off the top of the diagram. This is not really surprising in the light of the energy crisis and the North Sea discoveries of oil and gas. The rise in output for the industry as a whole is, of course, an average and conceals an enormous rise in the production of oil and natural gas and a decline in coal. Chemicals is the second industry whose output continued to grow relatively fast in the years up to 1984. It has, in fact, been a pacesetter since the end of the Second World War. Finally, there is the food, drink and tobacco industry, the only other industry to produce a larger output in 1984 than 1974. These products are less prone to decline in depressed economic conditions, though it can be seen that the industry's growth was relatively modest.

Fig 5.3 picks out only very broad industrial categories. However, there are several subgroups of industries which have grown relatively rapidly. Electrical engineering, for example, has enjoyed a fairly long upward trend in spite of the decline in engineering as a whole.

Contracting industries

The major industry groups shown in Fig 5.3 to have been contracting over the 10 years since 1974, are metals and clothing and textiles. Both have suffered from intense international competition, especially in iron and steel and textiles from Japan and developing countries. The engineering industry is also shown as contracting in the diagram. This is a very broad category. As already stated, parts of the engineering industry have done well. The chief poor performers are shipbuilding, vehicles and mechanical engineering. The first of the three has been on the decline for most of the present century, and would probably have disappeared entirely without government help. The decline in vehicle production, in contrast, is of more recent origin—it was one of the most rapidly expanding industries for some 20 years after the end of the Second World War—but has had to face intense competition from European manufacturers and from Japan.

Industrial productivity

Expansion in the volume of output can be traced to one of two causes:

- increases in the supply of factors of production
- improvements in their productivity arising from changes in the techniques of production and in factor performance

Increasing productivity has been a major source of rising living standards in most industrial countries for a very long time. This is not surprising since even an apparently modest rate of increase of output per man of 2 per cent per annum leads to a doubling of output every 35 years without any rise in the size of the labour force.

The most common measure of productivity is that obtained by dividing output by the number of workers employed, giving a figure of output per head. However, because of variations in hours worked, output per hour is probably a better measure of labour's productivity in the short-term. The procedure of measuring productivity is fraught with problems, especially when attempting to measure output in the service trades. It is therefore wise to treat estimates of productivity with caution and to regard only broad orders of magnitude as significant.

This warning is relevant when examining Fig 5.4, which gives an index of labour productivity (1950 = 100). Since it is restricted to productivity in the manufacturing sector, it is probably fairly reliable as far as long-term trends are concerned. It can be seen that output per unit of labour has risen fairly steadily since 1950 at an average rate of approximately $2\frac{1}{2}$ per cent per annum.

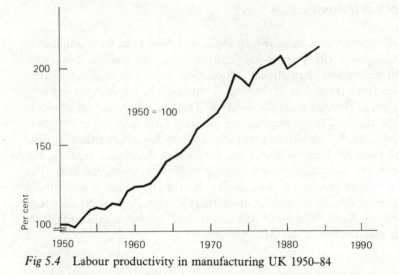

Fig 5.4 Labour productivity in manufacturing UK 1950–84

Productivity increases have varied widely from industry to industry, partly, of course, because of differences in the scope for the application of new technology. Computerisation, for example, is more easily applied to the chemical industry (which has had one of the fastest growth rates) than to the services of solicitors or hairdressers. In spite of certain exceptions, it is broadly true that productivity increases in manufacturing industry have tended to outstrip those in the tertiary (service) sector of the economy.

It is instructive to compare output per unit of labour in the UK with that in other countries. This calls for careful research in order to ensure that all data is on a comparable basis. A recent study has estimated that labour productivity in the USA was just over two and a half times that in the UK. The differential in favour of the US varied quite considerably from industry to industry, as Fig 5.5 shows, being as high as five to six-fold in ships and vehicles and less than two-fold in construction. The causes of the higher productivity per man in the US are complex. They reflect differences in the amount of capital per man, in the scale of output, in plant size, in industrial relations, etc.

The study referred to above also made comparisons between the UK and Germany, where the differential in favour of Germany turned out to be smaller than with the USA, though it was increasing. German output per man was, on average, about half as high again as British. Only in agriculture was productivity significantly greater in the UK. There is an obvious link between productivity and what is called R and D (research and development) which, prima facie, might be expected to lead to technical progress.

Research and development

The UK curently devotes about 2 per cent of its total output to R and D. This

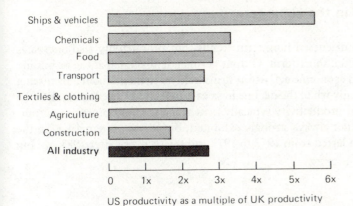

Fig 5.5 Comparative labour productivity, UK and USA 1976–77

is not far out of line with other countries such as Germany and Japan. However, about half of the expenditure is made by the government, which tends to concentrate on research in the field of defence, rather than in industry generally. Civil R and D expenditure benefits manufacturing industry for the most part, and Fig 5.6 shows its distribution. It can be seen that a relatively few industries are responsible for a disproportionate amount of the work, electrical engineering, aerospace and chemicals accounting for nearly three-quarters of the total. R and D tends to be concentrated in large firms which can afford the high costs involved in modern technological research, not to mention the willingness to accept the risks of failure. However, small firms have been responsible for some major innovations.

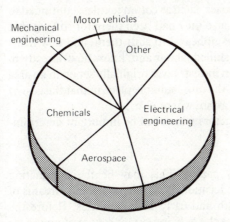

Fig 5.6 Research and development expenditure by manufacturing industry, UK 1981

Productivity in the short-term

So far we have discussed long-term trends, but productivity also fluctuates considerably in the short-term. Output per man tends to fall at the beginning of downturns in economic activity as firms hold on to their labour, dismissing the workforce only when the decline in sales is perceived to be lasting. For the opposite reason, productivity typically rises at the start of upturns in output. This pattern is not always strongly exhibited, but it was quite marked in the recession which lasted from 1973 to 1977 and the recovery after 1981 (*see* Fig 5.4).

The location of industry

It should be obvious that industry is not evenly spread over the whole of the country. Our knowledge of the geographical distribution of the population (*see* pages 45–7) should enable us to deduce that, since it is obvious that a district which is densely populated is likely to have more industry than a sparsely populated area, the map in Fig 3.5 showing the density of population is also a good guide to the location of industry. There is more to be said in explanation of the location of industry, however. Different regions tend to specialise in different industries and some, like textiles, are very highly concentrated in relatively few districts while others, like building, are more evenly spread over the country.

The reasons why certain districts specialise in particular industries are interesting, but they are usually also complex and could form the subject of profound study. Such a study would probably involve a great deal of historical research, for many of the older industries, such as cotton textiles, continued to be located in Lancashire largely because they had been there for so long that it would have required a tremendous upheaval to shift them, and new firms tended to be drawn by virtue of the skilled labour and 'know how' already in the area. Generally, we can say that an industry was originally set up in an area because at some time it was probably the most suitable place in that the cost of producing there was at least as low as anywhere else.

It is possible to distinguish four factors which can be important determinants of the location of industry:

1 *The need to be near a source of power* This may be the dominating influence. Witness, for instance, the location alongside rivers and streams of the cotton spinning mills in the 18th and early 19th centuries. Before the advent of the steam engine, water was the only important source of power for the factories. With greatly improved transport and the widespread distribution of electric power this restriction no longer prevails, but heavy industries,

like iron and steel, using a great deal of coal and coke which is fairly expensive to transport, still tend to be found near coalfields.

2 *The need to be near to the supply of a bulky raw material* This is closely related to the question of the availability of power. An example of this is to be found in the chemical industry, where an important section producing alkali (used in the manufacture of soap, rayon, glass and many other products) grew up in Cheshire near to supplies of brine, limestone and coal. The attraction of the nearness of raw material helps to explain a gradual change in the location of the iron and steel industry away from the coalfields and nearer to the iron ore supplies. As rich ore deposits were worked out the industry turned to deposits of a lower grade, such as those in Lincolnshire and Northamptonshire. Lower grade ore, however, means that much more of it has to be used to produce the same amount of steel, and it would be wasteful to transport the bulky ore a long way to the furnaces.

3 *The need for a ready supply of labour* This has become an important influence in the location of new factories since the Second World War. Although unemployed labour may often have been forced in the past to move to a district where employment was available, it has become increasingly difficult to induce people to leave their homes and move to totally different parts of the country. This is especially important if the labour required is highly skilled. We should not expect to find many precision instrument factories in the Scottish Highlands since, apart from anything else, it is not a place where one would look for skilled engineers and it is not easy to persuade them to move there.

4 *The desire to be near to a market where finished products are sold* This has the greatest bearing when the raw materials used are not bulky, since the cost of transporting them may well be offset by the advantage of being near to a market. The majority of industries do not, in fact, use bulky raw materials, and proximity to a market is probably the most important factor influencing the location of many factories. It is almost always true that to be near to a large market is to be near to a large town and thus, at the same time, to have the added advantage of a plentiful supply of labour. These two factors—nearness to markets and to a supply of labour—are the main reasons why industry has tended to concentrate itself in and around main cities. Whenever a new factory is built in a town it tends to attract people seeking employment. This in itself makes both the market and labour supply larger and may thus further increase the town's attractiveness.

Location of industry in Great Britain

There are two ways of looking at the location of industry in Great Britain. One is to concentrate on industries and examine, one by one, the extent to which each is spread over different regions in the country. The alternative, if it is carried out thoroughly, gives the same general picture. It is to look rather at the different districts and see how far each has specialised in particular industries. To do this really adequately would require a separate book, but we can get a good first approximation by dividing the country into the 12 standard geographical regions used in official statistics and examining the extent of concentration of particular industries in each.

Fig 5.8 has been drawn up to help in this exercise. It is based on the number of workers employed in each industry, and should be read alongside the adjoining map of Fig. 5.7. Each of the 12 areas has a column to itself, each space in which corresponds to an industrial group. Where this space is marked with a •, the percentage of the total area labour force in that industry is greater than the percentage in that industry for the country as a whole. Thus, wherever a • appears, the region is to some extent specialising in that particular industry. Wherever there is a blank space the region is not specialising in that industry although, of course, it may well be producing a certain amount of the goods in question.

Fig. 5.7 Standard regions UK 1984

There may be two possible reasons for non-specialisation. One is that the particular industry is one which happens to be concentrated in other areas. In that case, of course, there must be a ● against some other region or regions. The other explanation is that it is an industry in which no district is specialising for the simple reason that it is fairly evenly spread over the country. Thus there are no ●'s against gas, water and electricity, which are not highly concentrated in any regions.

	London	Rest of South East	East Anglia	South West	West Midlands	East Midlands	Yorkshire Humberside	North West	North	Wales	Scotland	Northern Ireland
Agriculture, forestry, fishing		●	●	●		●				●	●	●
Energy & water supply						●	●		●	●	●	
Metal manufacturing & chemicals					●	●	●	●	●	●		
Metal goods, engineering and vehicles		●			●	●		●				
Other manufacturing				●		●	●	●				
Construction						●	●		●	●	●	●
Wholesale distribution, hotels and catering	●				●	●						
Retail distribution	●	●	●						●	●	●	
Transport & communication	●											
Banking & finance	●											
Public administration & defence	●								●		●	●
Education, health & other services			●		●				●	●	●	●

Fig 5.8 Regional specialisation UK (● signifies that a region has more than the national average percentage of its labour force working in a particular industry)

The South East

The South East region employs over a third of the entire British labour force. Half the workers in the region are located in Greater London, which concentrates predominantly on non-manufacturing—hence the specialisation in finance, as so many offices of banks, insurance companies and other financial institutions are in the City. London is the pivot of road and rail networks, it is the chief shopping centre in the country and the site of many government departments.

The rest of the South East is second only to London in the size of its labour force. It is an important producer in agriculture, engineering and vehicles and employs more than the national average of its workforce in the distributive trades and education, health and other services.

East Anglia and the South West

East Anglia and the South West have much in common, despite their geographical separation. They are the foremost agricultural regions in England and Wales, employing some 6 and 3 per cent of their labour forces on the land, respectively. Both regions also specialise in food processing and contain important tourist resorts, which help to account for the fact that they have above average employment in the sector which includes hotels and catering. The South West is double the size of East Anglia in terms of total employment. Its industrial centre is Bristol. Although not specialising in terms of employment, engineering and aerospace equipment flourishes.

The Midlands

The Midlands is divided into East and West regions, the latter being substantially the larger. Both concentrate more on manufacturing than any other region. Both also specialise in metal manufacture. The West Midlands is the more important in the field of engineering, including (road) vehicles, much of the heavy sections of which are in the 'Black Country' around Birmingham and Wolverhampton. The East Midlands industry tends to be lighter and includes more clothing and textiles, and food, drink and tobacco. The East Midlands also has a sizeable agricultural sector, as well as taking in the coalfields of Derbyshire and Nottinghamshire.

Yorkshire and Humberside

This is a diversified, largely manufacturing region. Its specialisations include food, drink and tobacco, metal manufacture, and clothing and textiles, though there are more workers in engineering than in any of these industries. It is the largest employer, too, in coal mining.

The North West

The North West region, encompassing Manchester and Liverpool, is the second largest in Britain. It is also strongly industrial, specialising in all the major industries except metal manufacture. The region's traditional strength, Lancashire textiles, is now overshadowed by other industries including engineering, much of it heavy.

Northern England

Centred around Tyneside, the Northern region of England used to be particularly dependent on the heavy industries of coal, iron and steel, shipbuilding and chemicals. Almost a third of the labour force is still employed in manufacturing, which is now more diversified.

Wales

Wales is sparsely populated and largely mountainous. However it does have more than the national average percentage of workers in agriculture. It has traditionally been a coal mining area, although only about 3 per cent of the labour force remain in that industry now. Wales specialises in metal manufacture and chemicals, but iron and steel has been on the decline for several years. The range of manufacturing industry has, however, been widening to include engineering, plastics and clothing. Some decentralisation of government departments explains the specialisation in public administration and defence.

Scotland

Scotland is a good deal larger than Wales, but it also is sparsely populated and mountainous. A relatively high proportion of its labour force is in agriculture, and most industry is in the central lowlands, around Glasgow, with textiles in the Paisley area. Coal mining remains important and the exploitation of North Sea oil and gas accounts for the specialisation in energy and water supply.

Northern Ireland

Northern Ireland has the smallest number of employees of any of the regions of the UK—about half a million. Specialisation includes agriculture, food, drink and tobacco, and clothing and textiles. Many attempts have been made at industrial diversification in Northern Ireland, but the region has suffered for many years from both political unrest and the highest rate of unemployment in the UK.

Changes in location

This discussion of regional specialisation has failed to reveal one aspect of the location of industry. For the greater part of the century there has been considerable redeployment of industry over different parts of the country. In this connection, the decades between the two world wars were outstanding and witnessed a striking growth in the relative importance of Southern England and the Midlands at the expense of Northern England, Merseyside, South Wales and Scotland.

To account for these changes two main reasons may be offered. In the first place there was a tendency for industrialists to move southwards when erecting new factories, attracted by the growing market of Greater London. Moreover, the development of electricity as a source of power released them from the need to be near coalfields. The second explanation is the one that carries more weight. As we saw earlier, not all industries were expanding at the same rate and, in fact, some were declining. Most of the new and expanding industries, such as engineering, vehicles and electrical goods, were those in which the south and the Midlands were specialising, while the staple industries of the 19th century, especially textiles, coal and shipbuilding, were declining in importance and were largely concentrated in the North of England, Scotland and South Wales.

The period since the end of the Second World War has seen a continuation of the same broad trends, to which have been added more recent trends as some of the newer industries began to decline. Thus, the depressed state of the vehicle industry raised unemployment rates in the West Midlands from one of the lowest to one of the highest in Britain.

Government location policies

Heavy dependence of an area on one or more failing industries is naturally accompanied by serious local unemployment and it was not long before the government began to take steps to try to alleviate the problems of regions hit hardest during the inter-war years. The first step was taken in 1934 when certain 'special areas' were scheduled as depressed and commissioners were appointed to try to attract new industry to them. Post-war Distribution of Industry Acts reinforced this policy, giving powers to the government. These included building factories for letting in the areas (renamed **development areas**) and making loans and grants to encourage individual firms to go there.

In a negative way, too, the government's control over factory location was materially strengthened as a result of the Town and Country Planning Act 1947. By this Act new factories require planning permission from the local authority, and larger factories also require the granting of an Industrial Development Certificate. The government has, therefore, been in a position to influence the location of new plants by the withholding or granting of permission to develop particular sites—a powerful weapon.

The last 20 years have seen many variations in the policies of different governments aimed at preventing regional imbalance. In the 1960s Acts were passed giving the government power to make tax concessions and cash grants to firms locating in development areas. Special mention should be made of the **regional employment premium**. This was a measure, introduced in 1967 and lasting some 10 years, which offered financial aid related to the number of workers on a firm's books. It seemed to hit more directly at the problem of unemployment than that of making capital grants for new buildings and plant, which might be more likely to make capital intensive rather than labour intensive investment the more attractive.

In 1970 the Local Employment Act was passed, allowing for assistance to so-called **intermediate areas**, which were neither prosperous nor sufficiently depressed to qualify for development area status. However, the general policy continued in the 1970s of providing incentives for industries in 'assisted areas', which have included Scotland, Wales, Northern and North West England, Yorkshire and Humberside and parts of the Midlands and South West England, as well as Northern Ireland, an area of persistent problems and treated separately. Two recent developments have been the addition, since 1977, of run-down inner city centres to the category of areas eligible for support and the introduction, in 1980, of **enterprise zones.** Eleven were set up in that year, and by 1985, there were more than double that number. Firms in enterprise zones are exempt from rates (*see* page 234) and enjoy considerable freedom from government controls. The diagram, Fig 5.9, shows the location of enterprise zones, development areas and intermediate areas in 1985.

Regional unemployment rate differentials have tended to fall over the last two decades, though the extent to which this can be attributed to government policy is uncertain. However, the policy of the 1979 and 1983 Conservative administrations has reduced the scope of specially assisted areas in order to devote relatively more help to those in greatest need.

This section on regional policy ends by drawing attention to the fact that it has emphasised measures to encourage the movement of firms into declining areas. Such policies could be described as taking work to the workers and it would be wrong to ignore the obvious alternative of making it easier for workers to move to areas where jobs are available. Quite different problems have to be overcome with such policies. Not least is the fact that houses cannot be moved from place to place and people are often reluctant to move away from their friends and relatives. However, governments have not ignored the long-term support for regional policy that can come from measures to promote labour mobility by improving information about job availability and providing retraining facilities.

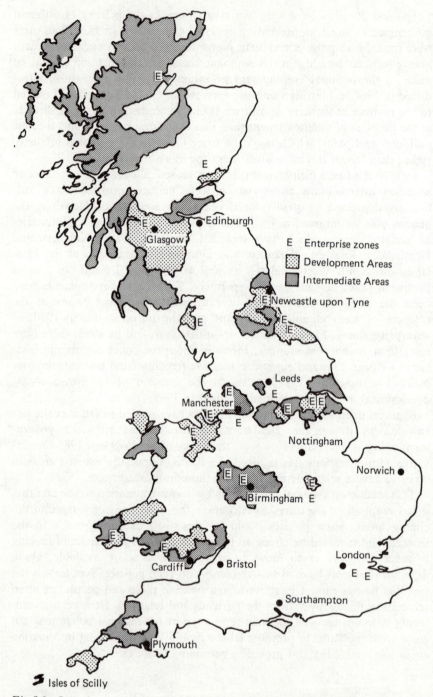

E Enterprise zones

Development Areas

Intermediate Areas

Edinburgh

Glasgow

Newcastle upon Tyne

Leeds

Manchester

Nottingham

Norwich

Birmingham

Cardiff

Bristol

London

Southampton

Plymouth

Isles of Scilly

Fig 5.9 Location of industry policy 1985; areas entitled to government aid

Industrial concentration

One of the outstanding features of industrial development in the past 100 years has been the growth in the size of firms and the extent to which industry has become concentrated in a relatively few large concerns. The days when the majority of goods were produced in a great number of small businesses have disappeared. The typical unit in many industries today is the giant **corporation**. There are many reasons for this development, but two deserve special attention.

Economies of large scale production

Over a wide section of industry, production in large units is more efficient than in small. Mass production has come about where it is both easier and cheaper to produce large quantities of standardised products in a factory than many slightly different ones in several small ones. This is, indeed, no more than an aspect of the specialisation among firms and among individuals noted at the beginning of this chapter. For as firms grow they are able to employ specialist personnel and equipment which is not worthwhile at a low level of output. Henry Ford achieved success by realising this and mass producing millions of motor cars, all exactly alike. Today, all the cheapest cars come from large factories. However, operation on a large scale often implies a degree of standardisation which may not be wanted by consumers, i.e. the scope for using mass production methods may be limited by the size of the market. We should note also that economies of large scale are not limited to production; they can be reflected in marketing, purchasing, financial, managerial or other costs.

Market power

Under private enterprise, if any firm comes to dominate the industry in one or more lines of business it is able to do things which the existence of effective competition from other firms might prevent, such as raising prices to the consumer, restricting output to maintain demand for its product, or stifling technical inventions which might make its product obsolete.

In the discussion which follows we should like to be able to attribute the growth of large-scale organisation in industry to a desire for more efficient production or for greater market control, although it may not always be clear how far each motive is responsible in every case.

The size of manufacturing establishments

In attempting to assess the importance of large- and small-scale production in present day Britain, it is wise to start by looking at the size of the individual factories, workshops, plants, etc., which are officially known as **establishments**. Although from the point of view of control the firm is the unit one should examine, the organisation of industry into establishments tells us something rather more basic, and may even help to distinguish between the two motives for expansion which have been mentioned.

If there are cost reductions to be realised within a factory one would not expect a firm to spread its output among several plants unless there are other advantages to be had. Hence, if economies of large-scale production are responsible for the concentration of an industry in large firms, they will tend to be associated with large establishments too. Large firms which operate several establishments may have grown in size for reasons other than the presence of falling costs of production in large plants. In such cases a desire for market control may be the dominant cause.

Fig 5.10 is based on information published by the government in the census of production and, although it is probably incomplete in its recording of very small establishments, it reveals that they are by far the most numerous. Of the total of about 100 000 manufacturing establishments covered in the census, over half employ 10 or fewer workers, while about 90 per cent employ under 100.

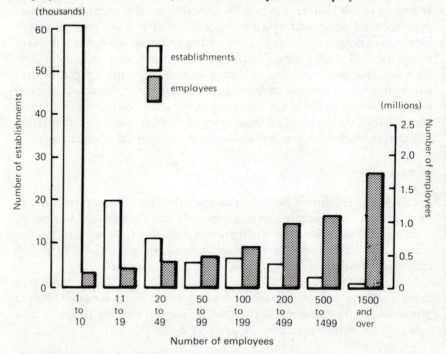

Fig 5.10 Size of establishments in manufacturing in the UK 1981 (establishments classified by number of employees)

This way of looking at the structure of industry conceals the more important fact that large-scale production is dominant in manufacturing. The 2000 establishments employing more than 500 workers each, which represent less than 2 per cent of the total, are so large that altogether they employ something like 50 per cent of the manufacturing labour force. Furthermore, the 436 largest establishments of all, each of which has more than 1500 workers on its payroll, account for nearly a third of total employment in manufacturing.

Large-scale production is, of course, much more common in some industries than in others. Some idea of this is given in Fig 5.11 which shows the percentage of total employment in establishments with 1500 or more employees. We find that the prime large-scale industry is vehicles, where large establishments are responsible for the employment of about three quarters of the labour force; in electrical engineering and metal manufacture for about half of total employment; and in chemicals and food, drink and tobacco, for about 40 per cent. The diagram shows, however, that there are industries, especially timber and furniture, metal goods and clothing, where large plants are relatively uncommon.

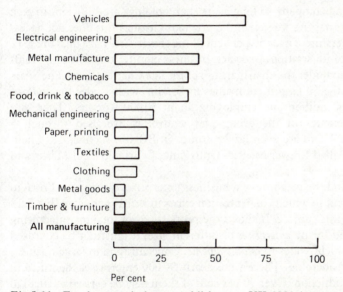

Fig 5.11 Employment in large establishments UK 1981 (percentage of total employment in establishments with 1500 or more workers)

The size of business enterprises

The concentration of industry in large establishments is, as we have just seen, considerable. However, we know that an individual company may own more than one establishment. This is particularly likely to be the case if the firm is a large one. The 1981 census tells us, for example, that the 100 largest businesses in manufacturing industry operated about 4000 establishments between them.

In order to see the full extent to which the control of business is concentrated it is necessary to move on from a consideration of the size of establishments to that of the size of businesses. The point should be made that individual firms are not necessarily independent of each other. A company may own other companies and we must examine the ways in which links between firms may be established.

Firms grow in two ways; by internal expansion and/or by the acquisition of other firms. Whichever way growth takes place a network of companies may be strung together creating a business empire. In such cases use is often made of the device of **holding companies**. Under this system the principal company, which is known as the parent company, owns a controlling interest in one or more other companies, which become its subsidiaries. The subsidiaries may, in their turn, own controlling interests in other companies, which are subsidiaries of the subsidiaries. In principle there is no limit to how far the process can go. A pyramid of companies can be built up, all ultimately controlled by the holding company so long as its shareholdings are sufficient to give controlling interests. (As we saw in the previous chapter, this does not necessarily mean ownership of over 50 per cent of the shares—*see* page 69.) Fig 5.12 shows, by way of illustration, one such business empire; that of Sears Holdings Ltd, built up under the chairmanship of the late Charles Clore. The Sears group is one of the 50 largest companies in Britain, with a sales turnover of more than £1500 million and employing about 50 000 workers. There are about 400 companies in the group and control is exercised through 5 pyramidal tiers. There are even larger groups in Britain, such as BP, Shell, ICI, Unilever, Allied Breweries, Rio-Tinto Zinc, Courtaulds and Marks and Spencer.

Bearing in mind the meaning of a business enterprise, we may next turn to examine the extent to which concentration exists in British industry. Fig 5.13 throws light on this subject. It shows the proportions of total manufacturing output accounted for by *enterprises* of different size; it must not be confused with Fig 5.10 which relates to *establishments*. Concentration in large business units is very considerable. There were nearly 90 000 enterprises identified in the census of production. Over 90 per cent of them may be classed as small in that they employed less than 100 workers each. They were, in the main, single establishment businesses and they accounted for not much more than 10 per cent of total manufacturing output in 1981. At the other end of the scale we can distinguish some 133 large enterprises each employing a minimum of 5000 workers. They represented less than 1 per cent of the total number of enterprises, but accounted for over 40 per cent of all production in manufacturing. Among them were 28 giants with at least 20 000 employees each, producing a fifth of total output.

The degree of concentration in individual industries, of course, varies as much when we take enterprises as our unit as when we take establishments. The measure of concentration in an industry is liable to be influenced by the

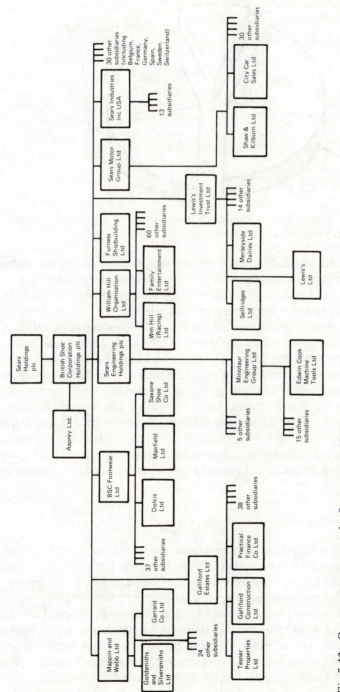

Fig 5.12 Company structure; the Sears group 1984

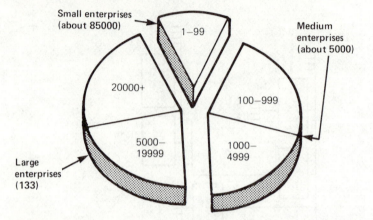

Fig 5.13 Concentration in manufacturing industry UK 1981 (shares of net output produced by enterprises of different size)

way in which the industry is defined—the more narrowly, the higher the degree of concentration. In order to illustrate some of the differences that do exist, Fig 5.14 has been prepared showing, for certain selected industries, the share of the largest 5 enterprises in total sales.

The diagram is based on what are known as **concentration ratios** (CRs). They are simply the percentage shares of the largest 5 enterprises in the total output of each industry group. The very wide range of CRs shown—from 10 to 100 per cent—is just one way of depicting the extent of differences in concentration. Thus, while there are highly concentrated industries, such as tobacco, man-made fibres and cement, there are others, like wooden furniture and machine tools, where the share of the largest 5 firms is much lower. It must be remembered that Fig 5.14 is confined to selected industries for purposes of illustration only and does not show all industry groups. Other products which are highly concentrated include, for example, man made fibres, margarine and asbestos.

Diversification

The great importance of large enterprises in British industry, brought out in Figs 5.13 and 5.14, is not open to doubt. However, it is necessary to recognise an additional feature of many of them; they are multi-product businesses. The Sears group of companies depicted in Fig 5.12 for example, has widely diversified interests including engineering, motor distribution, bookmaking, the gold and silver trade and the ownership of department stores, backing its main line in shoe retailing. Another example is Grand Metropolitan Ltd, whose chief interest in hotels is supplemented by others in breweries (Watney, Mann and Truman), milk supply (Express Dairies), bookmakers and Miss World (Mecca).

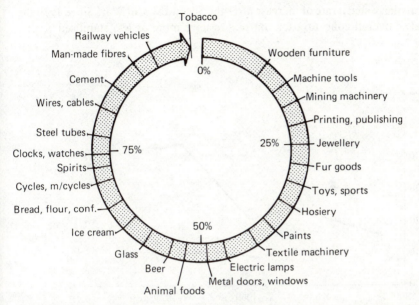

Fig 5.14 Large-scale enterprises UK 1981 (selected industries); percentage of total output by the 5 largest enterprises (percentages are measured separately for each industry clockwise from the 12 o'clock origin)

The extent of diversification among large corporations is not easily quantified. As in the case of the measurement of concentration itself, the results obtained by using various measures are liable to be sensitive to the way in which industry groups are defined. The more narrow the definitions the greater the observed diversification is likely to be. However, a recent study of the extent to which diversification has been increasing in British industry showed that, although there are a few sectors where diversification has declined, in the majority of cases it has increased. Moreover, plants owned by one or other of the largest 200 enterprises in manufacturing were to be found in every single one of the 120 or so separate industries in manufacturing industry.

Changes in concentration

Attention has so far been directed to the extent of concentration in British industry in the 1980s. It is time to look at trends over time in the degree of concentration, both overall and in different sectors. Fig 5.15 is based on information published in censuses of production since 1909 and shows the share of the largest 100 enterprises in total manufacturing output. It can be seen that the share of these giants rose from about 15 per cent in the first decade of the century to over 40 per cent at the end of the 1960s, with a particularly sharp rate of increase after the Second World War. Since 1970 the level of overall concentration appears to have more or less stabilised.

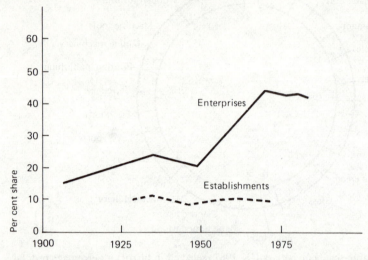

Fig 5.15 The growth of concentration in manufacturing industry UK 1909–81 (share of largest 100 enterprises and largest 100 establishments in total output of manufactures)

It is interesting to compare the rising share of the top 100 companies with that of the largest establishments, which is shown for a shorter period. The contrast between them could hardly be more marked. At the time when concentration in giant companies was proceeding most rapidly, the share of the largest establishments was virtually constant, at around 10 per cent. This suggests very strongly that whatever the cause of the increase in concentration, it was not substantially due to firms taking advantage of economies of scale associated with large plants.

Within the trend of increasing overall concentration of industry in relatively few businesses, it is necessary to look at what has been happening in different sectors. This is difficult to measure because of the changes that occur, particularly over long periods of time, in the nature of products offered for sale. However, studies based on the most comparable industry groups reach conclusions on trends in sectoral concentration that match those in overall concentration, as far as the time pattern is concerned (the size of the increases in concentration being rather less sharp). The post-war decade of most rapid concentration growth was the 1960s. One study estimated the *average* CR3 (i.e. for the largest 3 enterprises) in a sample of 42 industries to have been 29 per cent in 1951, 32 per cent in 1958, but 41 per cent in 1968. Since that date very little change was observed in sectoral concentration in the 1970s or early 1980s. It must be added that our summary runs only in terms of *average* concentration, and that all industries do not move in line together. Some sectors grew at above average rates and, even in the period of rapid growth of concentration, some industries experienced falling concentration (e.g. fruit and vegetable products and agricultural and electrical machinery).

Mergers

It was mentioned earlier that businesses can expand by internal growth or by the acquisition of other companies. While the former method has undoubtedly been an important one, especially in earlier times, growth by merger has been on the increase, and is estimated to have been the cause of at least half of the increase in concentration since the late 1950s. Mergers tend to come in waves. They were running at a rate of about 750 per annum from the early 1960s with peaks of more than 1000 in 1972 and 1973, before falling to less than half that figure after that.

Some mergers take place between companies of roughly equal size. In other cases a small firm may be taken over in such a way as to lose its identity virtually completely. From the point of view of concentration of the control of industry, however, the most important aspect of amalgamations between companies concerns the nature of the businesses. It is useful to distinguish three types of merger. They are known by the terms horizontal, vertical and conglomerate.

Horizontal mergers are those between firms producing similar products, such as the Dolcis and Manfield shoe chains in the Sears group, depicted in Fig 5.12. **Vertical mergers** involve the absorption of suppliers or outlets, such as the acquisition by Dunlop of rubber plantations or the purchase by a brewery of public houses which sell its beer direct to the public. The third type of merger, the **conglomerate merger**, is characterised by the fact that it leads to diversification of interests. The Sears group is a good example, since there is little in common with the product lines of some of its companies, e.g. shoe shops, bookmakers, engineering and property development. Nor is there reason to believe there is evidence in such cases of vertical integration.

One should be a little careful here for it is not always easy to place a particular merger in the correct category. Some amalgamations may not appear, on the surface, to have elements of either vertical or horizontal integration, but this may conceal less obvious matters, such as disposal of by-products or utilisation of expertise in a related field which might explain such otherwise unlikely combinations as detergents, plastics and ice cream manufacture in the Unilever group.

Horizontal mergers have been the predominant type in post-Second World War Britain, with vertical integration being insignificant. Conglomerate mergers gradually increased in importance in the 1960s and 1970s, accounting for about a third of the total by the late 'seventies, though falling back to about a quarter by 1983.

It is important to add that horizontal mergers and, to an extent, vertical ones tend to increase the power of a company over its market. Conglomerate mergers, on the other hand, have a prime aim in the diversification of activities either to reduce risks by spreading them or to move out of a declining industry into an expanding one. It is a controversial matter whether mere large size by itself strengthens a company's position, but there is no doubt that mergers of all kinds have been a major cause of the growth in the concentration of industry in the hands of the largest companies. Whether it has paid off or not is a different matter. Studies of the effect of mergers on company profits suggest that there were, on balance, few cases in which the post-merger financial situation was significantly improved.

Co-operation between firms

The emphasis so far in this section on industrial concentration has been on the power of business enterprises. It must not be forgotten, however, that there are avenues of co-operation open to separate firms which fall short of the full pooling of sovereignty involved in amalgamation. Some of the most common arrangements between firms take place through a **trade association**. This is a very wide term and includes any body of employers who have agreements with each other. The Confederation of British Industry (CBI) is one such example. It acts as industry's spokesman on economic and labour matters where a national voice is required.

In individual industries, trade associations usually have a more specific role. Their functions vary from industry to industry and include the carrying out of research and publicity. They may also cover activities such as regulating the output or fixing the price of products in the industry and organising the machinery for carrying through policies. Some trade associations have made arrangements for allocating shares of the market to constituent firms on a predetermined basis, involving the setting up of a central sales organisation, which is often referred to as a **cartel**. Agreements of this kind can have much the same effect as more complete mergers between firms insofar as the restriction of competition is concerned, although they may be less stable.

Legislation has been passed to try to limit the operation of restrictive agreements (*see* page 115). An example of a trade association which employed an elaborate system of devices to control the market—including the fixing of prices, the allocation of sales quotas to members punishable by a scale of fines and control of entry—is given in Fig 5.16. It also shows the known financial links between members of the Electric Lamp Manufacturers' Association in 1951. It is difficult to assess the effect that trade associations have on industrial concentration in the present state of knowledge about the precise nature of their activities. However, industries without a trade association are much in the minority and, where trade associations exist, membership is usually widespread.

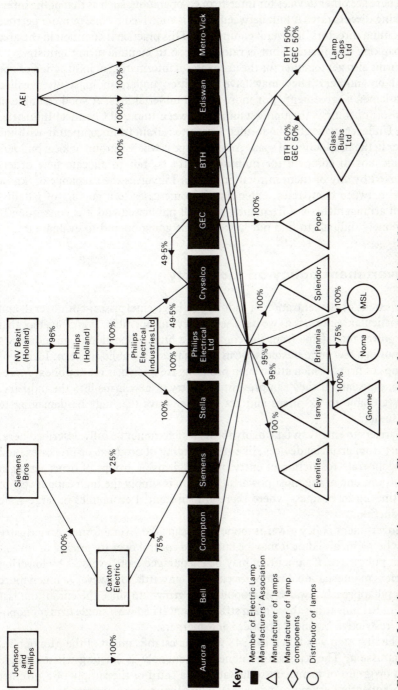

Fig 5.16 Links between members of the Electric Lamp Manufacturers' Association 1951

There are other devices for inter-firm co-operation, such as that of the **inter-locking directorate**. A link between firms is contrived by one or more persons becoming directors of several companies. This practice is common in the area of banking and finance, but is rather less so in manufacturing industry.

Firms also get together for the exchange of information or joint action of one kind or another. They may have unwritten understandings, often called 'gentlemen's agreements', or more formal undertakings. A good example of this sort of thing is the understanding between Imperial Chemical Industries and Unilever, whereby the former agreed to refrain from competing with the latter in the production of soap. Another type is where a group of local builders decide not to compete for building contracts, but to allocate new orders received by any of them in rotation. A third involves the exchange of 'know how' between companies, extending in some cases to a pooling of patents. Such arrangements are frequently not well publicised and it is consequently extremely difficult to find out how much is going on and to evaluate it.

Government policy on monopoly

The extent of concentration of industry in large enterprises, both overall and in particular sectors, is as we have seen, very considerable. It is clear, too, that the power that stems from the control of a high proportion of an industry's output in a few large businesses can be a matter for public concern. Firms, or groups of firms, which attain such positions are known as **monopolies**. Moreover, especially if they can prevent the entry of new firms into the industry, they are able to fix prices and act in other ways that may be damaging to consumers.

Barriers to entry can take many forms which cannot be fully described here. Apart from artificial devices, like the patenting of products or processes, and the deliberate restriction of entry by large firms or groups of firms acting in collusion, one of the most powerful barriers is simply the high capital cost of starting up in business where there are substantial economies of large-scale production.

Government policy towards monopolies can take several forms. An industry may be nationalised or it may be subject to control over its pricing or investment policy, etc. Competition may be encouraged from overseas by lowering barriers to international trade (*see* page 217 onwards). However, a much more general approach towards monopolies has grown up since the end of the last war in Britain. It has three main strands, concerned with single firm monopolies, restrictive business practices and mergers.

The first step was taken in 1948 with the establishment of the Monopolies Commission. The legislation defined a monopoly as existing when a single firm or group of firms controlled at least a third of the supply of a product (subsequently lowered to a quarter). The Monopolies Commission was given broad powers to inquire into industries where a monopoly was suspected, in order to ascertain if this was the case and, if so, whether or not the activities of businesses there operated against the public interest. In the years since it was set up the Commission made about 150 reports on industries from electric lamps to cross channel ferries. In the vast majority of cases it found some practices to be operating against the public interest, such as price-fixing and measures to prevent the entry of new firms.

The second strand in what has come to be called 'competition policy' concerns not so much monopolies as restrictive practices by *groups of firms*. The background to this development was the previous work of the Monopolies Commission uncovering practices in its early references which had been deemed to be contrary to the public interest and appeared to be widely prevalent. It was felt that the best way of tackling such practices was by special legislation. The Restrictive Practices Act of 1956 then followed. Under the provisions of the Act firms had to register a wide range of agreements affecting the supply of goods with a Registrar of Restrictive Practices, who could take proceedings against them to a Restrictive Practices Court. The presumption of the law is that all such agreements are contrary to the public interest unless special circumstances can be shown to exist, such as that they provide a substantial net benefit to the consuming public.

About 4500 agreements have been registered, although the vast majority have been subsequently abandoned voluntarily. Only a tiny proportion were contested before the Court, of which about a third were allowed to continue. The majority were found to be against the public interest and declared void, including the famous Cotton Yarn Spinners' Agreement: in spite of the fact that the Court accepted the argument that local unemployment would follow the abandonment of the agreement, it was held that this was not in itself sufficient to offset its detrimental effect of restricting competition.

Another development was the Resale Prices Act of 1964. The Act prohibited agreements, even by individual manufacturers, to fix minimum resale prices of their goods by retailers in advance, unless granted exemption by the Restrictive Practices Court. This piece of legislation was particularly effective. About 500 applications for exemption were made, the vast majority being refused. As a result of the Act the previously widespread practice of fixed prices for goods in all shops virtually disappeared from Britain; by shopping around, one can now usually buy most articles at a discount.

Later Acts added services as well as goods (1965) and nationalised industries (1980) to the references that could be made to the Monopolies Commission, and another class of agreements to those that should be registered (1968). These are so-called information agreements, whereby firms circulate price lists to others in the industry which, it has been argued, might be as effective in some circumstances as formal price-fixing agreements in preventing price competition.

The most important development, however, which represented the third strand in government policy, brought mergers into the net. As we saw earlier, a merger movement of very considerable proportions began in the 1960s and has been responsible for at least half the increase in industrial concentration since then. Many of such mergers may even have been stimulated by the effectiveness of the legislation outlawing restrictive practices *between* firms. The Monopolies and Mergers Act of 1965 was therefore introduced. It gave the Minister in charge of the appropriate government department (now the Secretary of State for Trade) the power to withhold permission for mergers which involved large companies (with assets in excess of £5 million) being taken over, or which would result in or intensify a monopoly. Such mergers could be referred to the Commission, renamed the Monopolies and Mergers Commission (MMC).

The policy on mergers has proved notably less effective than that directed towards restrictive practices. About 2000 mergers were caught by the legislation since 1970, but very few were referred to the Monopolies and Mergers Commission for report. It is true that a great many of these were either rejected or abandoned voluntarily. Others may not have seen the light of day because of the very existence of the Act, so it should certainly not be completely discounted.

The chief new features of competition policy in the 1970s were the creation of new machinery to bring together the various strands of government policy and the closing of some loopholes. The Fair Trading Act of 1973 established an Office of Fair Trading under a Director General of Fair Trading (DGFT). He became responsible, in consultation with the Secretary of State for Trade, for implementing both references to the MMC and for action on restrictive practices. A new Act in 1980 added to the powers of the DGFT, allowing him to institute preliminary investigations from his own office where there is a suspicion of the existence of so-called 'anti-competitive practices' not covered by the registration procedure of the Restrictive Practices Act. Anti-competitive practices are broadly defined to include such behaviour as the refusal of a firm to supply another—such as a discount store which might sell its products at 'cut', i.e. low, prices—and the tying of the sales of one product to those of another.

Seen as a whole British competition policy as it has developed represents a distinctive approach to the problems arising from the existence of monopoly power in the private sector of industry. In contrast to policy in other countries, particularly that in the USA, the underlying philosophy has been one of a case by case assessment whereby, except for certain registrable business practices, monopolies and mergers are recognised to have potential benefits as well as detriments for the public interest. Each case is judged on its merits before an overall assessment is made.

One consequence of this approach is that it tends to work slowly. Other criticisms have been made. The findings of the MMC do not have to stand up to public enquiry as do those of the Restrictive Practices Court. On the other hand, the government of the day has not always accepted the recommendations of the Commission and reliance has been placed on voluntary assurances from businesses after the publication of reports in most cases rather than on formal orders from the government for implementation.

Mergers policy has had to face peculiar problems of its own. Not least among them is that it has not been the only official policy towards industry. The government is also concerned to try to raise industrial efficiency. This can at times appear to cut across competition policy on mergers when it involves trying to stimulate increases in company size to realise economies of large-scale production. The Industrial Reorganisation Corporation, set up in 1966, and the National Enterprise Board 10 years later (*see* page 81) were both involved in exercises of this kind. A similar philosophy lay behind a White Paper, *An Approach to Industrial Strategy*, published in 1975. Reconciliation of such an approach with that of controlling merger activity is not always easy. On the other hand, the more recent 'privatisation' programme of the Conservative governments of 1979 and 1983, has contained elements designed to strengthen the competitive process. Examples are the Business Expansion Scheme to help small businesses (*see* page 83), and 'deregulation' measures, such as the virtual removal of licensing of long distance bus transport (1981) and the freeing of sales of spectacles (1984).

Finally, it is necessary to mention that Britain's membership of the European Economic Community (EEC) since 1973 (see pages 219–30) has meant that the Community's competition policy is applicable to businesses in Britain. EEC policy is not very different from that of the UK as far as restrictive practices are concerned. The rules, however, apply only where trade between different members of the EEC is involved. They came into prominence when it became known that the prices of certain cars were kept artificially high by firms refusing to allow right hand drive cars to be produced on the continent.

Exercises

For key to symbols indicating sources *see* pages xii–xiii.

1   From the library obtain a copy of the latest issue of *The Times 1000*, a publication containing details of the finances of the largest 1000 companies in Britain. Add the profits earned last year in the largest 20 profit earners. Next refer to the *Annual Abstract of Statistics* and extract the figure for the gross trading profits of companies for the same year. (Use the table headed Company Appropriation Account in the section 'National Income'.) Calculate the proportion of total company profits earned by the top 20 companies. Repeat the calculations for an earlier year. Does the degree of concentration in large companies appear to have changed at all between the 2 dates?

2   Find out how many people are employed in the firms in which 3 of your relatives or friends work. Assemble the information derived from the whole of your class and

prepare a table showing the size of firms for everyone concerned, grouping firms by size into the following classifications:

less than 100 employees   1000–20 000 employees
100–999 employees   over 20 000 employees

Calculate the percentage of the total in each group. Compare the results with those in Fig 5.13.

3 Using figures of numbers employed, calculate the proportion of the total number of workers in the engineering industry and in food, drink and tobacco accounted for by each sub-group under those headings. (For example, the group 'agriculture' consists of sub-groups agriculture, forestry, and fishing.) (*AS*)

4 Prepare 2 charts on the lines of Fig 5.2 showing the relative importance of the major manufacturing industries according to whichever of the following are available.

a the value of net output
b the value of sales
c the volume of employment

Use the latest figures available and compare your results. (*AS*)

5 List 6 of the most important industries in your locality. Can you offer suggestions as to why they were established there?

6 Using the oldest and latest figures you have available calculate the proportion of total wage earners in industrial groups according to whether you consider the product of that industry to be primary, secondary or tertiary in nature. Compare your results. (*AS, F*)

7 From the latest edition of *Who Owns Whom* in your local library prepare a chart on the lines of Fig 5.12 for 1 of the following companies:

Grand Metropolitan Ltd
Cadbury Schweppes Ltd
The Rank Organisation Ltd
Great Universal Stores Ltd
Courtaulds Ltd

8 Select 3 of the standard regions of the UK and make a note of their manufacturing specialisations (see Figs 5.7 and 5.8). Using the set of local telephone directories in the public library attempt to identify a number of companies in each region involved in its specialised product groups. Do your findings confirm the •'s in Fig 5.8?

9 Prepare a graph for as many years as you can of the numbers of companies acquired by merger in the UK. Is there evidence of any waves of merger activity? (*AS*)

10 Arrange a visit to 1 or 2 local factories. Try to find out in each case:

a how long it has been situated in its present site
b whether it is an independent company or a subsidiary of another
c what proportion of its output is exported
d how many employees it has on its books
e how fast its output has been growing

Where possible compare any answers you get with the average for the industry and for all industries together. (*AS*)

6 Labour

The first chapter in this book explained that the production of goods and services is achieved by a combined effort of many resources known as the factors of production. Among these are raw materials, land and buildings, machinery and equipment, and labour itself. Since goods are produced jointly by several factors of production working together, one cannot describe one factor as being more important than the others. There is a sense in which labour may be considered of primary importance in the production process, however, since other factors are useless if there is no labour to work with them, even if only to push a button; while even without machines men and women may be able to produce some things, if less efficiently. The reason for giving labour a chapter to itself is that inanimate factors are brought into use only as a result of decisions by people who own or manage them and it is only indirectly that human beings are involved. Workers, in contrast, enter directly into the production process and are, to an extent, able to control the use made of the labour services they supply.

We have already examined certain aspects of labour earlier in the book, for example when we looked at the size of the working population and the distribution of employment by industry and by occupation. We shall consider some others later. In this chapter we bring together some of the most important features of labour from an economic point of view—the level of wages and the extent of unemployment. This will involve the consideration of negotiations between labour and employers, the activities of trade unions and the problem of industrial disputes.

Wages

It is best to start a discussion of the structure of the earnings of labour by emphasising that a wage is really a price—the price of labour. In a market economy wages are settled, as explained in Chapter 1, by the forces of supply and demand. Workers are the suppliers in this case and the demand for labour comes from employers, and is derived from the demand for the product that labour produces. In competitive markets wage rates for different types of labour of varying skills will tend to settle at the level at which the forces of supply and demand are balanced. However, we know that Britain is a mixed economy and although market forces play a part in determining wages, other factors are also important. In particular the government, as we have seen, intervenes in the fixing of wages, and traditions built up over the years relating to wage differentials affect the pattern of wages.

Before examining labour incomes in detail it is necessary to cover a few technical matters. In particular we must distinguish between three terms which are often used loosely to mean the same thing—wages, earnings and salaries. There is nothing very complicated about the differences, but they should be understood.

Wages refer to the remuneration received by workers. Wages are calculated by reference to the 'wage rates' that are stipulated when employees are engaged for jobs. Wage rates are generally of two types: time rates and payment by results (PBR). **Time rates** are related to hours of employment and may vary according to the time and day of the week—i.e. a standard rate for 'normal hours' with provision for payment at higher rates for overtime, week-end and holiday work. **PBR** means no more than it says, that remuneration varies with output. There have been many systems of payment by results over the years designed to give special incentives to hard work. They enjoyed a wave of popularity after the end of the Second World War, when they applied to about a third of all wage earners. In recent years PBR has become less common. One of the reasons for this is probably the increasing use of mechanisation in industry and the associated difficulty of measuring output attributable to the effort of individual workers. This tends to make PBR rather pointless and potentially unfair.

Earnings are the total amount of money income received by workers. They take account of hours worked, or of output in PBR systems.

Salaries refer generally to the incomes of professional, technical and commercial workers. There is no hard and fast line between a wage and a salary, but a standard way of distinguishing between them is by reference to the length of contract agreed between employer and employee. Salaries are on an annual basis, usually paid monthly, while wages are on a weekly or daily basis.

Wage differences

Bearing in mind that workers are paid in a variety of ways and that this, in itself, is responsible for some of the variations between the earnings of individuals, we may nevertheless identify a number of causes of wage differences. Two groups can be distinguished relating to (a) the particular characteristics of individual workers and (b) the economic conditions of the industries and occupations in which they are employed.

One of the most important personal characteristics affecting earnings is ability, both innate and that acquired by education and training, which affects skill. Age and sex are significant influences as well as other factors, such as race, family background, and attitudes to work—which may lead one person to work longer hours than another, or to drive himself or herself to seek out more highly paid jobs. Though not strictly a personal characteristic, the weather can also affect earnings—people seem to work less hard in hot humid climates, understandably so.

Workers' earnings depend not only on their individual characteristics, but also on the demand for their services, deriving from their productivity and the demand for the product they help produce. The wage rates determined by the forces of supply and demand in factor markets, are influenced by economic conditions in different industries, different occupations, and different locations. It is important to note, too, that there are barriers to entry into many occupations; some are straightforward, like the possession of a particular skill, others are more contrived. Supply and demand for labour are also liable to be influenced by the relative bargaining power of employers and employees. This is where trade unions come into the picture.

Some of the causes of wage differences, e.g. innate ability and work attitudes, are almost impossible to quantify. We shall look at some of the most easily identifiable variations in wages, remembering, however, that they are not always simple to interpret.

Occupation differences

To a large extent occupational wage variations may be attributable to the skills needed to perform particular jobs. For example, the head chef at the Savoy Hotel is paid more than the unskilled cleaners and dishwashers there. It is hardly surprising that people with inborn skills and others who have acquired them should earn higher incomes. How much higher? That is not an easy question to which a general answer can be given because there is no unambiguous way of measuring the relative skills needed for different occupations.

One crude measure of the extra rewards paid for skills is to compare the earnings of manual and non-manual workers. In 1984, the average hourly earnings of adult male manual workers was £3.36, while that of non-manual workers was £5.36. Of course, these are average figures and conceal both larger and smaller differentials for specific skills. It is difficult to generalise further about present differentials, but more can be said about how these have changed over time.

Fig 6.1 shows the earnings of men in certain occupational groups expressed as percentages of average earnings in 1913 and 1978. The diagram is based on sample data published by the Royal Commission on the Distribution of Income and Wealth in the 1970s. Too much should not be read into evidence of this kind that extends over so long a period when so many conditions were changing. It serves one very useful purpose, however; that of emphasising that a long-term narrowing of differentials has been taking place. This trend

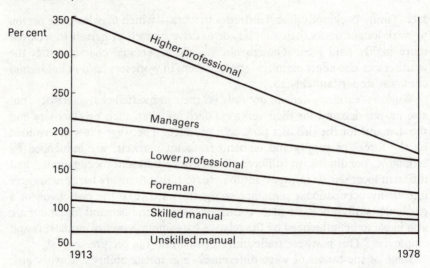

Fig 6.1 Occupational wage differences (males) 1913 and 1978 (the earnings for each occupation are shown as a percentage of average earnings of all male employees)

has been the result of changing forces on both the supply and demand sides of the labour market.

One supply side factor is increased labour mobility. The number of people acquiring qualifications is also greater now that it was near the beginning of the century. Moreover, although it is not visible from the diagram, the evidence suggests that the narrowing of differentials has recently slowed down, if not ceased altogether in some cases. This, too, may be partly due to market forces, but it must also be recognised that differentials built up over many years are not always easily eroded. They acquire a kind of status image that some of those engaged in wage bargaining are reluctant to see altered.

Wage differences by industry

A second source of differences in wages is related to the industry in which one works. Fig 6.2 shows details of the weekly earnings of workers in a selection of industries in October 1984. The average weekly pay of adult male manual workers at the time was £159. Compared with this, labour in the industries with the highest earnings were clocking up about 20 per cent more, whilst those in the industries at the bottom of the table were receiving about 20 per cent less. Too much attention should not be paid to the exact ordering of industries at that or any other particular time. There are often changes in relative position as businesses expand or contract, and are able or unable to pay higher wages. Indeed, these may be no more than the reflection of changing supply and demand conditions.

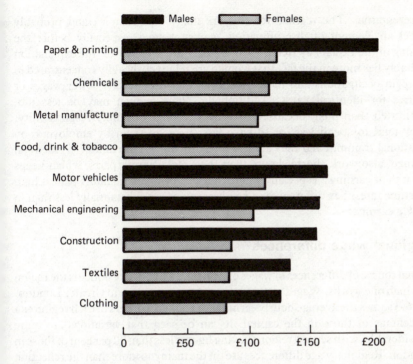

Fig 6.2 Average weekly earnings of manual workers in selected industries UK October 1984

A related matter is that differences in average hours worked may be associated with variations in economic conditions. Since overtime rates are usually higher than those for standard hours this would exaggerate differences in earnings. It should be emphasised, however, that observed inter-industry wage differences may, in part, reflect skill differences insofar as the proportions of skilled workers vary from one industry to another.

Age and sex differences in wages

It is commonly believed that people tend to be paid more as they get older. This is certainly true up to a point. The average earnings of male manual workers, aged 18–20, are less than two-thirds of the average for all workers.

What happens later on in life depends very much on the job, and it is dangerous to generalise. However, there is usually a plateau when earnings stop rising, or even fall. This is reached at younger age groups for manual workers than for non-manual, and earlier for women than for men.

As Fig 6.2 shows, a man is much more likely to earn more than a woman, regardless of the industry in which he works. Average earnings of women in all industries in October 1984 were between a half and two-thirds those of men, and although they differed from industry to industry, the figure is fairly representative. The reasons for this are many and complex and probably reflect an element of discrimination against women, especially before the passing of the Equal Pay Act of 1976 (*see* page 242). However, the explanation probably lies more in the fact that women are relatively heavily concentrated in low paid occupations and industries, than that they receive lower wages or salaries for identical work. Additionally, some women may be less job-committed than men, because of stronger feelings of family responsibility. They tend to spend less (or to have less spent on them by employers) on vocational training, and they are less likely to join a trade union. Women, on average, also work shorter hours than their male counterparts, which keeps down their earnings, especially where they decide to forego hours paid at high overtime rates. Sex differences in *hourly* earnings are substantially less than in *weekly* earnings.

Regional wage differences

A final source of differences in wages of which we should take notice is the region in which one works. Wages tend to be highest, on average, in Greater London. Fig 6.3 shows the average hourly earnings of manual workers in each region as a percentage of those in the capital. It can be seen that variations are quite considerable, with several regions having figures less than 90 per cent of those in London. Regional wage differences are, in the main, no more than the reflection of basic forces which we have mentioned earlier. Behind the statistics lies the fact that regions differ in the proportions of their labour forces in different industries. We have observed something of the extent of variations in earnings by industry, and these obviously affect the regional statistics. This is only part of the story, however. If we dig deeper we can appreciate that regional wage rates may be affected by the state of local labour markets. Employers in relatively prosperous areas, such as London, need to pay higher wages than those in others, such as Northern Ireland, which are relatively depressed.

Non-pecuniary advantages of occupations

A final word on the explanation of wage differences is in order before turning to our next subject; unemployment. The discussion so far has been entirely in terms of monetary earnings. Earnings are not the whole story. An early econo-mist coined the term 'non-pecuniary advantages and disadvantages' of different occupations in order to emphasise that some people would be happy with relatively low paid jobs if there were compensating (i.e. non-pecuniary) advantages to go with them. An outdoor job appeals to many people more than one in an office or factory; an interesting one (e.g. teaching!) more than a dull routine one; a job with long holidays rather than short; and so on. These and similar characteristics are difficult, if not impossible, to quantify, but there are other kinds of non-monetary rewards that can be quantified. They are

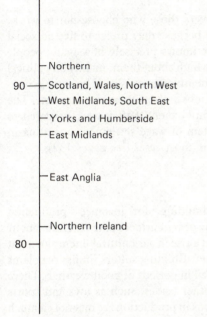

Fig 6.3 Regional wage differentials October 1984 (average hourly earnings of adult male manual workers for each region shown as a percentage of those in Greater London)

commonly referred to as **fringe benefits** and include such 'extras' as the use of a company car, subsidised lunches and housing, etc. The Royal Commission on the Distribution of Income and Wealth, mentioned earlier, made a special study of this subject in 1978 and found benefits over and above monetary remuneration to run from around a fifth to a third of total pay. It should be added that such fringe benefits may have been particularly high in that year for reasons associated with the government's policy of general pay restraint (see Ch 10, page 252), but they should not be overlooked at any time when discussing wage differentials.

Unemployment

Our consideration of wages ends for the moment. We shall return to the subject when we look at the activities of trade unions. First, however, we need to examine a matter which, at times, is as important to a worker as his pay— whether or not he has a job at all. It will help us to understand the picture of unemployment in Britain if we pause for a moment to consider the nature of unemployment and to distinguish between a number of different types.

1 Voluntary unemployment

The first category of unemployment covers those who choose not to work, either because they can afford not to, or because they prefer to live on social security benefits (see page 246). No one knows precisely how many people there are in this category, but feelings run high about them, mainly on political grounds. Indeed, the term 'voluntary' unemployment is used by some economists to include workers who cannot find jobs *at the going market wage rate*. The implication is that they could obtain employment if they were prepared to work for less than this, though the system of wage settlement operating in Britain must make this rather unlikely in most cases (*see* pages 139).

2 Seasonal unemployment

In some industries—agriculture and building, for instance—production varies greatly according to the time of the year. Farmers take on extra labour for the harvest, and we may expect to find a rise in agricultural unemployment as men are laid off when the harvest is over. Building suffers similar problems in as much as outside work is concentrated in periods of good weather. There are seasonal influences affecting many other trades, such as toys and sports goods. To some extent seasonal fluctuations in production are met not so much by actual unemployment as by workers going on overtime in the peak periods and on short-time in the slack periods.

3 Frictional unemployment

As we saw in Chapter 5, the structure of industry is constantly changing in that some industries are expanding while others are on the decline. Such changes can cause what is called **frictional unemployment** for, as an industry contracts, it is only to be expected that some workers may be unemployed until they find new jobs in other industries. While the period of unemployment is obviously not a happy one for the individuals concerned, a certain amount of frictional unemployment is something of a sign of a healthy economy—one that is adapting itself to changing circumstances.

It should also be recognised that people often prefer to stay out of work for a time rather than accept the first job offered. Others may even leave their existing employment in order to look for better pay and conditions. The chances of success may well depend on how much free time one has to search around. In a sense, unemployment of this kind may be considered frictional, but it is thought to have been on the increase in recent years so a new term has been found to cover it—**search unemployment**.

4 Structural unemployment

The next kind of unemployment does not differ, in principle, from frictional unemployment described in the last paragraph. Both arise from changes in the structure of the economy over time. The distinctive feature of structural unemployment is that it is caused by profound alterations which are long-lasting and severe in their effects. An example may help to clarify the distinction. If an office in the City of London closes down and dismisses its staff it may take a week or more for them to find jobs with other firms. Their unemployment might be described as frictional. In contrast, consider the case of the shipbuilding industry which, as we saw earlier, has been in a state of fairly steady decline for 50 or more years. As shipyards contract, or even close down, there may, in theory, be job vacancies elsewhere for redundant employees. In practice, such vacancies may not be suitable. They may require skills totally different from those of shipyard workers. Such unemployment is truly structural. The adjustment process may go on for years or even decades, helped in the main by natural 'wastage' as older workers retire and are not replaced (and perhaps also by some government cushioning by means of subsidies and the provision of retraining facilities).

Continuing with the illustration of the shipbuilding industry, there is a second reason why available job vacancies may be unsuitable for out of work employees. They may be in distant parts of the country to which the workers do not wish to move (or indeed cannot move because of housing and other financial problems). Circumstances like this give rise to a type of unemployment which is sometimes considered to be a class of its own—**localised unemployment**—and it may be very serious. Shipbuilding again provides a good example because of its heavy concentration in a few areas, e.g. on the Clyde, where alternative job opportunities for shipyard workers have been slight.

Looking ahead to the remaining years of the century, a second example of structural unemployment might be the situation which many people expect to follow the 'microchip revolution', including under that heading such machines as word processors. Insofar as this technological development brings about a fall in demand for the services of clerks, typists and other workers on a large scale, it may well be a potential creator of what should be called structural unemployment.

5 Demand-deficient unemployment

The final category of unemployment types to be considered is that called **demand-deficient**. Such unemployment is usually *general*, rather than in particular sectors of the economy. As its name implies, demand-deficient unemployment occurs when the level of aggregate demand is relatively low, with the result that there are not enough jobs available for all those who are looking for work. The circumstances which lead to such a situation were described in

Chapter 2 of this book, i.e. when the economy is generally depressed because of a deficiency of aggregate demand. Since market economies have historically experienced alternating periods of depressed and booming conditions, this type of unemployment is also known sometimes as **cyclical**.

Unemployment in Britain

After the brief survey of the main types of unemployment in the last few paragraphs we can now examine the pattern and extent of unemployment in Britain. It should, however, be made clear that the survey was intended as a guide to clear thinking. It is not a simple matter to decide how much of a particular kind of unemployment there is.

The absolute number of unemployed in a country is not, by itself, a very useful statistic. The figures of those out of work only acquire meaning and significance if they are compared with something else. Two measures are generally used. The first relates the numbers unemployed with the total of those available for work, to yield a **percentage rate of unemployment**. The second compares the numbers seeking jobs with the total of unfilled vacancies in the economy, to yield a ratio of one to the other known as the **u/v ratio**. (When the ratio has the value 1 the unemployed are equal in number to the unfilled vacancies, when it is greater than 1 the former outnumber the latter and vice versa.) Both measures have to be used carefully for a variety of reasons, the most important of which arises from the fact that there are problems in ascertaining precisely how many people really are seeking employment at any time. In practice statistics are based on something much easier to measure than this—namely the number of people actually registering for work at job centres or claiming benefit (*see* page 130).

Fig 6.4 has been prepared to outline the trends in the general level of unemployment in Britain since the 1920s. It is in two parts Fig 6.4(a) shows the unemployment rate in percentage terms as described in the previous paragraph; Fig 6.4(b) shows the number of registered unemployed and of notified vacancies. Ignoring, first, the earlier inter-war years, and concentrating on the period immediately following the Second World War, it can be seen that unemployment was relatively low as measured by either standard. The percentage rate for the country as a whole varied between $1\frac{1}{2}$ and $2\frac{1}{2}$ per cent of the labour force during most of the 1950s and 1960s. The numbers of unfilled vacancies also more or less matched the numbers out of work, for the first few years at any rate.

The picture began to alter towards the end of the 1960s and during the following decade, when unemployment rates rose, at first gradually, through 3, 4 and 5 per cent, and the gap between the jobless and unfilled vacancies widened. By the middle of 1980, the rate topped 8 per cent while the numbers out of work passed the 2 million mark. There were nearly 20 men and women recorded as seeking jobs for every vacancy notified to job centres throughout

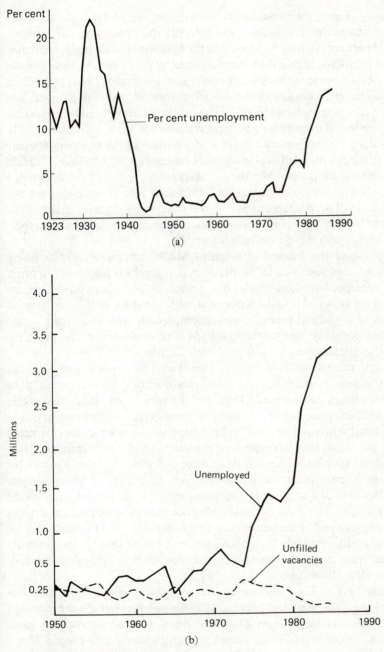

Fig 6.4 Unemployment in Great Britain 1923–84
a Percentage unemployment rates 1923–84
b Numbers of registered unemployed 1923–84 and numbers of unfilled vacancies
1948–80

the country. Barely two years later, towards the end of 1982, the numbers unemployed exceeded 3 million, and by 1985 the unemployment rate was about 13½ per cent. It must be added that the 'true' level of unemployment may well have been even higher than that suggested by the figures, because gloomy job prospects deter some people (especially married women) from looking for work. Moreover, a change in the official method of counting the numbers unemployed was introduced in 1982. The new basis substituted benefit claimants for registered unemployed persons available for work. Its use resulted in an immediate drop of nearly a quarter of a million in the numbers *officially* jobless. Although disabled unemployed are counted for the first time, the main difference between the new and the old bases relates to those (mainly married women) who do not claim benefit on losing their jobs because they are not entitled to it. The probable effect of the change has been to increase the number of hidden unemployed, but neither series of statistics (nor any other) is completely accurate or easy to interpret.

Estimation of the amount of so-called **hidden unemployment** resulting from the matters described in the previous paragraphs is not an easy matter. Several attempts have been made, but there is no agreement on the precise amount that exists. All that can be said with certainty is that the relative reliability of the official estimates varies considerably with underlying conditions of the economy, and that comparisons of unemployment rates over time and among countries must be treated with caution.

Trying to fit real observed unemployment into the types described in the previous section, is a difficult and controversial matter. Several explanations have been offered and debated. Three may be mentioned. In the first place, part of the rising general level of unemployment in recent years may be due to frictional and structural causes. Technological advances have not only made obsolete old skills; they have involved automation and computerisation leading to labour saving on a large scale in some industries. A second reason for high rates of unemployment is the relatively high level of social security payments which, it is argued, do not encourage those out of work to look hard enough for jobs. The third explanation, which undoubtedly ranks as a major one for the very end of the period under consideration (and probably also for some years with relatively high unemployment before then) is the generally depressed state of the economy—what was described as cyclical or demand-deficient unemployment.

Looking back at Fig 6.4(a) we can see a similarity between the inter-war years and the 1980s. Between 1919 and 1939 the numbers out of work exceeded 1 million in every single year. The worst times were in the so-called 'great depression' in the early 1930s, when the unemployment rate topped 22 per cent and the absolute number of jobless passed the 2½ million mark. (These are annual average figures. The worst month was January 1933, when almost 3 million were recorded as out of work.)

Comparisons between the 1930s and the 1980s should be made with caution.

For one thing, the labour force itself was much smaller in the inter-war years, so that a given number of unemployed represented a significantly higher *percentage rate* in the earlier period than it does today. There are also the problems mentioned above of how the actual number unemployed are counted, which have indeed changed over the past 50 years. However, there can be no room for doubt that, although structural and other causes of unemployment were present in both periods, a deficiency of total demand was of major importance in the very high rates in the 1930s and in the 1980s. One interesting difference between the 2 periods is the extent to which governments might have been able to control the situation through their economic policies. We shall consider this question in Chapter 10. Meanwhile there are some characteristics of the distribution of unemployment, that should be considered.

Distribution of unemployment

When unemployment strikes, its impact does not fall evenly among the population, but bears much more heavily on some groups than on others.

Regional unemployment

A feature of the incidence of unemployment which must be considered is the extent to which it varies in different parts of the country. Fig 6.5 shows the rates of unemployment in each of the standard regions of Britain in January 1985, a date at which the average for the country as a whole was $13\frac{1}{2}$ per cent. It can be seen that local variation was considerable.

Those with the lowest levels were the South East, East Anglia and the South West. Those with the highest were Northern and North West England, Scotland, Wales and Northern Ireland. It is no coincidence that most of these areas happen to have relatively heavy concentrations of the labour force in declining industries such as shipbuilding, steel and textiles (*see* page 99). The unemployment rate in the West Midlands, which is a major producer of cars, illustrates the same point. During the first 20 years after the end of the Second World War the vehicle industry flourished and unemployment rates in the West Midlands were relatively low. In 1985 the car industry was depressed and the region's rate of unemployment was well above the national average.

Unemployment by ethnic group

Unemployment rates vary with characteristics other than the region in which workers happen to live. One of some social significance is ethnic origin. Fig 6.6 which is based on a survey made in 1982 shows that non-whites, especially

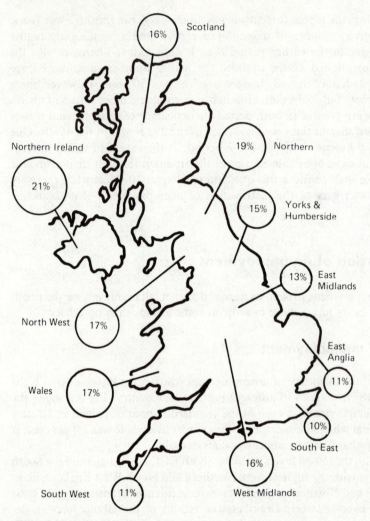

Fig 6.5 Regional unemployment UK January 1985 (percentage of employees registered as unemployed)

those of West Indian and Guyanese origin, had substantially higher unemployment rates, on average, than whites. Although some part of the differentials in the diagram may be explained by differences in age, qualification and region, a significant difference remains when these factors are taken into account.

The duration of unemployment

One of the reasons why the high level of general unemployment in Britain in the 1980s causes particular social concern, is that it tends to be concentrated on

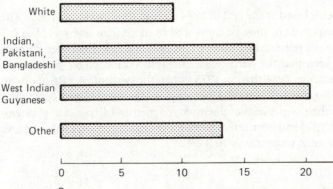

Fig 6.6 Unemployed rates by ethnic origin UK 1982

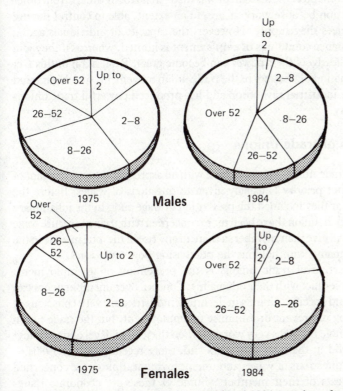

Fig 6.7 Duration of unemployment 1975 and 1984; number of weeks out of work.

the young, and that those thrown out of work have tended to stay unemployed for long periods.

The way in which the young have borne a disproportionate share of the burden, is evidenced by the fact that no less than one in five men, and one in four women, unemployed at the end of 1984 were in the 20–24 age group. The duration of unemployment may be measured in more than one way. Fig 6.7 shows how long those persons unemployed, in 1975 and 1984, had been without work. It can be seen that the percentage unemployed for longer periods was substantially greater in 1984 than in 1975 (when the percentage rate of unemployment was also much lower—$4\frac{1}{2}$ per cent as against $13\frac{1}{2}$ per cent). For example, no less than 44 per cent of unemployed men and 30 per cent of unemployed women in 1984 had been out of work for over a year, compared to figures of 30 and 15 per cent respectively in 1975.

Trade unions

At the start of this chapter, the statement was made that labour differs from other factors of production because workers are, to an extent, able to control the use made of the services they supply. However, the capacity of individuals acting separately to influence conditions of employment is limited, whereas if they join forces and act collectively their power can become great. Realisation of this fact led to the combination of workers in the trade union movement, which gathered strength with the industrial revolution and has produced powerful trade unions in the present day.

The functions of trade unions

The activities of trade unions are concerned with all aspects of the employment of their members, but priority is usually given to questions of wages. Before the Second World War they included the prevention of wage cuts. In the inflationary conditions since then, unions have been more concerned with trying to secure wage increases which will give their members a share in any rise in the total income in the country or, minimally, with holding the purchasing power of wages.

A second objective of trade unions is the prevention of unemployment, although this can conflict with their other aims. Concern over unemployment can be both general and specific. Unions in declining industries are very conscious of their role of trying to prevent or minimise unemployment, but the trade union movement as a whole becomes very worried when the general level of unemployment rises as it did in the inter-war years and, more recently, in the 1980s.

In addition to questions of wages and unemployment, unions are concerned with other interests of their members. Some of these are economic issues related to wages; e.g. fringe benefits, like cheap company goods, medical care and holidays. Hours of work may come into this category, since one union objective may be securing higher earnings through reductions in normal, or standard, hours with corresponding increases in hours paid at, higher, overtime rates. Normal hours have come down from about 48 per week to less than 40 in many occupations since before the war. Average hours worked have fallen less. Those worked by adult males remained at about 46 per week, until weak economic conditions in the 1980s brought them down (to 44 in 1984).

A rather different category of trade union objectives is managerial issues which go beyond financial rewards, fringe benefits etc, and are concerned with how workers are treated in their jobs. Examples are safety and general working conditions, recruitment, promotion and dismissal procedures, methods of supervision, discipline and the provision of time off for training and union meetings etc. Some unions also try to obtain increased influence in the management of a business by securing union representation on the board of directors. Finally, British trade unions have political aims of wide general significance. They play an important part in the formation of Labour Party policy and several trade union officials have become Members of Parliament.

The finance for trade union activities comes mainly from subscriptions from members plus income from accumulated funds which, for some unions, are substantial. For the individual, however, union dues are, on average, only a few pounds a year per member. However, they vary widely from one union to another, largely as a result of differences in the range of benefits provided, but also varying to some extent with the level of workers' incomes. Many so-called 'friendly benefits', e.g. for unemployment and sickness, which were traditionally provided by trade unions, lost significance with the growth in the public provision of social services after the Second World War. Nevertheless most unions offer some such benefits, especially superannuation in the case of certain craft unions. Dispute benefit is another matter and the reserve funds are available to subsidise members for loss of pay during strikes.

The growth of trade unions

The early history of trade unionism, from the first local trade clubs in the 18th century, was one of tremendous struggle by working men to gain recognition for their organisations, for the law was not always on their side. Anti-combination Acts were passed in 1799 and 1800 inflicting severe penalties on workmen who tried to form a union, and many suffered before public opinion was won round and changes in the law were made.

No sooner had legal victory been gained by a number of Acts of Parliament between 1824 and 1876 than trade union membership grew with rapid strides, from something under a million members in 1870 to a pre-war peak of over 8 million in 1920. The years between the two world wars, however, were times of depressed industrial activity, whereas trade unionism flourishes in periods of general prosperity. Membership, consequently, began to fall off in the 1920s and 1930s and at its lowest ebb in 1933 was little more than half the 1920 figure. With the revival in activity in the later 1930s, however, trade unionism increased again as Fig 6.8 shows. The 1920 peak was passed soon after the end of the war. Membership continued to increase in the years up to 1980, when a new peak of 13 million was reached. Thereafter, in the more recent period of low economic activity, the number of unionised workers began once more to fall, to 11¼ million by 1983. Part of this decline can also be explained by changes in the structure of the economy, and the fall in employment in particular industries, e.g. manufacturing, where trade unionism is strong.

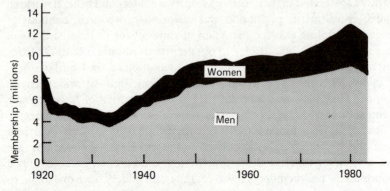

Fig 6.8 Trade union membership UK 1920–83

Trade union strength

Trade union membership, of around 11 million, is less than half of the total number of employees in the UK, though the proportion of men joining unions is considerably higher than that of women (over two thirds compared to two fifths). The difference is to some extent explained by the fact that more women work part-time, and a higher proportion of them than of men in small establishments, where unionism tends to be weak. When allowance is made for these factors, membership differences are slighter. However, it has been traditionally more difficult to recruit women into trade unions. This may be due to differences in work attitudes between men and women, reflecting, perhaps, the fact that many women intend to leave the labour force, for several years at least, to raise families.

Unionism varies also in strength from industry to industry. It is difficult to illustrate this from available statistics, partly because data is available only for broad groups and partly because some of the largest unions have members extending over a range of industries.

With these reservations in mind, we may nevertheless draw some tentative conclusions about union strength from Fig 6.9 which confirms the relative weakness of trade unions in agriculture and the distributive trades compared to engineering and transport, for example, though the great strength of unionism in coal mining, government service and the railways is not brought out in the diagram. Special historical circumstances account for much of the difference in trade union membership in different industries, but the degree of strength is an important factor when negotiations with employers are in progress. Unions are particularly powerful in industries where closed shops operate. These are arrangements, agreed with employers, where only union members may be employed. Closed shops may be either 'pre-entry', where the workers must be a member of the union before being taken on, or 'post-entry' where the worker joins the union on being employed. About a quarter of the workforce in 1980 was in closed shop industries, but only about 15 per cent of these were in pre-entry closed shops. Moreover, legislation to protect workers with conscientious objections to joining a trade union was introduced in the early 1980s (*see* page 141).

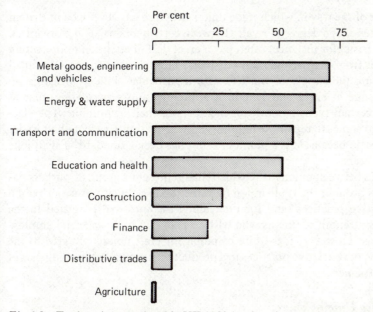

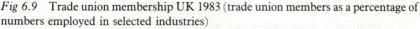

Fig 6.9   Trade union membership UK 1983 (trade union members as a percentage of numbers employed in selected industries)

An important recent trend that should be mentioned is the growth of so-called 'white collar' unionism over the last 25 years. Office workers have been recruited in substantially larger numbers than previously. This has been of considerable help to the trade union movement in maintaining, and even increasing, total union membership during a period when the traditional areas of union strength have been declining.

Trade union structure

The total number of trade unions in existence in 1983 was fewer than 400, and most of these were very small. Over half had fewer than 1000 members each, while the 23 largest accounted for about 80 per cent of the total membership. In the main, these very large unions have grown over the years as a result of amalgamations. Some unions are organised on an industry basis, such as the

National Union of Mineworkers and the Union of Communication Workers. Others, especially the older ones, are organised on a craft basis, like the National Graphical Association. However, the largest unions of all are either general unions covering a wide range of industries and/or occupations, such as the Transport and General Workers' Union with nearly 2 million members, or multi-craft unions like the Amalgamated Union of Engineering Workers.

Union demarcations

One result of the way in which trade union structure has developed in Britain is the existence of a degree of rivalry between certain unions. Those organised on a craft basis, for instance, often pay a great deal of attention to protecting their trades from encroachment by outsiders. This takes two forms, one aimed at restricting the supply of workers with a particular skill, by insisting on minimum age at entry and length of apprenticeship service; the other at reserving certain types of work for members of their own union. The electrician who comes to repair the lighting and will not tighten a loose bolt under the washbasin because it is a plumber's job, has been a standard, if sick, joke for many years.

Disputes between unions as to which shall represent a group of workers has sometimes brought the trade union movement bad publicity. A major reason for restrictive practices (and for inter-union disputes too) is related to the bargaining strength of unions who wish to maintain both wage and employment levels. However, it is quite common for craft unions to agree to the elimination of restrictive practices in a productivity agreement forming part of a wage settlement.

The Trades Union Congress

The central body of the trade union movement is known as the Trades Union Congress (TUC). Established in 1868 in Manchester, primarily for political purposes, its activities were restricted in the 19th century, and it was not until the 1920s that it began to assume the importance that it undoubtedly has today.

Like most trade unions the TUC has a full-time salaried General Secretary. The other members of the General Council consist of part-time officials from individual unions, who are elected at the annual conference, when delegates attend to discuss the current business. All large unions, including those of white collar workers, are affiliated to the TUC and have a say in the formation of general policy. Voting is on what is known as a 'block' basis whereby each delegate is allowed a number of votes roughly corresponding to the membership of the union he represents. Control of policy is thus effectively in the hands of the largest unions.

The TUC has come increasingly to be regarded as the representative voice of the trade unions. The government frequently consults it on questions of national policy, not only on such matters as factory legislation, health, pensions and national insurance, but also on general economic issues, where its support for the policies of the government of the day may be critical. However, the formal powers of the TUC are surprisingly limited. There is, for example, no obligation on individual unions to observe decisions taken at the annual conference. This considerable weakness is the result of the traditional reluctance of many unions to sacrifice their independence and it is not impossible that the powers of the TUC might sometime be increased.

Collective bargaining

Most wages are settled by collective bargaining between the appropriate union or unions and employers. In the inflationary times in which we live negotiations usually take place at least annually and lead to a series of 'wage rounds' of pay increases. Comparability with workers in similar industries or occupations and the profitability of the business are among the major issues discussed.

In the majority of cases negotiations are successful in that the bargaining sessions produce an agreed wage package, sometimes, as stated earlier, associated with productivity commitments on the part of unions. Negotiations take place at many levels and can cover a variety of subjects. Wages are usually the central issue, but hours and conditions of work, redundancy, allegations of victimisation of individual workers by management, etc., may also be involved.

Disputes

If the parties fail to agree, an industrial dispute follows. At such a time, the union may call on its members to come out on strike or to take other action, such as refusing to work overtime. Employers, on the other side, may decide to close down the business, dismiss staff or implement their offer even when it has not been agreed.

Disputes, of course, involve loss of production and Fig 6.10 shows the number of days lost as a result of stoppages of work since 1911. Three observations should be made about the trends shown in the diagram. First, the average number of days lost is substantially lower in the post-war period than in the 1920s. Second, notice the tendency for disputes to involve substantially more disruption in some years since the 1970s than in earlier post-war years. Third, a high proportion of the total number of days lost is often attributable to a very few disputes. Of the 27 million days lost in 1984, for example, 22 million can be put down to the strike in the coal industry.

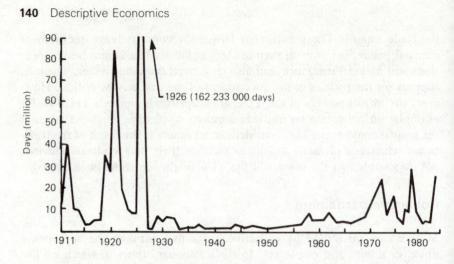

1926 (162 233 000 days)

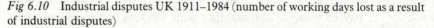

Fig 6.10 Industrial disputes UK 1911–1984 (number of working days lost as a result of industrial disputes)

It may be worthwhile adding a general comment on where Britain fits into the international scene. The strike record in Britain is often regarded as something of a national disgrace. It is, however, important to realise that the record is not as dreadful as some people believe. Although statistics on disputes are collected on differing bases in individual countries, and are not therefore strictly comparable, it is nevertheless true that many countries have no better records than Britain. One should add that this includes countries such as Canada, Australia and the United States, which are sometimes held up as models. However, strikes tend to come in waves and, when they do, their effects can be widespread and serious, particularly if they involve wholesale disruption of power and communication services, thereby threatening indirectly both industry and the home.

Government intervention

The settlement of wages in the UK has for long been based upon the principle of free collective bargaining. There has, however, always been a public interest in helping to achieve a fair balance between the parties and in avoiding disputes. An early measure was the establishment of **joint industrial councils** for industries which had not by then provided their own negotiating machinery. More recently, in 1974, an independent **Advisory Conciliation and Arbitration Service (ACAS)** was set up, together with a permanent **Central Arbitration Committee (CAC)** to which disputes may be referred by agreement. In the most serious cases the Secretary of State for Employment can appoint a special court of inquiry or committee of investigation. Their recommendations are not legally binding, but often lead to settlements. (For disputes involving individual workers and dealing with cases of unfair dismissal, sex and social discrimination etc., there are industrial tribunals and an Employment Appeals Tribunal.)

Many and varied attempts have been made to influence the legal and institutional background within which collective bargaining takes place. Invariably they reflect the philosophy of the governments which made them.

In 1971 a Conservative government brought in an Industrial Relations Act which was bitterly opposed by the trade unions. It followed some of the recommendations of a Royal Commission on Trade Unions (the Donovan Commission) which had reported in 1969. The Donovan Report favoured a strategy of non-legalistic voluntary reform but identified so-called unofficial strikes (called by shop stewards at the place of work without official support from the union headquarters) as a major source of trouble in industrial relations. A **Commission on Industrial Relations (CIR)** was also recommended and established.

The industrial Relations Act of 1971 tried to create a new legal framework for industrial relations. The CIR was retained and given some teeth. In addition, the Act set up a registration system for unions, a National Industrial Relations Court with power to order 'cooling off' periods and strike ballots, financial penalties for unions (including damages, resulting from strikes) and a new concept of unfair industrial practices, covering closed shops and the calling of strikes by unauthorised union officials. The Act tried to limit participation in disputes to the unions *directly* involved.

In 1974, a Labour government repealed the Industrial Relations Act and substituted the Trade Union and Labour Relations Act and the Employment Protection Act, the following year. These pieces of legislation were less hostile towards the trade unions. Included, for example, was a provision requiring employers to supply unions with certain information during pay negotiations.

Conservative governments were elected in 1979 and 1983. They did not immediately reinstate the full provisions of the 1971 Industrial Relations Act, partly because of opposition from the unions, but also because management had not taken any great advantage of it. However, three important new pieces of legislation were brought in, in 1980, 1982 and 1984.

The first two, the Employment Acts of 1980 and 1982, limited lawful picketing to one's own workplace and restricted the scope for secondary strike actions. They also protect employees who do not wish to join a union against unfair dismissal, e.g. where a closed shop agreement has not been approved by at least 80 per cent of the workers in secret ballots taken in the previous 5 years. Finally, the Acts greatly weakened the special immunities for trade unions provided by law and gave employers the right to seek injunctions and damages in the courts against trade unions themselves (as well as union officials) arising from cases involving commercial deals and industrial action—something which had not been possible since 1906. For the first time unions could be sued for unlawful acts unconnected with industrial action, e.g. libel, negligence and nuisance.

Later, the Trade Union Act, 1984, was passed, directed at union management and organisation. The most publicised provision of this Act relates to the calling of strike action, making union immunity for organising industrial action conditional on the holding of secret and properly conducted ballots. The 1984 Act also provides for secret ballots for the election of individual members of union governing bodies, and allows union members to be consulted at regular intervals on whether union funds should be spent on party political matters.

Exercises

For key to symbols indicating sources *see* pages xii–xiii.

1 Obtain figures of the average weekly earnings of the following groups of full-time adult workers last year and 5 years ago. Calculate the percentage change for each group and compare your results. (*AS*)

Manual workers, male	Salaried workers, male
Manual workers, female	Salaried workers, female

2 Prepare a graph for a recent year showing the relationship between age and average weekly earnings for full-time adult males and females. (Use the horizontal axis to measure age and the vertical axis for earnings.) Does the age-earnings profile differ between the sexes? (*AS, F*)

3 Prepare a chart on the lines of Fig 6.1 showing the percentage change in earnings of workers in each of the following industries over the last 5 years. Which have changed most and what differences in rank order are there? (*AS*)

Food, drink and tobacco	Coal
Metal manufacturing	Textiles
Mechanical engineering	Chemicals

4 Construct a chart showing the average weekly hours worked by adult men and women since 1970 for as many years as you can obtain statistics. (*AS, F*)

5 For the most recent year for which statistics are available find out the total number of workers and the total number of unemployed in each of the following industries:

Agriculture and horticulture	Metal goods
Bread, biscuits and confectionery	Electrical engineering
Hotels and catering	Clocks and watches
Chemicals	Motor vehicles and parts
Retail distribution	Shipbuilding
Footwear	Woollen and worsted

Work out the percentage unemployment in each case and compare your results. (*AS*)

6 Prepare graphs showing the percentage of the working population that was unemployed in the United Kingdom in the following years: 1924, 1929, 1932, 1937, 1955, 1965, 1975 and 1985 and a more recent year, if available. (*KS, AS* or *MDS*)

7 Prepare a graph showing the excess or deficit of employment vacancies unfilled over the total number of registered unemployed in Britain for each of the last 12 months. (*ET* or *MDS*)

8 Trace an outline map of Great Britain from an atlas and divide it roughly into regions. Shade areas where unemployment rates are equal to the average for the whole country, and hatch those where they are below. Compare the result with Fig 6.5. (*ET* or *MDS*)

9 Prepare a table for the last 2 years showing

a the number of workers unemployed
b the number working overtime
c the number on short-time.

Calculate the percentage changes from one year to the other. Which appear to change more similarly, *a* and *b* or *a* and *c*? Have you any idea why? (*MDS*)

10 Find out the number of trade unionists belonging to unions with 100 000 or more members in 1975 and the most recent year available. Express the numbers as percentages of total trade union membership. How has the share in the total enjoyed by these large unions changed? (*AS, F*)

11 Collect figures showing the number of industrial stoppages of work in the main industrial groups in Britain for the past 2 calendar years. Work out the proportion of total stoppages accounted for by each group and compare your results. Are there any great changes, and do you know why? (*AS*)

7 National income and the price level

A great deal of our description of features of the British economy so far in this book has been concerned with what we called microeconomic aspects in Chapter 1 (*see* page 2). You will remember that the microeconomic approach focuses attention on the allocation of resources, which is what we did when we looked at the structure of industry in Chapter 5, and at the distribution of unemployment in Chapter 6, for example. In this chapter, in contrast, we shall be more concerned with a macroeconomic viewpoint (*see* Chapter 2 page 19). This approach looks at the economy as a whole, rather than at its constituent parts. Here, we shall focus on the level of total output in the economy, or, as it is better known, the national income.

The national income

The national income was defined in Chapter 2 (*see* page 20). It is a measure of the sum total of all goods and services which are produced during a given period of time, usually a year. The national income is expressed in money terms, because money values provide the most convenient way of adding together all the outputs of the various goods and services produced—tons of steel, gallons of milk, computers, restaurant meals, and so forth. We take the volumes of output in every sector and multiply them by their price in order to arrive at their money value. The total gives us the value of the national income.

Measuring the national income

There are a great many problems that beset the economic statistician engaged in trying to estimate the size of the national income in any year, and its trend over a period of time. Many are of a statistical or technical nature and will not concern us. However, those faced with the task of measurement are aided by the knowledge that they have a choice of three different methods to use. They can measure either the total flow of incomes, of outputs or of expenditures. As we explained in Chapter 2 (*see* page 20-1), income and expenditure flow in a circular fashion to create the identity that national income equals national output and also equals national expenditure. The explanation of these identities will not be repeated here, but it is helpful to understand that statisticians have three avenues of approach. All are used; and they act, to some extent, as cross checks on each other.

It should, however, always be remembered that statistics of national income are only estimates. One should not be misled by the apparent precision of published numbers and assume that these are accurate. Sometimes they are much more reliable than at others. To illustrate this point, consider the figures of the growth rate of national income from one year to the next. In theory, estimates of national income growth rates should be the same whether based on income, output or expenditure data. But, if we look at these estimates over a run of years in the 1970s and 1980s, we find that sometimes the three approaches give very similar results, e.g. in 1982–3, all three measures estimate the growth of national income at between 2.9 and 3.4 per cent for the year. In other years, the differences in growth rates using the three methods can be larger, sometimes much larger. In 1976–77, for example, national income appeared to have grown by 3.7 per cent using income based data, whereas, using expenditure based data, the growth rate was a mere 1.1 per cent.

Living standards

We now know national income to be a measure of the goods and services produced in a country. It would not be unreasonable to imagine that it is, therefore, a good indicator of the standard of living there. If we divide the national income, or product, by the number of people living in a country we obtain a figure of income per head (or *per capita*) of the population, which is fairly closely related to living standards. However, it would be dangerous to take the analogy too far.

The national income does not measure *everything* that contributes to living standards. There are many differences between the two concepts, and we can do no more than mention some of the most important here. Nearly all arise from the fact that the only goods and services that are included in the national income are those that are bought and sold in the market place, or provided by the state (in which case, incidentally, they are mostly valued at cost). Things that are excluded, therefore, include the beauty of the environment, the pleasures of a good climate and all the cultural legacies inherited from the past. A different type of exclusion is the leisure that is enjoyed. Insofar as people in a country decide to produce no more goods and services, but to spend more time at home or on holiday, for example, their living standards may be considered to have risen while the national income remains unchanged. Finally, there is a group of exclusions that are simply due to the nature of economic organisation in the country. Some services, for example, are performed without any money transactions taking place, while others, which may be equally important, go unrecorded. Principal among the former, are the services of housewives as distinct from those of paid housekeepers, the do-it-yourself jobs undertaken by men and women rather than paying for the work to be done, and the unrecorded transactions typified by work done for 'cash only' by individuals who wish to evade paying tax in what has come to be called the 'black economy'. The last of these have become increasingly common in recent years. No one knows precisely how much all these would add up to if they could be counted, valued and added into the national income as conventionally defined. Estimates of the size of the black economy put it at around 5 per cent of the total, but this is not a firm figure, of course.

The only conclusion that can be drawn from all this is that there are substantial differences between the real national income and what goes to make up the standard of living of the population. We must therefore treat the statistics with caution, especially if there are grounds for believing that there have been any significant changes in the circumstances affecting either.

One last consideration deserves comment. The matters mentioned so far tend to suggest that living standards may be higher than would be indicated by the size of the national income. There are, however, some reasons why the opposite may be true. The most important is the existence of what have rather unfortunately been called economic 'bads' (the use of the word 'bads' is analogous to that of the word 'goods'—both imply value judgments on the part of society). These are things like pollution and spoilation of the environment that have sometimes been observed to accompany rapid economic growth. They can lower the standard of living even though the national income appears to be rising.

The national income of the UK

We are now ready to take a look at the size and composition of the national income of the UK. As a starting point, we may observe that the total value of all goods and services included in the national product in 1983 stood at a figure of about £300 000 million, which works out at approximately £6000 per head of the population. Later, we shall see how representative this average figure is. First the total needs to be broken down into major components.

As mentioned earlier (and explained in Chapter 2), the national income can be measured in three ways, corresponding to the sum of all incomes, all output, or all expenditures, each of which is equal to the others. Fig 7.1 shows these three measures, together with their main constituents. We have already dealt at length (in Chapter 5) with the breakdown of national output by major industry group; hence we concentrate here on the expenditure and income measures.

National expenditure

The left-hand column in Fig 7.1 shows the major components of national expenditure. Two of the principal categories are consumption and investment. The

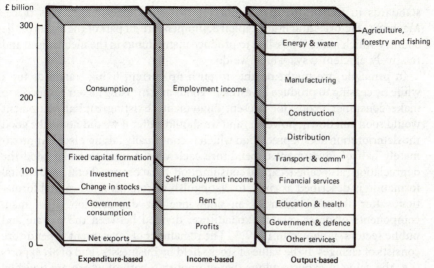

Fig 7.1 National income, output and expenditure UK 1983

difference between these is that expenditure on consumption is made by consumers when they buy goods and services for their own sake (e.g. food, drink and tobacco, clothing, household goods etc.), while expenditure on investment is made by businesses and includes the purchase of capital goods, such as plant and machinery, which are not wanted for *present* consumption, but to aid in production. Investment expenditure also includes *changes* in the values of stocks held by businesses.

As can be seen in Fig 7.1, private consumption expenditure is the largest category, and accounts for about 60 per cent of the total. The main classes of consumption expenditure are shown in Fig 7.2.

The second major category of expenditure is that on investment, known also as capital formation. If the nation wishes to enjoy at least its present living

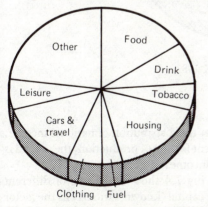

Fig 7.2 Consumer expenditure UK 1983

standards in the future it is important that such investment takes place. Machines, factories and other capital equipment are all part of the assets of the country which make it possible to produce many things in the mechanised and relatively efficient ways which we do.

In principle, we might be able to push up current living standards for a while by ceasing to produce investment goods and by using all our resources to make consumer goods for present enjoyment. Existing capital equipment would soon run down, however, and we should suffer if we did not make good the deterioration and depreciation which is continually taking place. Approximately half of investment expenditure each year is used to make good the depreciation (also called 'capital consumption') that occurs. Total fixed capital formation is described as *gross*, to distinguish it from *net* fixed capital formation, after the deduction of an allowance for depreciation. The main components of gross capital expenditure, divided between the private and public sectors, is shown in Fig 7.3. The remainder of investment expenditure consists of changes in the value of stocks held by businesses, and of *net* exports (i.e. the value of exports minus that of imports), both of which are typically small relative to the other components.

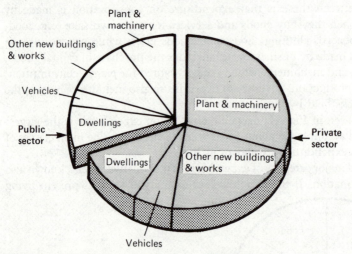

Fig 7.3 Gross fixed capital formations UK 1983

National income distribution

There are two distinct ways of looking at the distribution of national income. One is to observe the shares of the different factors of production, the second is to note the distribution by the size of incomes of persons.

The middle column of Fig 7.1 and Fig 7.4 show the shares of different factors of production—land, labour and capital (known variously as the factor or functional distribution of income). It must, however, be understood that the divisions in the diagram (derived from published statistics), do not correspond at all precisely to the shares of factors of production as defined in economic theory. They come closest in the case of income from employment, which group encompasses wages and salaries in the public and private sectors of the economy. Profits are gross, before the deduction of depreciation allowances (*see* page 148), and include interest on capital, providing, thus, the pool from which dividends and interest are paid. Self-employment income is usually shown as a separate category in the national accounts. It covers two somewhat different groups. One is professional workers, who are in business on their own account as accountants, authors, architects, lawyers, and so on. They do not receive regular wages or salaries, but are paid fees or royalties for their work. The second group is composed of small businesses, such as independent retailers, which are not organised as joint stock companies. The income of the self-employed, especially those in the second category, cannot be regarded as the reward to a single factor of production, as with the first two main categories; it is rather a mixture. Part represents income for work done and part a return on capital invested, either in a business or in education and training to acquire the qualifications without which such professional earnings would not accrue.

The largest share, about two-thirds in 1983, accrued to labour in the form of wages and salaries. Rent took about a tenth as much as this; self-employment income accounted for about 10 per cent of the total, and the rest is accounted for by gross trading profits.

Trends in the shares of factor incomes

Fig 7.4 showed the shares of the chief factors of production as they existed in one particular year—1983. These shares are not always exactly the same. The share of capital tends to be high in years of prosperity, when profits are high. Labour's share falls accordingly in such boom periods and rises, for the opposite reason, when trade is less flourishing. That is not to say that wages are necessarily high in depressions, only that the *share* of employment incomes is large. In absolute terms, wages may be low.

Apart from short-term fluctuations some long-term trends are observable in factor shares. If we look back to the 1870s we can see a fairly stable share of wages alone which persisted until about the middle of the present century. It should be added, however, that the number of wage earners was falling at the same time. Taking account of all incomes from employment the share of wages *and* salaries rose by about 10 percentage points over this long period although towards the end there may have been a slight fall.

The share of self-employment income is of rather less interest, consisting as it does of a mixture of employment and other factor incomes. The long-term trend was downward during the period of growth of joint stock companies. In more recent times self-employment income has accounted for between 8 and

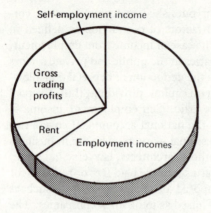

Fig 7.4 Factor distribution of income 1983

11 per cent of the total of factor incomes. One reason for variations lies in the way in which taxes are levied on people. There have been changes from time to time in the advantages that accrue from being treated for tax purposes as a self-employed person as against a wage or salary earner or the owner of a business organised as a joint stock company. Another is the level of unemployment in the country. When it is high, people may seek to set themselves up in small businesses, often assisted by payments made in compensation for being declared redundant.

The size of incomes

So far we have been concerned with the way in which incomes are distributed to people in return for their services as *factors* of production. This does not, however, reveal much about the actual distribution of *personal* incomes—an important matter. It usually matters less to an individual whether his income is called wages, rent or profit than whether he earns £10 000 a year or £100 000.

Our next task, therefore, is to examine the distribution of personal incomes. This differs from the distribution of factor incomes for three main reasons. In the first place wages, profits, etc. vary from one individual to another (*see* pages 120–5 for a discussion of the causes of wage differences). In the second place, it must be appreciated that the incomes of many persons are derived from more than one source, e.g. wages or salaries from employment, interest or dividends from the ownership of capital, etc. Lastly, some incomes do not accrue from the services of factors of production but as a result of government payments designed to provide some income for the poor, sick, elderly and the out of work. Social security benefits, such as retirement pensions and unemployment benefit, are known as **transfer payments** because they are transfers made through the machinery of government. They must be included in the discussion of the size distribution of income.

We present a description of the size distribution of personal incomes in the UK by means of a rather unusual type of diagram, often used to portray degrees of equality and inequality—Fig 7.5.

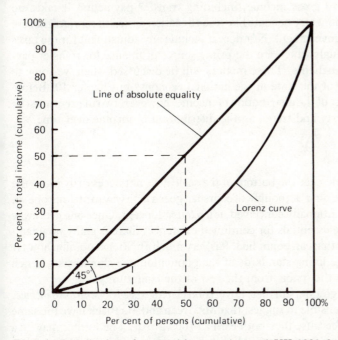

Fig 7.5   Distribution of personal incomes (pre-tax) UK 1981–2

This diagram measures inequality with what is known as a **Lorenz curve**, which shows how much of total income is accounted for by given proportions of persons. The percentages measured on both axes are *cumulative*, so as we move along the horizontal axis we look at the shares of the bottom 1, 2, 3, etc. per cent of the population and then read off their shares on the vertical axis. For example, the bottom 30 per cent of persons received about 10 per cent of total income, the bottom 50 per cent about 23 per cent of income and so on. We can compare the Lorenz curve at any time with the *line of absolute equality*. This is drawn in the diagram as the diagonal going through the origin. It indicates absolute equality because all points along it show that a given percentage of the population receive exactly the same percentage of total income, i.e. the bottom 1 per cent receive 1 per cent of total income, the bottom 5 per cent receive 5 per cent, etc. Hence the further the Lorenz curve bends away from the diagonal, the greater the degree of inequality.

The simple single line of the Lorenz curve gives a full description of the distribution of income among persons (strictly speaking the data refers not to persons but to 'tax units' whereby the incomes of most husbands and wives are counted as one). It shows, for example, that the top 30 per cent of the population receive about 45 per cent of total income while the bottom 20 per cent receive only about 5 per cent.

It is necessary to emphasise that the distribution of personal incomes in Fig 7.5 relates only to gross income, including transfer payments. It takes no account of non-monetary benefits like free education or health services that are provided by the government. Nor does it include any adjustment for the taxes levied on individuals which are the prime source of finance for transfer payments and other benefits. These matters will be discussed when we come to examine the role of the state in the national economy in Chapter 10. Before leaving the subject of the distribution of income, however, two matters must be mentioned; poverty and trends in the distribution of income over time.

Poverty

To have an income near the bottom of the scale does not necessarily mean the same thing as to be poor, although, of course, it goes a long way to making one so. Poverty, as conventionally conceived, is a *relative* concept. Once one gets away from the absolute essentials for continued existence, there is really no unambiguous standard that can be applied. It is very much a matter of opinion how far below the average living standards of the population one should set a bench mark to separate the 'poor' from the rest of the community.

It is possible to go a step further. Poverty is related to *needs* as well as to *income*. It would not be sensible to suggest that Mr Green and Ms Black have the same living standards because they both earn £10 000 a year. The former may be a single man with no dependents. Ms Black may be a disabled woman, whose husband has left her with 5 children and a widowed mother. The example is deliberately extreme to emphasise how varied individuals' circumstances can be. This is not a subject that we can go into in any detail in this book. However, one guideline which might be accepted as a starting point of poverty by many people is the income at which one begins to qualify for social security relief, known as **supplementary benefit** (*see* page 235).

This is still an arbitrary standard, but recent estimates of the numbers living on or below the poverty line, measured as the level of income at which supplementary benefit is payable, are of the order of 7 to 8 million people, representing nearly 5 million families, or 10 to 15 per cent of the population. Of this total, over half were below the supplementary benefit level. These people were, of course, eligible for social security but for some reason or other preferred not to claim it.

The numbers of persons entitled to supplementary benefit has risen since the early 1970s, as the level of unemployment has increased. However, it is important to note that the data by themselves do not quantify the size of the poverty problem, since they do not take account of how far below the benchmark the poor are living, nor the extent to which there is a hard core of permanently poor rather than a changing number of people in temporarily reduced circumstances.

While there may be differences of opinion as to *how many* people should be counted as 'poor', there is less room for argument about *who* they are. Poverty is associated with being unemployed, with age (especially with being old, but also with being very young and with workers over 50), with being female, with being sick or disabled, with having little education or ability, and with family size (single-parent families in particular). Poverty also varies regionally, the South West, East Anglia and Scotland having the highest proportions of poor. What is not fully understood is whether the underlying causes of poverty are to be found mainly in individual personal characteristics or in the structure of jobs. There is a good deal of evidence of the existence of a dual labour market in countries like the UK—a primary market, where pay and employment prospects are good, a secondary market with high unemployment and low pay—and little movement between them, with many of the poor trapped in the secondary market.

Trends in the size distribution of income

As often in this book, we have looked at a characteristic of the economy by reference to the situation in a recent year. Fig 7.5 related specifically to the distribution of income in the year 1981–2. We ought to consider how far that year was typical and whether there have been changes in income distribution in recent times.

We know that it is often difficult to make comparisons of economic circumstances over long periods. Nowhere is this more true than when comparing income distributions. Indeed, the need for comprehensive reliable information on the subject was considered so great that the government set up a standing Royal Commission on the Distribution of Income and Wealth (the Diamond Commission) in 1974 simply to report on the facts of the situation. The Commission produced eight lengthy and complex reports which are capable of more than one interpretation and are difficult to summarise. However, they did observe a long-term decline in the share of the highest income groups in the period between the late 1940s and the 1970s. The decline was greatest for the groups with the highest incomes. Those in the top percentile, as it is called (i.e. with incomes which put them in the top 1 per cent of the population) suffered a virtual halving of their share of total income, from about 11 per cent to about $5\frac{1}{2}$ per cent of the total. Those in the top 10 per cent (including of course the top 1 per cent) suffered a fall in their share from about a third to a quarter of total income.

If the highest income classes lost, other groups must have gained and it seems clear that the chief beneficiaries were middle income groups. Within the top half of income earners, those lower down the scale gained approximately as much as the top 10 per cent lost, so that the share of the top half of income earners as a whole remained virtually unchanged (at about three quarters of total income). The lowest half of the population neither gained nor lost on balance over this long period. Both at the beginning and at the end they were receiving about a quarter of total income. Let it be clear that these are long-term changes. In the short-term, from year to year, the experience at times has been different. Recent data relating to the period since the Diamond Commission was disbanded, 1978–79 to 1981–82, show some reversal of the trends, in that the top 10 per cent of the distribution increased their share of the total, while the share of the lower half of the population fell.

The changing shares described in this section relate to gross incomes before tax. We shall consider the effects of taxation on the distribution of personal income when we come to the role of the state in the economy in Chapter 10. It follows, however, that explanations of the changing distribution of income that we have observed must lie elsewhere than in changing taxes. In fact, we cannot offer simple reasons for the changes that have taken place. This subject is a complex one, and we can only point to relevant matters such as trends in the supply of and demand for, labour with different skills, and the overall state of the economy, including the general level of unemployment, which are likely to be important. We should also recognise the relevance of the social and demographic structure of the population in this connection. Insofar as income is related to age and education, for example, changes in the proportion of the population engaged in full-time education, or over retirement age, will be likely to have an effect on the size distribution of income. Finally, we have to take account of the fact that income is partly derived from the ownership of capital assets which bring in income, and that this, too, is liable to change over time.

Wealth

Whilst considering the accounts of joint stock companies, in Chapter 4, attention was drawn to the fact that the record of income and expenditure for any year, in the Profit and Loss Account, was a much better guide to the financial condition of a company if it was studied in conjunction with the Balance Sheet statement of assets, or stock of wealth, which the company owned. The same thing is true for a person. When we think of someone as being rich or poor we should not restrict ourselves to a consideration of the income which he or she currently earns, but should include the amount of property, or capital, which has been accumulated in the past. It is a combination of income *and* wealth which is relevant.

The national capital

The identical argument applies also to a nation. It was pointed out at the beginning of this chapter, that Britain has been devoting about a fifth of the national income in recent years to the renewal and accumulation of capital and that this helps to promote economic growth. The value of the nation's capital stock is very large, in the mid-1980s running to a figure with nine noughts. It is difficult to appreciate the significance of such a magnitude. One way of putting it into perspective is to consider that it represents something like the total output of the entire economy for 4 to 5 years.

Fig 7.6 shows the breakdown of the tangible assets of the community, with buildings as the largest item. Notice also that dwellings account for nearly a third of the total assets. These, it is true, are not capital goods of the kind we described. However, they are long-lasting and, in the sense that they help to provide for enjoyment in the future, they are usually regarded as part of the nation's capital resources.

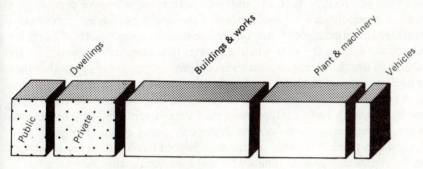

Fig 7.6 Gross capital stock UK 1983

Tangible assets are not the only components of the national wealth. Some assets are locked up, for example, in the skills acquired by education and training. They are known as '**human capital**'. Such intangible assets are hard to evaluate in money terms and they are not included in Fig 7.6.

Personal property

When we turn from a consideration of the wealth of the nation to the personal ownership of property we must introduce an important distinction, since a person's wealth may take one of two principal forms:

1 It may, like the national wealth, take the form of real items of property, such as houses, machinery or other business assets. The only point to be made here is that it is dangerous to assume that the apparent holder of such property is, in fact, its owner. It is common to find a person living in a house which is legally his, and yet the 'owner' may only have been able to buy it by borrowing from some other person or institution. Until the loan has been repaid the entire value of the house cannot truly be counted as the occupier's property.

2 The second form which property may take consists not of tangible assets but of paper tokens which may, however, be just as valuable. A paper token may have value for the simple reason that it is the document giving legal

ownership to a certain tangible asset. In the previous example of a house, the document giving title or legal ownership to it is called a deed. This would be retained by the institution providing the loan until it had been fully repaid. Similar paper claims to wealth are the share certificates given to those who have put money into joint stock companies. For the value of all the share capital of a business is closely related to the value of the assets of that business which, in the last resort, it represents.

It is necessary to point out, however, that some property consisting only of paper claims is of value in spite of the fact that the documents do not directly represent any real assets. Cash, in the form of notes or coin or deposits in a bank, is generally acceptable as a means of payment for goods and services and provides a good example of this. Government securities are another. These are offered for sale by the state when it decides to borrow money, and they are similar to the debentures issued by a company (*see* pages 65–6) in that they carry fixed rates of interest. Insofar as some government securities have been used to pay for past wars, and the guns, shells, etc. on which the money was spent have long since disappeared, they do not represent any underlying assets. Securities, such as war loans, are only paper claims. However, they have value so long as the state continues to honour its obligation to pay interest on them annually to individuals who still hold such securities.

A person derives two distinct benefits from the ownership of property. In the first place, he has a reserve of capital which can always be used to maintain his standard of living. Even if he is unemployed he can allow his bank balance to run down, sell some of his houses, land or shares, while he may be earning nothing at all. The second benefit which accrues to a person owning property shows that this last possibility is not, in fact, likely to occur, since the possession of most property (other than cash and personal effects) usually involves the receipt of income as a direct result. This is obvious in the case of a landlord who lets his house or farm in return for rent, but it is also true of other property such as shares in joint stock companies and holdings of government securities, as we have seen earlier. Even a deposit in a savings bank earns interest. It is true that the yield from the ownership of capital tends not infrequently to be greater the larger the amount of property one possesses, but this does not affect the general principle.

The distribution of personal property

The total of all personal wealth differs, as we have seen, from the real value of the nation's stock of capital because of the existence of certain classes of property consisting of paper claims which, nevertheless, are of value to an individual. It must be added that some of the nation's assets, such as those of the nationalised industries, are not owned by any individuals, but by the state. However, the ownership of wealth usually brings with it the receipt of income to those persons who own it, and it is generally considered important for policy making to know something about how equally or unequally personal wealth is distributed.

A census of personal wealth has not been taken in modern Britain and it is necessary to rely on estimates of the shares of different groups in the total. This is a particularly difficult exercise and results tend to be highly controversial. It was one of the tasks given to the Royal Commission on the Distribution of Income and Wealth (*see* page 153). The Commission admitted that it could make no single unambiguous statement on the ownership of personal property for many reasons, not the least being the difficulty of quantifying the property of the lowest groups of wealth holders. Several estimates were therefore presented of the distribution of personal wealth based on different assumptions. Fig 7.7 uses figures chosen from among them. It should, therefore, be treated with caution as far as precise figures are concerned, but it serves to emphasise one undisputed feature; that the degree of inequality in the distribution of personal wealth is substantially greater than that of personal income. For example, whereas the top 10 per cent of *income units* receive roughly a quarter of total income, the share of the top 10 per cent of *wealth holders* in total wealth is nearer to double that figure.

The concentration of personal wealth in relatively few hands is no new feature of society. It results from many factors, of which inheritance and the

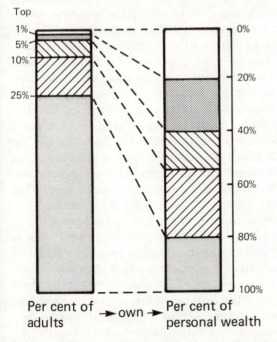

Fig 7.7 The ownership of personal wealth Great Britain 1982

tendency for people to accumulate wealth during their working lives and decumulate it after retirement, are the most important. The distribution is liable to change as the prices of the different assets comprising wealth alter over time. Chief among them are land, houses, shares and other securities, which are held in different proportions by rich and poor. Year to year fluctuations in the distribution of wealth can be very considerable, but one can discern a long-term reduction in the degree of inequality, particularly as measured by a declining share of the top 1 per cent of wealth holders in the total wealth during the present century. To the extent that this is partly offset by an increasing share of other wealth holders within the top 20 per cent, it might indicate a spread of wealth within families rather than a more general redistribution.

National income and the price level

The reader may have noticed that the earlier discussion of the size of the national income barely mentioned past trends. This was certainly not because it is unimportant to examine the growth of the national income over time. This question was left on one side because there are some particularly difficult problems associated with it; we shall now face them.

Some of the difficulties revolve around the problem of knowing how best to allow for changes in the *quality* of goods and services and of their prices. A switch from black and white to colour television, for example, is widely regarded as raising the quality of satisfaction derived from watching TV, but it is not automatically catered for adequately in the national accounts. Moreover, as the price of colour television sets has come down (reaping economies of large-scale production) the national output does not really fall in one sense, although as conventionally measured it does.

There is, however, another basic difficulty which stems from the fact that, as we know, the national income is a measure in money terms of the output of goods and services in the economy. Everyone is aware, however, that the value of money—the price at which the national output is valued—has not been stable for a long time. We live in an inflationary age. If we are to be able to estimate the changes in the volume of physical output during times when the price level is changing, we must make an allowance for inflation.

The method of allowing for inflation is to measure national output using *constant prices*, i.e. the prices ruling in a particular year. When we do this we obtain estimates of the *real* value of output, as distinct from the *nominal* (or money) value of output measured at the current prices of each year.

Fig 7.8 makes abundantly clear why an adjustment of this kind has been needed in recent times. There are two lines on the graph, showing the course of nominal and of real income in the two and a half decades since 1960. Nominal income in 1983 was over ten times its level almost quarter of a century earlier. Real income, in contrast, valued throughout in the prices

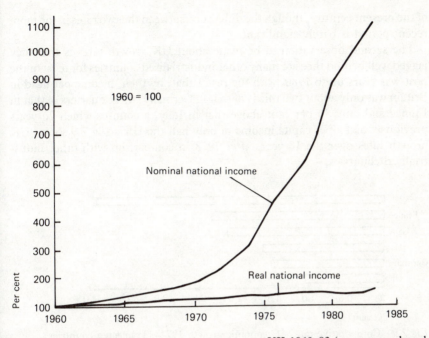

Fig 7.8 National income in real and money terms UK 1960–83 (percentages based on national income in 1960)

ruling in 1960, was up by only about 50 per cent. The difference between the two series is the result of inflation, which we discuss further below.

Economic growth

Now that we are able to make allowance for changes in the general price level, we can look at the rate of growth in real output that has taken place in the UK.

As we saw in the previous section, real output grew by about 50 per cent in the years between 1960 and 1983 (*see* Fig 7.8). This works out at an *annual* growth rate of a little more than 2 per cent, and is a fraction below the longer term rate of growth since the end of the Second World War, which is about $2\frac{1}{2}$ per cent per annum. It may seem low by some standards but it is higher than the average rate of growth earlier in the century, which was around 1 per cent before the First World War and 2 per cent in the inter-war period.

Two observations should be made about the growth rates described in the previous paragraph. First, the rates cited are of total output, and take no account of population changes. As we know from Chapter 3, the population of Britain grew rapidly in the first few decades of the century, though it has been virtually stable since 1970. Growth rates of output *per capita*, are, therefore, bound to be lower than growth rates of total output for the first three quarters of the present century, though the difference between the two rates in the more recent period is barely significant.

The second observation to be made about UK growth rates is that they lagged well behind those of many other industrialised countries for most of the post-war years up to 1980, with the result that, by then, income per head in Britain was only about two thirds of that in Germany, three quarters of that in France and only 30 per cent above that in Italy, a country which 20 years previously had a per capita income of only half the UK's Fig 7.9 shows UK growth rates over the 10 years after 1973 in comparison with other industrialised countries.

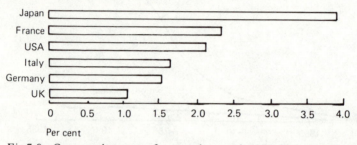

Per cent

Fig 7.9 Comparative rates of economic growth 1974–83 (selected countries)

The reasons for international differences in growth rates are complex. Growth depends ultimately on the quantity and quality of the factors of production available and on the efficiency with which they are combined. Observers often blame the UK's poor showing on its relatively low proportion of national income devoted to investment (and correspondingly high proportion devoted to consumption). Fig 7.10 shows these proportions for the same six countries as in Fig 7.9. Since the correlation between high investment and

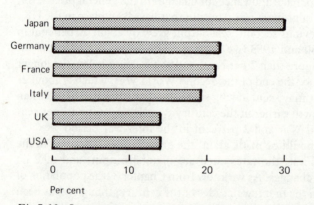

Per cent

Fig 7.10 Investment as a percentage of gross national product 1980–83 average (selected countries)

high growth rates is not perfect, it is clear that other forces are also at work. It is also important to remember that high growth is only one of several policy goals. When others, such as quality of life and reduction of pollution, come into conflict with the goal of high growth, some compromise has to be sought.

Inflation

As we learnt in Chapter 2, inflation is defined as a rise in the general level of prices. Although there have been a large number of occasions in the past when the price level rose, the period since the end of the Second World War has often been called 'the inflationary age'. This is partly because inflation has been more persistent for longer than at any other time for at least 150 years, and partly because the rate of inflation began to accelerate, especially in the 1970s.

Shortly after the war, in the 1950s, the price level rose relatively moderately, by about 3 to 5 per cent per annum. In the 1960s the inflation rate rose a little, prices being about 50 per cent higher by the end of the decade. The 1970s then witnessed a significant upsurge in the rate of inflation, especially after 1973–4 when the price of oil charged by the so-called OPEC group of oil exporters quadrupled. What has come to be known as 'double digit inflation', i.e. 10 per cent per annum or more, first occurred in 1974, and the rate subsequently accelerated, reaching 24 per cent the following year. Over the decade of the 1970s, prices rose on average by 250 per cent. Inflation continued into the 1980s, though the rate had fallen back to the single digit level by 1982, since when it has stayed around 5 per cent. Over the whole period 1960–85 the level of prices was on average about 6 times higher at the end than at the beginning of the period. A pound in 1985 was worth about 17 pence in terms of its 1960 purchasing power. Fig 7.11 shows the annual rates of inflation in the UK since 1960.

Fig 7.11 Inflation in the UK 1960–84 (percentage changes in retail prices from year to year)

The effects of inflation

Inflation has many consequences. It encourages people to seek channels for their savings which at least keep pace with rising prices, e.g. buying postage stamps and works of art, rather than investing in productive outlets. When the rate of inflation is variable, it makes it difficult for businesses, and households, to plan with confidence for the future; and inflation may affect the balance of payments (*see* page 209).

One of the main effects of inflation, however, is redistributive. Redistribution comes about in two ways. The first arises from the fact that the money incomes of different sections of the population do not move together in line with inflation. We know from Chapter 6, for example, that wage rates tend to be adjusted (usually annually) in modern times, as a result of bargaining between employers and employees. Strength at the negotiating table differs from one group of workers to another; those who are in strong bargaining positions keep their incomes at least abreast of rising prices and do not lose from inflation. Some may even gain. Others in weaker positions lose if their incomes lag behind the rate of increase of prices. No general indication can be given of who the winners and losers are, except to say that anyone whose income is fixed in money terms is bound to be a loser. As inflation has become accepted as a more or less permanent feature of life, more and more incomes tend to be tied in some way to prices. If the link is a formal one then **indexation** is said to be applied to them. Any individuals who are unfortunate enough not to have any kind of adjustment to their incomes when prices rise are bound to lose. Owners of securities who receive a fixed rate of interest on their capital are one example.

The second way in which inflation can cause a redistribution of income arises from the fact that when the average general level of prices rises, the prices of some goods and services rise faster, sometimes much faster, than others. Hence, those persons who are in the habit of buying relatively large amounts of goods which have risen greatly in price, tend to suffer, compared to others who tend to buy those which have risen relatively little.

Movements in the *average* level of prices are usually measured by what is called the **Retail Price Index** (**RPI**), published monthly by the government. This index shows what is happening to the cost of living as represented by the prices of a typical 'basket' of goods and services bought by the average household. In the basket are the goods most commonly consumed, with 'weights' attached to them representing their relative importance in the average household budget.

Movements in the RPI record changes in the cost of living between two dates for an average family. Such a family spends about 20 per cent of its income on food, about 15 per cent on transport and vehicles, and on housing, 10 per cent on alcohol and tobacco, and 6–7 per cent on each of clothing, fuel and light and durable household goods. The average family is, of course, a statistical artefact. For any individuals or groups the index may not accurately portray *their* cost of living. That will depend on their own expenditure pattern because all prices do not move in line together.

Fig 7.12 shows price level changes for different commodity groups between 1974 and 1984. During this period the index number for the *average* price level (RPI) was 359 on the base of 1974. However, as can be seen, the price indices for fuel and light and for tobacco were both around 500, while those for clothing and durable household goods were both under 300.

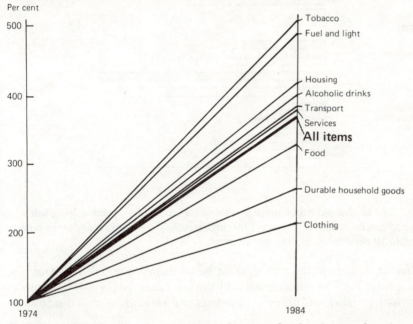

Fig 7.12 Index of retail prices: percentage increase of major classes, of goods, and services in 1984 compared with 1974

The effect of these wide variations in the rate of inflation for different commodity groups on the distribution of real income depends, of course, on the relative importance of each of these items in household budgets. Fig 7.13, by way of illustration, shows how households at three different income levels were affected. We can see that the three classes of goods which rose most in price between 1974 and 1984 (fuel and light, tobacco, and housing) were relatively more important in the budget of low income groups than of high ones. At the same time, the two classes of goods which rose least in price during the same period (clothing and durable household goods) were relatively more important in the budget of high income groups.

One should be careful before concluding from the information in Figs 7.12 and 7.13 that relative price changes have had an inegalitarian influence. The effect of changing relative prices is a complex matter and the full effect of

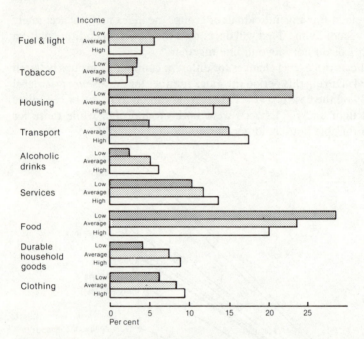

Fig 7.13 Household expenditure at different income levels; percentage of total expenditure on commodity groups 1983 (high income = top 20 per cent; low income = bottom 10 per cent of income distribution).

different weights in the indices must be taken into account. Moreover the evidence of Fig 7.12 relates specifically to a precise period (1974–84). Choice of alternative periods and different base dates could lead to different conclusions.

Appendix

The national accounts

Statistics of the national income of the UK are published in several standard forms. It is useful to be familiar with these and to understand the relationship between the most common measures, which appear in Fig 7.14.

The top row in the diagram shows total *domestic* expenditure, broken down in the manner to which we have become accustomed, i.e. into consumption, investment and government sectors. However, we need to take account of exports and imports. To derive *total* expenditure on UK products, it is necessary to add expenditure by non-residents on UK exports to domestic expenditure. This gives **Total Final Expenditure (TFE)**. To obtain a measure of total UK *output*, it is necessary to deduct expenditure on imports. This total is known as **Gross Domestic Product (GDP)**.

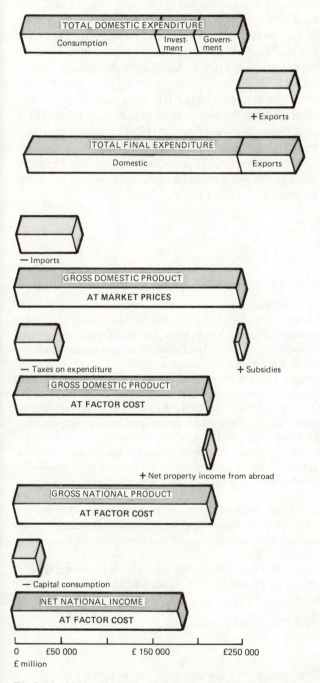

Fig 7.14 National income and product 1983; relationship between major definitions

It will be noticed that the wording in the bar in the third row of Fig 7.14 is: **GDP at market prices**. These, however, reflect taxes on expenditure, e.g. on tobacco, and subsidies, e.g. on housing. Taxes cause market values to exceed factor earnings, while subsidies allow market values to be less than earnings. To convert GDP at market prices to GDP at factor cost, these taxes must be subtracted while the subsidies are added. This yields **GDP at factor cost**.

The national income of the residents of the UK must take account of receipts (net) of income derived from the ownership of property overseas. This is added to the GDP to yield **Gross National Product (GNP)** in the fourth row of Fig 7.14, which has been termed *gross*. When capital consumption (depreciation allowances) have been deducted, the measures become *net*. Thus, the bottom bar in the diagram shows **net national income** (or **product**) as a result of subtracting capital consumption from **GNP**.

Exercises

For key to symbols indicating sources *see* pages xii–xiii.

1 How much did the national income increase last year *a* in money terms, *b* in real terms? Calculate the changes which took place in the real national product for each of the last 5 years compared with the previous year. How does the average compare with the post-war trend mentioned in the chapter? (Use figures for gross domestic product— GNP less overseas income—if others are not available.) (*MDS, ET, AS*)

2 Draw a graph to show the division of the national income between consumption and investment for the last 5 years. Compare your results with Fig 7.1. (*MDS, AS, F*)

3 Prepare a graph on the lines of Fig 7.1 showing the shares of wages and salaries, rent, interest and profits and self-employment income of total income last year and 5 years previously. Have the shares changed at all? (*AS*)

4 Find out the weekly unemployment benefit for a married man without children. Turn it into an annual rate and estimate approximately the number of incomes below this figure. Does the number give you any indication of the extent of poverty in Britain? (*WA, AS*)

5 Refer to a table which gives details of the numbers of incomes in different size classes. Group the data into three size classes, low, medium and high incomes (on any reasonable basis). Calculate the percentage of the total numbers of incomes and of total income in each size class. (*AS, ET*)

6 Compile a table for a recent month and for the same month a year ago showing average weekly wage rates of all manual workers. Compare this with the changes in prices over the same period:

a of all items in the retail price index
b of foodstuffs
c of housing (*MDS*)

7 Compile a 'league table' showing the average annual rate of increase of consumer prices for a recent year and for 5 years previously for each of the following countries.

Rank them according to their performance in the 2 years. Has the UK changed its position in the table?

France	Japan
Germany	UK
Italy	USA

Now repeat the same exercise, ranking the same countries according to their growth rates. (*N*)

8 Try to find out how your weekly family income is distributed among the main groups of items of expenditure in the index of retail prices. Assemble the information for the whole class and compare your own family's pattern of expenditure with the average for the class and with the national average. Are any differences a result of your family income being higher or lower than the average? (*AS, MDS, F*)

8 Money and finance

Almost every economic activity in Britain involves money, for although the production and distribution of goods and services could in theory be carried on without it, money is an indispensable part of the equipment of an advanced economy.

The functions of money

Money is said to perform three functions—to act as a *medium of exchange*, as a unit of account, and as a store of value. The first of these is, in many ways, the key function.

The best way to understand the significance of money is to imagine what life would be like without it. In our complex society things would be completely unmanageable. Production could, in principle, still continue, but problems would abound. How, for example, would the businessman pay for his raw materials and labour? The farmer might conceivably obtain machinery in exchange for farm produce and offer to engage labour on the same terms, but he would nevertheless be unlikely to find individuals who would agree to be paid in foodstuffs alone. Everyone would prefer payment in terms of money, part of which they could use to buy food and part to purchase other things. Most manufacturing businesses would be even worse off. Who would go to work in a coal mine to cart a load of coal home every pay day, or to a steelworks to be paid so many iron bars per year? Clearly, unless one could buy food and clothing for lumps of coal or iron bars in the market, coal miners and steel-workers would starve and would, therefore, rather stay at home and cultivate their own garden plots for nourishment, while their wives spun and wove simple woollen garments to clothe them. We should, in other words, be back in a primitive society where there was no specialisation and where the standard of living was accordingly low.

The difficulties involved in a society where exchange takes place only directly between commodities are real enough to need no exaggeration. They could be overcome only by the introduction of a means of payment which is generally acceptable to everyone, and through the medium of which any commodity could be exchanged for any other. Money is just such a means of payment although, in the past, man has employed a variety of other things for the same purpose; from seashells to cattle and, during the war, cigarettes, which often served in prisoner-of-war camps where real money was not available. The one essential feature of all these means of payment was that anyone would accept them in payment of wages or debts, since in doing so he knew that he could use them to purchase anything he happened to want.

All that the function of money as a medium of exchange means, is that it is generally *acceptable* as payment for debts and other transactions. Its existence facilitates the complex economic life of present day Britain. It avoids the need for anyone who has something to sell having to hunt around for someone else who will offer him in exchange just what he happens to want. He can sell his commodity for money to anyone who will buy it and can use money to buy anything he needs.

Money's other two functions are more easily described. We saw how it is used as a *unit of account* in Chapter 7, where money values are employed to add together the various goods and services which make up the national income. Money also helps the business man to assess how well his business is doing, when he draws up his profit and loss account and balance sheet (*see* pages 61–4). Money's *store of value* function is fairly obvious. Holding money is a convenient, though by no means the only way, of storing one's accumulated wealth.

Forms of money

In modern times we no longer employ any of the primitive forms of money, but there are more types of money in use than we might perhaps at first imagine. A good way of illustrating this is to consider the various ways in which we might pay for what we buy.

Coins

If the sum involved is a small one, the most likely way of making payment is with coins. Gold and silver used to circulate in Britain before the First World War. Today, coins are made of bronze or of alloys of copper and nickel. They are manufactured by the Royal Mint and are legally acceptable up to certain amounts, known as **legal tender**, e.g. pound coins are legal tender up to any amount, 50p and 20p coins up to £10, and 10p and 5p coins up to £5.

Notes

For larger debts it is much more common to pay in notes. Bank notes, or paper money as it is sometimes called, have an interesting origin. In England in the 17th century the most general form of money was the gold coin. Rather than keep a large quantity of gold at home, people naturally used to take it for safe keeping to local goldsmiths, who were the first bankers. In return for the gold the goldsmith issued a receipt, on which it was stated that he promised to pay on demand to the holder of the receipt the amount of gold mentioned. Following upon this, the custom grew for individuals to accept such receipts or notes in payment for debts, since with the signature of a reputable goldsmith, and later a banker, they were in fact 'as good as gold'.

Today, bank notes are the principal form of currency, although it is no longer open to any banker or goldsmith to issue them. In England and Wales this right is now exclusively reserved for the Bank of England (*see* page 186). Bank notes, however, still retain their original form. If you look at a £5 note you will still find printed there a statement which no longer has any real meaning (since gold is no longer obtainable on demand in exchange for notes), but which is signed by the Chief Cashier on behalf of the Bank of England and reads 'Promise to pay the bearer on demand the sum of five pounds'. The notes in general use at present are for £5, £10, £20 and £50. All bank notes are legal tender up to any amount.

Bank deposits

By far the most important means of settling debts today does not involve the handling of notes or coin, but is carried out with the assistance of banks and usually involves the drawing of cheques. Cheques originated at roughly the same time as bank notes. After depositing gold in a local bank or with a goldsmith it became common for a person to write a letter to his banker instructing him to pay a sum of money to a person he would name. He would then give the letter not to his banker, but to the person to whom he owed money. The latter would then dispatch it to his banker who would arrange to collect the cash and hold it for him. Quite soon, this form of settling debts became so important that it was unnecessary to write a special letter every time one wanted to make a payment, as the banks themselves began to print letter forms, known as cheques. These only need the insertion of the amount, the date, the name of the payee and the signature of the person making the payment. Today, banks issue books containing such cheques to their customers, although there are other means of transferring money in bank accounts.

The advantages of making payments through banks are simplicity and safety, especially when the sum involved is large. All businesses use banks. So do many private individuals. The great importance of bank deposits in comparison with the volume of notes and coin in circulation is shown in Fig 8.1.

Notice, two types of bank deposits shown in the diagram—**sight deposits**, kept in current accounts, and **time deposits**, kept in deposit accounts. Sight deposits are withdrawable on demand and without notice, merely by presenting a cheque. Traditionally they used not to earn interest, but a recent

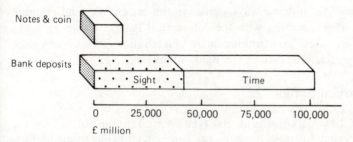

Notes & coin

Bank deposits

0   25,000   50,000   75,000   100,000
£ million

Fig 8.1   Money supply UK January 1985

development has been the growth of some interest-bearing sight deposits—they increased by almost 40 per cent in 1984. Banks usually charge customers for the office work involved in running such accounts, especially small ones.

Most businesses do not keep all their money on current account; they put some of it in a deposit account. Here it earns interest, but seven days' notice is legally required for its withdrawal. In practice, however, banks seldom object if customers make transfers of reasonable amounts from deposit to current account for immediate payment. For this reason time deposits may be considered, for some purposes, as part of the money stock. (*See* pages 190–1.)

Other means of payment

Fig 8.1 includes only bank deposits held in sterling. However, businesses and individuals may decide to hold some of their cash balances in foreign currencies, either to make payments overseas, or to convert them into sterling when circumstances are favourable. In January 1985 foreign currency bank deposits in the UK amounted to about £20 000 million—about half the total of sterling sight deposits. The proportion of total money assets held in foreign currencies varies widely, however. It was high in January 1985, reflecting, among other things, the strength of the US dollar and the corresponding weakness of the pound sterling (*see* pages 216).

Payments may also be effected in a variety of other ways besides the use of currency and bank deposits. There are a number of financial institutions, such as building societies (*see* below) which offer facilities similar to the banks. The Post Office operates a National Giro for the transfer of money through post offices. Settlements may also be made using credit cards, IOUs, promissory notes, etc., though in such cases they are only temporary as far as the payer is concerned.

The banking system

The importance of banks has already been mentioned in connection with the supply of money. There are, however, several types of financial institutions which have functions in some ways similar to the banks. We shall examine them in some detail, starting with the commercial banks, and going on to consider what are called 'non-banking financial institutions'. Finally, we shall discuss a very special institution, the Bank of England.

The commercial banks

For well over 100 years the principal type of banking institution for the conduct of everyday business has been the commercial bank, formed on the lines of a joint stock company. This has not always been the case; previously the joint stock form of organisation had been prohibited to banks, leaving the business in the hands of a multitude of small private partnership concerns and the Bank of England, founded by Royal Charter (*see* pages 185–8). It took a year of financial crisis, in 1825, to bring about a change in the law.

Bank mergers in the 19th century, during the First World War and in the 1970s, brought the number of banks down to the present level. Four large banks—Barclays, Lloyds, Midland and the National Westminster (Nat-West)—now account for well over 90 per cent of the total business of the London clearing banks (*see* below).

Bank clearing

Every time someone draws a cheque in favour of another person it is necessary to transfer the amount of money involved. If the two people both happen to have accounts at the same bank, it is a simple matter. All that happens is that the bank makes entries in the accounts of the two people concerned, debiting the one and crediting the other. If they have accounts at different banks this is not possible. The most straightforward solution is for the bank of the person making the payment to hand over to the other bank the sum of money in question. This is what happened in the past. Soon, however, bank clerks who used to travel around the City of London collecting such money realised that a lot of work would be saved if they met to sort out the payments that were due. For it often happened that a bank clerk was collecting from one bank while his counterpart was round at his office on a similar mission. Obviously, if the amounts involved were identical there was no need for either of them to be collecting at all. Even if the amounts were not equal the smaller could be offset against the larger, and the clerk from the latter bank could collect the difference, still cutting the work in half.

The essential requirement for the successful working of this system of offsetting claims against one another and leaving only residual amounts to be collected, now known as **clearing**, was simply that the clerks should all meet together for a 'grand sort out'. In the early days in the 18th century the clerks took this upon themselves and began to meet informally, but today there exists a bankers' clearing house in the City of London where computerised data on the transfer of sums between different banks are reconciled and the subsequent differences between the banks settled.

The business of banking

Commercial banks are in business to make a profit. They are essentially borrowing and lending institutions; that is, they borrow as cheaply as possible from one set of people and lend to others at a profit. How is it possible for a bank to lend other people's money, which it is supposed to be holding in safe custody? What happens if the people who have deposited money in the bank demand payment and the banks are unable to satisfy them? The answer to these questions revolves around a fact which the earliest goldsmith-bankers did not take long to realise, namely that it is very rare for all their customers to demand money *at the same time*. Consequently, all the banker has to do is to keep a reserve immediately available to cover the proportion of his customers whom he thinks might demand payment at one time. Moreover, he can keep this cash reserve at a minimum by relying also on a second line of defence by holding some financial assets which earn only a small rate of interest but which are, so to speak, 'near money' in the sense of being speedily and easily exchangeable for cash. So protected, the banker can make loans to other individuals and institutions at a rate of interest which allows him to make a profit. The best proportions of cash and **liquid assets**—as money and near money assets are called—to deposits were evolved as a result of experience. Traditionally a ratio of cash to total liabilities (deposits) of 8 per cent used to be observed by the banks. We shall examine their liquid asset holdings in a moment. It is relevant to know that the proportions in which the banks divide their assets is not nowadays something over which they have complete freedom; they are subject to control in this and certain other matters by the Bank of England, in ways which will also be discussed later.

Fig 8.2 shows the two sides of the banks' business. On the left-hand side stand their deposits. These constitute the total of their liabilities—credit standing in the accounts of customers, some of which may be demanded at any time. These also constitute the resources out of which the banks may make loans. The distribution of their assets is shown on the right-hand side of the chart.

Liabilities

The liabilities, which we have already mentioned, consist almost wholly of current and deposit accounts standing to the credit of their customers. The difference between them has been explained earlier (*see* page 170).

There are two sets of liabilities included in the 'other' category of Fig 8.2. One consists of liabilities to the banks' shareholders, while the other is **certificates of deposit**. These are notes (receipts) issued by the banks and which

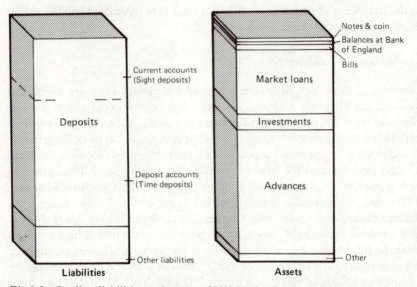

Fig 8.2   Sterling liabilities and assets of UK banks October 1984

are in circulation in the money market; they have to be paid when presented by a holder at the maturity date.

Assets

The asset side of the balance sheet of the clearing banks may best be examined using the concepts of profitability and **liquidity**, the latter referring to the speed and ease with which an asset may be turned into cash.

Notes and coin held in the vaults are the banks' first line of reserve—they are perfectly liquid and earn no return at all.

Accounts at the Bank of England are the credit balances of the clearing banks at the Bank of England which, among other things, acts as the 'bankers' bank'. The deposits kept there by the clearing banks are of two basic kinds. The first are the balances which the banks freely decide to hold at the Bank of England for their own convenience. The second are balances which the banks are required to hold there by the government, as decided by the Bank of England itself. The latter are also of two types:

Special deposits are non-interest bearing frozen assets called for and released at the direction of the Bank of England.

Cash ratio deposits are also in a sense frozen assets, although they do earn interest. They are the result of undertakings by the banks to hold a small percentage of their liabilities in their Bank of England accounts (the percentage in early 1985 was less than 1 per cent of so-called 'eligible liabilities'—mainly sterling deposits). These are related to monetary policy, which is discussed later in this chapter.

Bills There are two rather different assets included under this heading: bills of exchange and Treasury bills. Both are fairly liquid, consisting as they do of loans made for short periods to traders and to the government. The principle of discounting a bill of exchange may be illustrated with an example from international trade.

Suppose a trader in one country sells goods to a purchaser in another and the latter does not receive the goods for a considerable time after they have left the seller's premises. The purchaser may not want, or be able, to pay for the goods until they arrive, but the seller may, at the same time, not wish to have to wait for payment. A solution is for the seller to draw up a bill of exchange which he sends to the debtor for signature. The debtor writes 'accepted' across the bill, signifying that he has agreed to make the payment, and returns it to the drawer. As bills are usually drawn to be paid at a specified date in the future (3 months is not uncommon), the seller does not receive his payment immediately. He can, however, sell the bill through his bank to one of the specialised financial institutions who look after such transactions, and receive cash immediately, even though the purchaser of the goods (who is the 'acceptor' of the bill) has not yet paid over the money. The sale of the bill by the trader is known as 'discounting' and the amount he receives depends on the discount rate. If a seller discounts a bill worth, for example, £100 in 3 months' time and the discount rate is 12 per cent per annum, he will have to forgo a quarter of £12 and will get only £97 when he discounts the bill.

Bills of exchange were very common, especially in international trade before the First World War, but they are less so today. The banks still hold a substantial number of bills, however, although some are of a special type known as **Treasury bills**. These are similar to trade bills in that they are promises to pay a sum of money at a future date, but the promissor in the case of a Treasury bill is the government, which issues a number of them every week in order to finance current expenditure.

Market loans are assets with a high degree of liquidity comprising short-term loans to city financial institutions, including the discount houses in the money market.

Investments All the assets listed so far are more or less liquid, in the sense that they are either cash itself or are easily converted into cash. The group described as investments covers a wide range of assets, some of which may be as liquid as Treasury bills and others which are relatively illiquid.

Bank investments are held in the form of government securities. These are sold by the state when it needs to borrow from the private sector of the economy on fairly long-term. They are redeemable (if at all) a good many years after issue.

The liquidity of the securities in the banks' portfolios, therefore, depends on how long they have to run to maturity. Those which are almost due for redemption by the government are regarded as being highly liquid. Others are less so. Of course, a government security can always be sold at the current market price, but this can vary greatly, and liquidity is related to the certainty of the amount of money that can be realised on a sale as well as to mere marketability. We cannot go into details of the precise holdings by banks of securities of different maturity. Current practice is to split them into two groups according to whether they mature in more or less than twelve months, the latter being considered 'liquid'.

Advances The largest group of assets held by banks are loans and advances to customers, as can be seen in Fig 8.2. This is where local bank managers may play a key role. Businessmen wanting credit to expand their operations, for example, must make their propositions appear sound. Sometimes banks require some security, or 'collateral', such as share certificates, and they have a distinct preference for loans of relatively short duration, such as those made to finance seasonal fluctuations in trade. In any event, outstanding loans are reviewed annually. Straightforward personal loans for fixed sums are made, but advances are commonly on an 'overdraft' basis. Under this system permission is given to the customer to draw cheques up to a certain stipulated amount. The procedure is very convenient, especially for borrowers whose needs are liable to fluctuate. It avoids borrowing a larger sum than is necessary and it tends to be cheaper, since interest is payable only on the amount overdrawn and not on the limit of the overdraft.

The rate of interest charged by the banks on advances is subject to considerable variation from time to time, and is partly affected by the risk attaching to particular loans. They are all, however, related to what the banks call their **base lending rate**. It is important to realise that advances are the most profitable of the undertakings that the banks engage in. They are, at the same time, regarded as illiquid assets because it is impossible to call all of them in at short notice, even though there are always some being repaid. The distribution of advances among the main types of borrowers is shown in Fig 8.3.

Other assets The other assets of the banks are a miscellaneous category and include bank premises and equipment. We must, however, mention that the classification used for Fig 8.2 and the accompanying text neglects certain formal distinctions between what are known as **eligible assets** and **liabilities**. These are part of the mechanism of monetary policy and will be explained later (*see* page 190).

We conclude our description for the time being of the work of the commercial banks with a general comment. All the ways in which the banks use their resources (except only holding cash) involve the sacrifice of ready money for some asset which will bring in a larger sum at a future date. As a general principle it may be said that the longer the wait and the greater the risk, the more profitable the loan is likely to be. To sacrifice all for the chance of large profits, however, would soon lead to the collapse of a bank, and it is the maintenance of a portfolio which shows a nice balance between profitability and ready cash which is the art of banking.

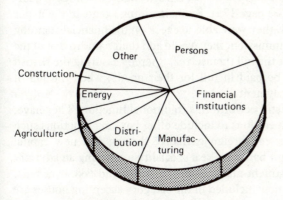

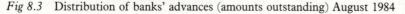

Fig 8.3 Distribution of banks' advances (amounts outstanding) August 1984

The UK banking sector

The London clearing banks form the major part of what is known as the UK monetary sector, although there are other clearing banks in Scotland and Northern Ireland. There are also banking institutions which perform similar functions to them. Since 1983, UK banks have been classified in three categories—retail banks, overseas banks, and accepting houses.

Retail banks

This is the term used to describe banks which either have extensive branch networks in the UK or participate in a UK clearing system. Hence, the clearing banks are retail banks; so are the Trustee Savings Bank, the National Giro and a few other similar institutions.

Overseas banks

The number of foreign banks maintaining branches in the UK has risen very greatly, by a factor of four, in the past 25 years. This is partly a reflection of the growth of international trade and partly due to the increasing tendency of investors in the UK to hold foreign securities.

Accepting houses

The third category of banks is known as **accepting houses**, or **merchant banks**. The term sprang originally from the role played by financial houses with well-known names such as Baring, Hambros, Lazard and Rothschild, in guaranteeing bills of exchange (*see* page 175). By maintaining agents in the major trading centres of the world, they were able to check on the financial standing of traders. In return for a commission, they would add their name to that of the original acceptors (or accept the bill themselves), thereby assuring the British exporters that they would be paid in full for their goods, when the bill of exchange became due for payment.

Modern merchant banks still perform this traditional function. They have, however, diversified their operations to include other banking functions such as making loans to businesses, foreign exchange dealing and new capital issues. Many major merchant banks make a speciality of offering an advisory service with regard to investment management, mergers and take-over bids. Other financial institutions now included in the category accepting houses are finance houses, whose traditional business of providing finance for hire-purchase and credit sales and leasing of cars and equipment, has been widened to cover some other normal banking functions.

Non-banking financial institutions

The prime importance of the banking system stems from the fact that bank deposits are widely used to pay for transactions in the economy. In this connection, as we have seen, the banks function as lending organisations. However, there are other financial institutions which channel borrowing and supply credit to those who are prepared to pay for it: they make their living from the margin between the rates of interest they charge and receive. These institutions differ from the banks in that individually they are often smaller in size but also, more significantly, because each type of institution tends to specialise in a particular class of financial business, borrowing and lending either on short- or long-term, and supplying credit, e.g. to agriculture, industry, house purchasers, for hire-purchase, etc. The important institutions which will now be considered are discount houses, building societies, insurance companies and pension funds.

Discount houses

As their name implies, these are businesses which do most of the discounting of bills of exchange and Treasury bills. When they do so either for the government or for a private trader they must, of course, have a supply of cash which they borrow, largely from the banks on short-term. (These are included in the bank assets described as **market loans**, *see* Fig 8.2.) Banks lend at fairly low rates of interest, and the discount houses are able to make a profit by charging a rate for discounting slightly above the rate which they have to pay for this accommodation.

Although the bills which they discount usually become due for payment only after anything from two to six months, and the money which they borrow is repayable at shorter notice, the discount houses are not usually left short of funds since it generally happens that when one bank is calling in its loans another is offering more to the discount market. Even if this is not the case the discount houses can always turn to the Bank of England as the *lender of last resort*. As they may have to borrow here at relatively high rates of interest they will probably show a loss on these transactions, which they naturally try to avoid. The frequency with which the discount houses are forced 'into the Bank' depends upon the general financial state of the country and the monetary policy of the government (*see* below).

The discount houses hold a considerable number of the bills which they discount until maturity, but they also rediscount some with the banks which, as we have seen, like to keep a proportion of their assets in this form. In fairly recent times they have also become quite important dealers in other government securities as these approach maturity.

Ten London discount houses are members of the **London Discount Market Association**. Their freedom of action is limited by controls similar to those on banks. Since 1981, for instance, they must hold minimum percentages of their assets on deposit at the Bank of England (*see* page 190).

Building societies

In terms of sheer size, the largest category of non-banking financial institutions is the building societies. Their total accumulated funds in 1984 amounted to about £90 000 million, a figure comparable with the sterling deposits of the clearing and other retail banks.

The societies have a history going back to the 18th century, when many were founded locally by small groups of people to finance the building of their own houses. Today there are about 200 building societies, although the number has been decreasing for some time as the smaller ones have been absorbed by the rapidly expanding societies. Over half of the business is in the hands of half a dozen companies, of which the Halifax and the Abbey National are the largest.

The prime function of building societies is not the building of houses but the lending of money to borrowers for house purchase; about 80 per cent of their funds is used in this way. The method of borrowing money from a building society is known as obtaining a **mortgage**. An individual desirous of buying a house obtains a loan for a period of years by surrendering to the society the title deed of the house and by paying interest on the sum involved at a rate varying with conditions in the market. For suitable house property in first class condition societies are, in normal times, prepared to lend about 90 per cent of the value of the house. The borrower then has only the balance to find immediately from his own resources and can pay off the mortgage over a period, generally 15 or 20 years or even longer.

Building societies obtain the money which they lend to house purchasers by borrowing from members of the general public at a lower rate of interest, and in this they are assisted by a legal concession which makes them liable to income tax at a reduced rate. Money is lent to them either on deposit or in return for shares in the society. Shares earn a slightly higher rate of interest than deposits, but they must not be confused with shares in joint stock companies. The distinction between building society shares and deposits is much closer to that between deposit account and current account deposits with clearing banks. Withdrawal of funds in the form of shares may formally require notice but shareholders, like those with deposit accounts at the commercial banks, can normally make withdrawals much more quickly. Indeed, people have come to treat such accounts with building societies as more or less liquid assets with the effect that the societies have themselves taken on some of the characteristics of commercial banks. Some building societies even offer chequing accounts. One result has been that they have been included in some of the controls used by the Bank of England, which were formerly restricted to the banks (*see* page 190).

A noticeable feature of the flow of funds into building societies is associated with the fact that their interest rates often tend to lag behind those in other parts of the market. Consequently, when interest rates are rising generally, the societies tend to experience a shortage of funds and it becomes difficult for would be borrowers to obtain mortgages, and vice versa at other times. The ease with which mortgages are obtainable is, moreover, a very important factor affecting the price of houses. Some house purchase is, however, financed by other institutions including local authorities, banks and insurance companies.

Insurance companies

The business of insurance companies is to take over from individuals or firms specific risks in which they are involved in return for a relatively small payment, known as a **premium**. They are able to do this because, although something may be completely uncertain for an individual, it is not so for a company which specialises in risks of a particular type. A businessman can have no idea whether his factory will have a serious fire next year, nor can any motorist know whether he will meet with an accident on the roads. However, an insurance company dealing with thousands of these risks is in an entirely different position, for the law of averages works very well with large numbers.

On the basis of claims experience and detailed statistical analysis, insurers are able to assess such risks; the essential principle of insurance being the pooling of risks and their proper classification into groups. For example, the premium to insure family cars used for social and domestic purposes is very different from that to insure high speed sports cars owned by youthful drivers.

There are several types of insurance to be distinguished. Marine insurance covers ships and cargoes for maritime perils. Much of this business is done through the institution known as Lloyds, where the enormous risks involved with single vessels are spread among a large number of **underwriters**. Fire insurance covers material loss to buildings and contents from fire and kindred perils. Accident insurance means what it says, the principal class being cover for motor vehicles.

The most important single category of insurance from the viewpoint of sources of finance is life assurance. This differs from the other types in an important respect. Whereas in the case of fire or accident there is uncertainty as to whether the incident will take place, in the case of life assurance there is no doubt as to whether one will die. The uncertainty is *when* the unfortunate event will take place. Life assurance, however, is attractive for an individual because he may wish to cover his relatives in the event of his early death or provide for his own retirement if he lives to enjoy it. The life assurance companies have data on the risk attaching to individual lives. They know the risk varies with age and premiums rise accordingly, so that the older a person is when he or she takes out a life assurance policy, the higher the rate of premium.

The importance of the funds of the life offices should now be evident. The companies accumulate sums of money over long periods from a large number of people. They then invest the funds in such a way as to yield the maximum return consistent with the need to pay out the capital sums assured on the deaths of policy holders, or on their maturity in the case of so-called endowment policies, when this occurs before death. The total accumulated funds of insurance companies at the end of 1983, stood at over £110 000 million. Their distribution over different types of asset is shown in Fig 8.4. Government securities used to be the most important group, but about a third of the total now comprises shares in private industry. It is the fact that the bulk of these are ordinary shares which accounts for the significant role of insurance companies in the ownership of many British companies as mentioned in Chapter 4 (*see* page 68).

Pension funds

Employers in the public sector and many privately owned companies provide their employees with pensions on retirement. So do some trade unions, as we saw in Chapter 6. In certain pension schemes employees make contributions as well as employers. Pension (or superannuation) funds accumulate from the contributions made during the working life of employees and they are used to earn interest and dividends by the purchase of securities and shares in British companies. Pensions funds may be self-administered or handled by insurance companies or banks. Total funds in 1983 were only a little less than those of

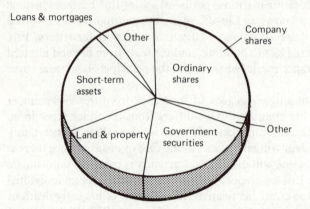

Fig 8.4   Insurance companies UK end 1983 (distribution of total assets)

insurance companies, and nearly half of the assets of such funds consisted of ordinary shares in joint stock companies. The managers of pension funds, therefore, play a role similar to that of their counterparts in insurance companies. Both are described as institutional shareholders and can be influential.

The Stock Exchange

Our description of the major financial institutions is nearly complete. One unique institution is next on our list—the Stock Exchange.

The Stock Exchange is a specialised market where shares and bonds issued by joint-stock companies and securities issued by the government are bought and sold. As we learned in Chapter 4, the popularity of joint stock companies leapt forward at the time the Companies Acts allowed them limited liability, the advantage of which depends on the presence of a market place where shares can be traded. Thus the modern stock exchange began to develop rather more than 100 years ago, when those first Companies Acts were passed. That is not to say that the Stock Exchange has a history no longer than that of limited liability. Business in shares had been transacted for many years before the early stockbrokers began to meet regularly, as did so many other financiers, in a convenient coffee house—Jonathan's in Exchange Alley—in the 18th century.

The nature of the Stock Exchange

The Stock Exchange is not an open market where the general public is free to buy and sell; it is more like a club open only to members. The nature of the Stock Exchange is, however, expected to change, probably dramatically, as this book goes to press. This is because of a number of changes in the regulations governing membership and trading, to be introduced in 1986.

Traditionally, membership of the Stock Exchange has been restricted to private individuals, who were in one or other of two groups, known as *brokers* and *jobbers*. The distinction between them resembled that between retailers (brokers), who deal with the general public, and wholesalers (jobbers) who deal only with retailers in any trade. However, the division is expected to disappear with the removal, in 1986, of a ban on members entering each others' preserves.

A second major change introduced in the same year is admission to membership of corporations, who are expected to replace the private members who for centuries have been the only dealers allowed on the Stock Exchange. The new structure of the market cannot be predicted with certainty, but will probably see the emergence of a number of large finance corporations, including international banks and stockbroking firms (e.g. Bank of America and Merril Lynch, the American brokers) playing a dominant role.

A third innovation is the establishment of a new Securities and Investment Board (SIB)—an official body given the task of licensing institutions and regulating stock market dealings, which were previously subject only to self-control by the Stock Exchange itself.

Types of investors

The prices of securities on the Stock Exchange are liable to fluctuate daily with changes in reports of the profitability of particular companies and with the general state of optimism or pessimism in the market. For investors who intend to hold shares for a number of years in order to receive an income from the dividends, such fluctuations are not of great significance. There is, however, a class of investor who buys shares without intending to keep them but to make a profit by buying at a lower price than that at which he sells. A person who anticipates that a particular company's shares will shortly rise in price and buys them in the hope of selling later at a profit is known as a **bull**. His opposite, the **bear**, believes that there will be a fall in price and therefore sells, hoping that before he is called upon to deliver the shares he will be able to buy them for less than the price at which he sold. A third Stock Exchange 'animal', known as a **stag**, applies for new shares before they are issued, intending to sell them as soon as dealing begins, hoping, of course, for a rise in price. It should be remembered, however, that by no means all investors are persons; the financial institutions which we have discussed have become of outstanding importance in view of the substantial funds of which they dispose.

Settlement of accounts takes place fortnightly. Each successful bull or bear then receives from his broker a sum equal to the difference between the price at which he bought and that at which he sold his shares. If the change in price hoped for did not materialise the investor may wish to postpone settlement. In the case of an unsuccessful bull this may be done by payment of a rate of interest known as a 'contango'. If the supply of shares is very short, however, an unsuccessful bear will be called upon to pay 'backwardation'. It is also possible to deal in 'future' securities, by purchasing an **option** to 'put' or 'call' shares at a date in the future, often three months.

Types of securities

The Stock Exchange deals in stocks and shares. There is no more than a superficial difference between these names that a company can give to the capital it issues, except that **shares** are in fixed units of nominal value, such as £100 or £1 while **stock** can be bought or sold in odd amounts, such as £743.50. Securities traded on the Stock Exchange include shares and debentures of public companies and bonds issued by British and foreign governments. UK government securities are known as 'gilt-edged' because the likelihood of bankruptcy is virtually nil. Shares in the largest and best-known companies are called 'blue chips' and are considered sound, because there is always an active market in them. Not every public company's shares are dealt in on the Stock Exchange. To earn the right to a full Stock Exchange quotation, companies must comply with certain rules, including the offer of a minimum proportion of its shares to the general public. However, to attract smaller, and mainly new, companies an Unlisted Securities Market was established in 1980, with less restrictive regulations.

Investors who wish to minimise risk can buy shares in **investment trust** companies which carry a range of shares. Alternatively they can buy units in a **unit trust**. This is an organisation which holds a portfolio of securities, so that the purchaser of a unit participates in the benefits and risks attaching to all the shares in the portfolio. These units are especially attractive to small savers and can be bought and sold in small denominations and with a minimum of formality, without necessarily going through the Stock Exchange.

New issues

The principal business of the Stock Exchange is in existing securities. However, the Stock Exchange is involved in new capital issues mainly because the council of that body decides whether permission shall be granted for shares to be dealt in. It is vitally important for the success of an issue to be assured of this permission. The council sometimes suspends dealings in the shares of a company if there is suspicion of illegal trading and while takeover bids are in progress. Detailed rules for procedure in such matters are contained in the City Code on Takeovers and Mergers.

Four main methods are used to raise new capital (other than the ploughing back of profits, *see* page 67). The first, a **public issue**, is a straightforward offer of shares to the general public. This is usually done in co-operation with a specialist financial institution, such as a merchant bank or a stockbroker. There are also a number of issuing houses which make it a wholetime function. An advertisement is placed in the press, outlining details of the company, voting rights, etc., and calling for applications for shares, which are then allotted. It is common to have such issues 'underwritten' by an issuing house in return for a commission. This guarantees that all the new shares will be bought regardless of the amount of applications. A second method, known as an **offer for sale**, is where the company sells shares directly to an issuing house, which then disposes of them to the public. Third, there is a **placing**, which is a way of making, especially, small issues of shares by finding a number of investors who agree to buy the shares privately.

Companies may also offer additional shares, at below current market prices, to existing share-holders in what is called a **rights issue**. This method tends to keep the costs of the issue down, but the shares have usually to be offered on favourable terms.

The UK monetary sector

The way in which the UK financial system has been described in this chapter might suggest that it is composed of a number of clearly distinct types of institution, each with its own function. Such was not too far from the case in the past. However the last 25 years or so have seen certain important changes in the nature of the financial system. Concentration in fewer and fewer firms has been accompanied by diversification and the extension of international links, so that the dividing lines between the different types of institution have become blurred. Much of this is the result of mergers. For instance in 1984, Hambro Life Assurance announced plans to merge with merchant bankers Charterhouse J Rothschild, and Mercantile House took over Alexander Discount plc. There have also been several moves by clearing and merchant banks to acquire an interest in firms on the Stock Exchange (*see* page 183). For example, in 1984, the Midland Bank linked up with stockbrokers Greenwell, Morgan Grenfell with stockjobbers Pinchin Denny, and other links have involved UK and foreign firms.

The Bank of England

The Bank of England is the financial institution that we have left until the end of this chapter. The reason is that it stands apart from all the rest which we have discussed, and which are all privately owned by commercial bodies. The Bank of England is unlike these. It is the **central bank** of the UK, owned by, and operated on behalf of, the government.

The history of the Bank of England goes back to 1694 when it was founded by Royal Charter. Originally a private concern owned by its shareholders, its great importance led to its nationalisation in 1946, when the shares were taken over by the government. A few relics of its earlier ordinary banking business remain, but today the Bank is on an entirely different footing from the commercial banks, over which it exercises a profound influence. The Bank of England controls the currency and acts as banker both to the government and to the commercial banks. It also plays a key role in the government's monetary policy, and its activities may be discussed under the headings of the two main departments into which it was divided by the Bank Charter Act of 1844.

The Issue Department

The monopoly of the note issue in England and Wales which the Bank of England enjoys is traceable to the 1844 Act, although the process of taking over the issuing rights of other banks was a gradual business. This means that, apart from a few banks in Scotland and Northern Ireland which still retain their old privileges, the Bank of England is the only institution which is allowed by law to issue bank notes.

The work of this department of the Bank is illustrated by the weekly statement of its activities, the chief items of which are as follows:

Bank of England

Issue Department 19 December 1984
(£ million)

Notes in circulation	12 610	Government securities	1 888
Notes in Banking Dept	10	Other assets	10 732
	12 620		12 620

At one time the amount of notes which the Bank was allowed to issue was closely related to the value of the gold in its vaults. Today only a minute fraction is covered by gold, but the note issue is not unlimited. The remainder, which is known as the 'fiduciary issue' (from the Latin *fiducia* meaning 'trust'), is covered by government securities of unimpeachable standing. The amount of the fiduciary issue is subject to considerable variation from time to time in accordance with the public's need for cash. It is traditionally raised, for example, at Christmas time, when the demand for money increases. On 19 December 1984 the Bank had issued over £12 000 million in notes, most of which were held by the general public.

The Banking Department

The more important as well as the more interesting of the Bank of England's activities concern the Banking Department. Here it is that the Bank functions as the government's bank and the bankers' bank. The similarity between Fig 8.5, which shows the operations of the Banking Department, and Fig 8.2 is more apparent than real for, although the Bank of England, like the commercial banks, is concerned with the lending and borrowing of money, it is not primarily in business to make a profit but to serve certain needs of other City institutions, to act as banker to the government, and to implement its monetary policy (*see* below).

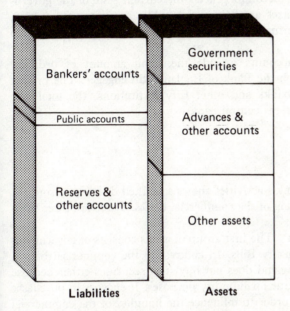

Liabilities   Assets

Fig 8.5 Bank of England (Banking Department) liabilities and assets, 19 December 1984

Liabilities
There are three main groups of accounts which constitute the liabilities of the Bank of England—bankers' accounts, public accounts and reserves and accounts.

Bankers' accounts

These accounts relate to the Bank of England's function as the bankers' bank. They are the credits standing on deposit in favour of the clearing banks and discount houses, i.e. credits to them but liabilities to the Bank of England. They consist of two types of deposit. **Operational deposits** are working balances held mainly for settling debts among the London clearing banks.

Non-operational, non-interest bearing **deposits** have been required since August 1981 to fulfil the cash reserve requirement that the banks (and the discount houses) must hold against their liabilities. Included in this category would also be the cash ratio and special deposits referred to earlier (*see* page 174).

Public accounts   The second, smaller, group of deposits stems from the Bank's function as the government's banker. These are called the public accounts, and it is under this title that the government banks its money. The balance of the public accounts reflects the current state of the government's finances. When taxes are flowing in, public accounts tend to rise, whilst when the government is spending faster than receipts they tend to fall.

Reserves and other accounts include the small amount of ordinary banking business in which the Bank of England still engages. The private customers are overseas banks and other City institutions, the total also covering liabilities to overseas central banks.

Assets

The assets side of the Bank's activities shows a marked difference from the search for profitable lending of the commercial banks. There are three principal groups of assets.

Government securities   The first group of assets consists of government securities, including Treasury Bills. In contrast to the commercial banks, however, the Bank of England does not buy such securities either because of the interest they carry, or for liquidity purposes. It engages in purchases and sales of securities in order to influence the liquidity of the commercial banks, as we shall shortly see.

Advances and other accounts   Small, but nonetheless important, are the advances made by the Bank of England. Some are made to its ordinary customers but the most significant are those made to banks and other financial institutions. The Bank of England, in fact, operates as a 'lender of last resort' and is always prepared to make advances to such institutions if they are in temporary need of cash. It is prepared to discount bills of exchange and Treasury Bills, although in doing so it may charge a rate of interest which is high, even penal, which is in excess of the current market rate. Such loans are, therefore, regarded by borrowers as temporary expedients to be avoided as far as possible.

Other assets   These include a small amount of notes and coins which are in no way a safety reserve to fall back upon as are the commercial banks' cash holdings, for the Bank of England can always have more notes printed if it is short of cash. They are, rather, the carry-over of the note issue from the Issue Department, and are available for release at any time, as required.

Monetary policy

A major function of the Bank of England relates to its role as the institution which puts into effect the monetary policy of the government.

Monetary policy is one of the set of instruments that are used to try and stabilise the level of expenditure in the economy in pursuit of the goals of full employment, economic growth and price stability (i.e. the control of inflation). The reasons why such stabilisation may be desirable were explained in Chapter 2 (*see* pages 36–7); the other sets of instruments will be discussed in Chapter 10 (*see* page 248ff). At this point, we are concerned only with describing the basic techniques of monetary policy, as it is carried out by the central bank—the Bank of England.

The way in which monetary policy can be used to influence the level of aggregate expenditure is through the level of lending undertaken by the banks and other financial institutions. The volume of bank lending depends on both the willingness of the banks, etc, to lend and their customers to borrow. These supply and demand aspects roughly correspond to the two main techniques available to the Bank. The first involves what are called **open market operations**, which bring about changes in the liquidity of the banks. The second, acting through **interest rates**, is directed more to the amount of borrowing.

Open market operations

It will be remembered that both the Bank of England and the commercial banks hold short-term government securities called **Treasury Bills** in their portfolios. The Bank actively engages in the purchase or sale of these Bills in order to affect bank liquidity. Suppose, for example, the government wishes to put pressure on bank liquidity. The Bank of England then sells some of its Treasury Bills on the open market. These may be bought by the banks (or their customers) and paid for out of the balances standing to the credit of the banks at the Bank of England. Such balances are, as stated earlier, regarded as highly liquid. Insofar as their liquidity is thereby lowered, the banks may be induced to reduce their loans and advances, which will in turn lead to a fall in total deposits, i.e. in the quantity of money. In different circumstances, when the government is trying to increase spending, the appropriate policy would be for the Bank to buy securities, thereby increasing bank liquidity.

The technicalities of monetary policy are complex and have changed substantially over the years. No attempt can be made here to offer a comprehensive description of all of them. There have, however, been two landmarks in recent years which are notable for signifying changes in the emphasis of different facets of monetary control techniques. They occurred in 1971 and 1981 when the Bank of England published two important papers, entitled *Competition and Credit Control* and *Monetary Control—Provisions*, respectively.

Competition and Credit Control concentrated on the liquidity of the banks in a wide sense. A new concept was introduced—that of so-called **eligible reserve assets**. Certain of the banks' assets were declared to be 'reserve assets' and the banks were required to hold a minimum of $12\frac{1}{2}$ per cent of their total sterling liabilities in one or other of them. The assets included were credit balances at the Bank of England (other than Special Deposits—*see* page 174), money market loans, Treasury bills, a proportion of commercial bills of exchange and British government securities with less than 12 months to run to maturity.

The reserve asset system weakened the control of the Bank of England over credit creation by the commercial banks. This was because many of the reserve assets were also held by the non-banking private sector, thus the commercial banks could always replenish their reserves by buying some of the required assets from other private-sector sources. Indeed, the introduction of the system was accompanied by an unparalleled increase in the UK money supply.

The reserve asset system operated for nearly 10 years until 1981, when *Monetary Control—Provisions* shifted the emphasis of the techniques of monetary policy towards the control of the growth of money and credit created by the banking system.

The 1981 provisions were not limited to the clearing banks, but apply to a wider range of institutions, including also other retail banks, accepting houses and other 'licensed deposit takers'. The revised rules also require the holding of minimum percentages of eligible deposits with members of the London Discount Market Association (*see* page 179) and as call money with institutions in the London money market. The latter provisions are designed to broaden the market for bills in which the Bank of England engages in open market operations. (Eligible liabilities are defined slightly differently for the clearing banks and for the other financial institutions. For the former they are sterling deposits, other than those arising from loans for more than two years.)

One problem which faces those in charge of monetary policy must be mentioned: that of deciding on which of several available 'monetary targets' it should focus attention. For, although we began this chapter with a definition of money which seemed perhaps, simple enough, as we progressed we saw that many things may be considered as money—notes and coin, certainly, but also bank deposits. Even the latter is not a simple concept as we know there are sight deposits and time deposits of the clearing banks, as well as deposits of building societies, overseas banks, etc.

Which of these kinds of money should be the focus on which the monetary authorities at the Bank of England concentrate? There is no single answer to this question. There are several monetary targets at which they can aim. Each corresponds to a different definition of the supply of money. They are set out in Fig 8.6, and range from the narrow MO (comprising notes and coin held by the banks and the public plus bankers' operational balances at the

Bank of England), through the often quoted sterling M3, to the much rarer and very broad PSL2. (The precise definitions of each measure of the money supply in Fig 8.6 is in an appendix to this chapter.) Most monetary targets have been used at some time or other. The most recent of them is MO, added in 1983.

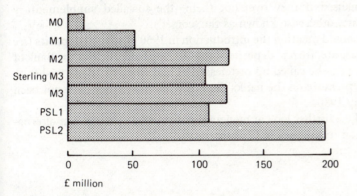

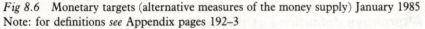

Fig 8.6 Monetary targets (alternative measures of the money supply) January 1985
Note: for definitions *see* Appendix pages 192–3

Interest rate policy

The arrangements summarised in the previous section relate to the way in which the Bank exercises control over the money supply. Control over lending through interest rates was demoted by the 1981 paper. Traditionally the Bank had the power to change interest rates directly and thereby influence the demand for borrowing. This power arose from the Bank's function as 'lender of last resort'. In times of cash shortage, for example, the Bank could charge a rate of interest above the market rate, and this higher interest rate would then filter through to the rest of the financial system. Indeed, for over 200 years the weekly announcement of **bank rate,** the rate of interest at which the Bank of England was prepared to rediscount eligible bills of exchange (such as Treasury bills), was watched closely by financial institutions all over the world. After 1972 the bank rate became known as **minimum lending rate (MLR)**, but any changes announced by the Bank were still regarded as evidence of whether the government wanted to see interest rates rise or fall generally. In 1981, however, this use of MLR was abandoned, though it can be restored in special circumstances, and was in early 1985 to help support the £–$ exchange rate (*see* pages 216). This emphasised the relative importance newly attached to control of the supply of money rather than demand for it. The Bank continues to provide funds to the discount houses when they are in need, but does not normally publicise the rate at which it is prepared to do so, though this may often be inferred from its activities.

Other techniques of monetary policy

Other techniques of monetary policy have been used from time to time. Ceilings have been placed on bank advances, and informal requests to banks to restrict lending have been employed. A system was also in use between 1973 and 1980 whereby the banks were set target rates of growth for their deposits and were penalised if they overshot them (the so-called **supplementary deposit scheme**, otherwise known as the 'corset').

Finally we should mention the introduction in 1960 of **special deposits** (*see* page 174). These are 'frozen' deposits of the clearing banks held at the Bank of England. They can be called up or released as and when the Bank wishes to raise or lower pressure on the banks' liquidity, although they have not been used since July 1980.

We shall take a further look at monetary policy, when we consider alternative stabilisation techniques in Chapter 10.

Appendix

Alternative definitions of the money supply

Fig 8.6 provided information on a number of alternative definitions of the money supply which may be used as monetary targets. The definitions of each of them are as follows:

M0   This is the narrowest measure of the money supply. M0 is almost entirely made up of notes and coin held by the public and the banks. The small residue consists of working balances held by the commercial banks with the Bank of England (*see* pages 187–8).

M1   This comprises notes and coin plus the sterling sight deposits of the private sector with UK banks. Less attention had recently been paid to M1 than to M0, because of the growth of interest-bearing sight deposits referred to above (*see* page 171).

M2   This is a monetary measure introduced in an attempt to find one that better captured all money that could fairly readily be used for transactions purposes. M2 consists of notes and coin and non-interest bearing sight deposits of the banks, *plus* deposits with building societies (*see* pages 179–80) that are easily withdrawable.

£M3   This is M1 plus sterling time deposits of the private sector plus sterling sight and time deposits of the public sector.

M3   This is sterling (£) M3 plus UK residents' deposits in other currencies.

PSL1   This includes notes and coin, time and sight deposits of the private sector plus what are known as 'other money-market instruments', of which the largest are deposits with local authorities and certificates of tax deposit. (PSL stands for private sector liquidity.)

PSL2   This is the broadest measure of all and includes deposits with building societies, National Savings and Trustee Savings Banks, in addition to those items listed under PSL1.

DCE   Finally there is **domestic credit expansion (DCE)**. This is a measure of *changes* in the money supply (adjusted for international transactions), and must not be confused with the above definitions which quantify the money stock itself. (DCE consists of changes in the following: notes and coin, bank lending to the public and private sectors, and external financing of the public sector.)

Exercises

For key to symbols indicating sources *see* pages xii–xiii.

1   Prepare a table showing for the last 10 years:

a   the total currency (notes and coin) in circulation
b   the total of clearing bank deposits
c   the gross national product

Calculate the ratio of *a* plus *b* to *c*. What trends do you observe? (*AS*) Try to find figures for a year before 1970. Was the ratio very different then? (*KS*)

2   Obtain a copy of the latest balance sheet of any large commercial bank. Group the assets into the main categories listed on pages 174–6. Calculate the percentage of each group in the total. Compare the results with Fig 8.2.

3   Using a recent weekly return of the Bank of England prepare a chart on the lines of Fig 8.5 showing the size of the various deposits and assets in the Banking Department. (*FS, FT, T* or the Quarterly Bulletin of the Bank of England)

4   Imagine that you want to borrow money in the London money market:

a   to discount 3 month Treasury bills to the value of £10 000 issued today
b   to discount a 6 month commercial bill for £1000 issued 3 months ago
c   to discount with the Bank of England a 3 month commercial bill for £300 issued today
d   to borrow £10 000 for 24 hours

How much would you have to pay in interest at current market rates in each case? (*FS, T, FT*)

5   Draw a graph showing the trends of total advances and total deposits of the London clearing banks:

a   for the past 10 years (*AS, KS*)
b   for the past 12 months (*ET, FS, MDS*)

6   Make a list of all building societies whose assets exceed (*i*) £1000 million and (*ii*) £100 million. Then calculate the percentage of (*a*) total assets and (*b*) the total number of societies represented by (*i*) and (*ii*). (*WA*)

7   Imagine that you have £10 000 to invest; £1000 in each of the following groups of securities:

British government stock

Foreign government stock

Textile companies

Mining companies

Steel and engineering companies

Oil companies

Retail shops and stores

Vehicle manufacturers

Breweries

Miscellaneous industrials

Select a class of shares of a company in each group and calculate how much profit or loss you would show if you bought the shares today and sold them in 3 weeks' time. Would you have done better to sell today and buy in 3 weeks' time? (Disregard stamp duties, stockbrokers' commissions, contangos, etc.) (*E, FT or T*)

8 Prepare a graph showing the course of the following over the past 5 or more years:

M1

£M3

MO

RPI (retail price index)

Can you tell which of the measures of the money supply is best correlated with the rate of inflation?(*N*)

9 Prepare a graph showing the trends in the following interest rates over the last 5 years on:

a the average yield on industrial ordinary shares

b the average yield on long-dated British government securities

Are the movements associated in any way? (*AS, FS*)

9 The international economy

Reference has been made in earlier chapters to the part that specialisation plays in the promotion of economic efficiency in Britain. Individuals specialise in different occupations, firms in various branches of production, and regions tend to concentrate to an extent on particular industries. Nations, however, differ from each other in certain fundamental respects more than regions. These are largely political in origin. The most important arise first from the fact that factors of production are on the whole able to move more freely within countries than between them and, second, from the existence of separate currencies which nearly all nations possess. There are additional matters, like variations in taxation, economic and social policies and in life styles which add strength to the differences.

Specialisation and trade

It is a small step from regional specialisation to the specialisation which takes place between countries. Nations, like individuals and regions, usually find that they are best suited to particular lines of production, and international trade exists to effect the exchange of the products of one nation for those of another.

Some interchange of goods takes place because most nations are incapable of satisfying their needs for every product. In the main, this is due either to the uneven dispersion of minerals over the world or to the existence of regional variations in climate. Canada, for example, is rich in nickel deposits, Spain and Italy in mercury and South Africa in gold, while Britain has virtually none of these metals. Again, climatic differences are responsible for the inability to produce certain agricultural crops. Britain with her temperate climate cannot grow such tropical and sub-tropical products as coffee, tea, cotton, rubber or cocoa. The only way in which she can obtain these and certain other agricultural and mineral products which are not produced in the country is by importing them from abroad in exchange for goods which Britain produces for export.

Apart from virtual inability to produce certain goods, a major part of international specialisation and consequent trade springs up because nations find that, although they can produce many different types of goods, they are nevertheless much better at producing some than others. These differences tend to be reflected in relative prices and it is sensible for a country to concentrate on producing those goods for which it is best suited. It can produce more than is needed for home consumption and can export the surplus to other countries, importing in exchange goods which other nations are in a more advantageous position to produce.

International differences in the size of the labour force and in its particular skills, in the amount and fertility of the land, and in the quantity of capital equipment that has been accumulated over past years, are the principal reasons why such specialisation is profitable. They explain why, although Britain has its own sheep, it is more profitable to buy some lamb from countries like New Zealand, where land is more plentiful, and export those manufactured goods, which Britain's labour and accumulated equipment and skill enable her to do relatively more efficiently. That is not to say that most of Britain's trade is of this kind, although it used to be. A great deal of international trade consists of exports and imports of manufactured goods, each country specialising to an extent in different products. Britain exports a great deal of aerospace equipment, for example, and imports cameras from Japan and cars from Italy.

The pattern of world trade

It will help us to appreciate the significance of Britain's foreign trade if we start from a broad basis, taking the world as our canvas. It is important to realise which are the major world trading nations. Fig 9.1 sets out details of the value of the total imports and exports of the 10 leading countries which together are

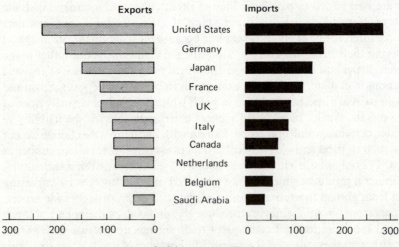

Fig 9.1 Major trading nations 1983 (values of exports and imports in US dollars)

responsible for about two thirds of all international trade. Between these lead-ers, however, it is immediately apparent that there are great differences. The scene is dominated by the United States, Germany and Japan which together account for about 30 per cent of world exports.

The UK occupies the fifth position, in both import and export trade. This is a very different picture from that of earlier years, for Britain's importance in world trade has been undergoing a period of long-term decline. This downward trend is of special significance in the case of exports of manufactured goods, where Britain traditionally dominated the field. At the beginning of the present century the UK was responsible for no less than a third of the world total. As Fig 9.2 shows, however, the last 30 years have witnessed a fairly steady fall in Britain's share. Although the rate of decline tailed off during the 1970s, the UK's share in 1984 was at an all-time low of less than 8 per cent. In that year Germany and the United States each had more than double, and Japan almost treble, Britain's share, and together these three countries accounted for over half the world total.

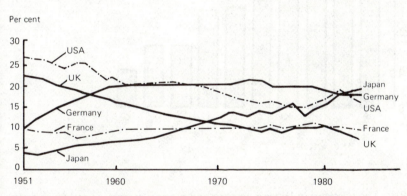

Fig 9.2 Percentage shares in world trade in manufactures 1951–84

The size of a country's exports or imports can be very misleading as a guide to the significance of foreign trade to that nation. A very large country can have an extensive foreign trade, which is nevertheless disproportionately small in comparison with that of a much less important nation. The relationship between the value of imports and national income, which is shown for a number of countries in Fig 9.3, is one indicator of the wide differences which exist. Thus, the USA, which is the world's leading importing country, depends much less on imports than the majority of others. Only about 10 per cent of her total income is spent on imported goods, whilst a relatively small country like Norway spends about 40 per cent, and Belgium is even more dependent on trade and spends over half of its income on imports. Britain spends about a quarter. Thus although a decline of, say, 50 per cent in foreign trade in the United States would make a fair hole in the total volume of world trade, it would make comparatively little difference to the United States itself. On the other hand, the complete cessation of imports by Norway would have barely a 1 per cent effect on world trade as a whole, but it would very gravely disrupt the Norwegian economy.

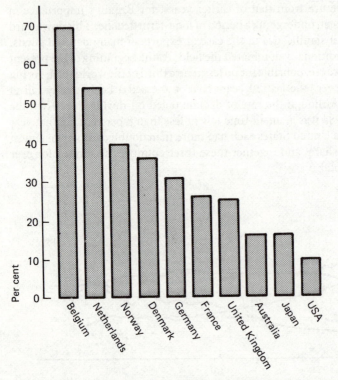

Fig 9.3 The relationship between imports and national income, selected countries, 1983 imports as a percentage of national income

The trade of the United Kingdom

We can obtain a rough guide to the importance of foreign trade to a country by comparing the value of its imports with its total income. The only thorough way of assessing this, however, is to consider in detail the goods which it imports and exports and the various countries with which it trades. We shall therefore proceed to examine the commodity structure and regional distribution of the trade of the United Kingdom.

Commodity trade

The principal goods which Britain imports and exports may first be discussed with reference to Fig 9.4.

Imports

The traditional picture of Britain in the world economy in the past was characterised by her great dependence upon foreign sources of supply for essential raw materials and foodstuffs paid for by the export of manufactured products. This is no longer the case. The importance of primary products in the import bill has greatly diminished as a result of many factors, including the development of synthetics and the decline of some raw material using industries such as textiles.

In the 1930s foodstuffs and basic materials, other than fuel, used to account for well over two thirds of the value of Britain's imports. This pattern began to change shortly after the Second World War, and by the early 1980s, the same group of products accounted for only about a fifth of the total. Food, beverages and tobacco imports are now considerably greater in value than crude materials—the reverse of the previous situation. The former group make up around 15 per cent of imports, meat being the largest category, followed by beverages (including wine), coffee, fruit and vegetables. Other important items are cereals, dairy produce, sugar, tobacco and fish.

Fuel imports are, of course, almost entirely petroleum, mostly in its crude state. This was the largest single item in the import list in several years in the 1970s, but as North Sea oil began to yield substantial quantities of oil, Britain moved into self-sufficiency in the early 1980s, even becoming an oil exporter. The crude material imports include iron and other ores, wood and pulp (for furniture, paper and other industries), textile fibres, hides and skins, crude fertilisers, natural and synthetic rubber among many others.

Manufactured goods accounted for about two thirds of total imports in 1983. Over half of these were of finished goods, the remainder being made up of semi-manufactures, such as chemicals which are further processed in Britain.

Exports

In contrast to imports the pattern of British exports has not changed fundamentally during the century in the sense that manufactures still provide the solid backbone of this country's export trade. There have, however, been substantial shifts in their composition. These reflect, in part, changes in the structure of British industry itself noted in Chapter 4. Textiles and iron and steel, for example, made up approximately half of total exports in 1913. By 1983 their share had dropped to a mere 5 per cent and their place had been taken by machinery, vehicles, transport equipment and chemicals, as Fig 9.4 shows.

Import penetration and export sales ratios

The description of the commodity composition of UK trade in the previous section might be summarised by saying that it now consists of the exchange of manufactured goods with other countries. It is, therefore, interesting to look at the extent to which foreign imports compete with domestic production, and

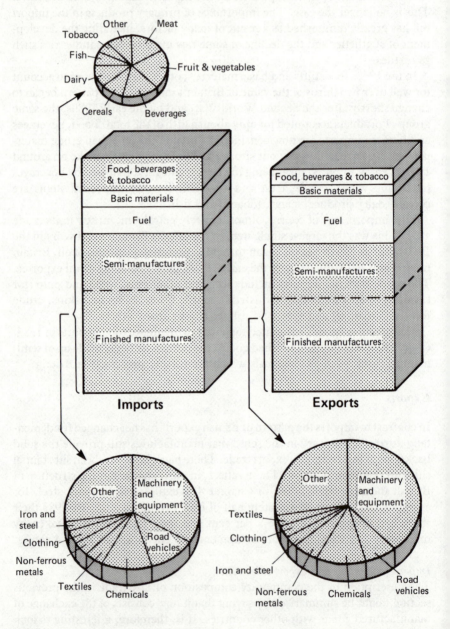

Fig 9.4 Commodity trade UK 1983

the relative importance of exports to domestic production in different sectors of manufacturing industry.

Fig 9.5 throws light on both these matters for a selection of industries, which are listed in order of import penetration. Instrument engineering and motor vehicles, at the top of the list, are industries where the foreign share of the domestic UK market exceeds 50 per cent, while penetration exceeds a third for the next four industries shown—electrical engineering, textiles, clothing and chemicals.

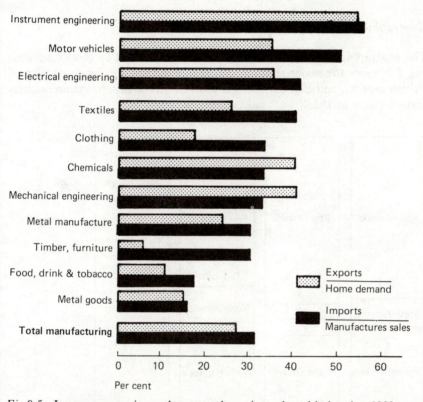

Fig 9.5 Import penetration and export sales ratios, selected industries, 1983

The large share of the British market taken by foreign suppliers is not necessarily a cause for concern. One should look also at the export performance of British industries, shown in the diagram by the ratio of exports to total sales. We find, in fact, that some of the industries where there is heavy import penetration are also ones where exports account for high proportions of output by UK firms. Instrument engineering, for example, exports over half its production, and the chemical industry's export sales ratio (over 40 per cent) exceeds the import penetration ratio (under 35 per cent).

Fig 9.5 presents only a snapshot picture of the situation in a single recent year. It should be added that the trends in both import penetration and export sales ratios have been of steady and appreciable increases in both figures. For manufacturing industry as a whole, import penetration rose from 17 to 31 per cent between 1971 and 1983 while exports as a percentage of sales rose from 19 to 27 per cent over the same period. In the previous section we described British foreign trade as being characterised nowadays by an interchange of manufactures. We see now that this applies as much *within* industry groups as to exports of manufactures as a whole.

Geographical distribution of UK trade

The geographical composition of UK trade is illustrated by three diagrams; Fig 9.6 traces the major shifts in percentage distribution by destination of British exports, and Figs 9.7 and 9.8 show details of Britain's main markets and suppliers in 1983.

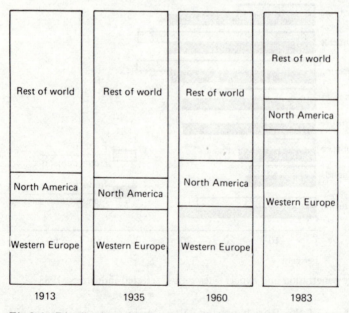

Fig 9.6 Distribution of UK exports, 1913–83 (selected years)

Europe

The nations of Europe, taken as a whole, are at once the largest group both as suppliers and as markets for the UK. In 1983 they bought well over half of British exports and provided an even higher proportion of the country's imports. This has not always been the situation, however. The importance of

Europe as a trading partner has increased substantially and fairly steadily, since the Second World War. The growth can be attributed principally to the changed structure of UK trade—the fall in importance of imports of primary products relative to manufactured goods—and to declining trading links between Britain and the Commonwealth, which used to occupy the dominant trading position. The postwar trend towards increasing European trade received a boost in 1973 when the United Kingdom joined the countries of the Common Market in the European Economic Community (EEC) (*see* below).

Figs 9.7 and 9.8 divide Europe into two parts—members of the EEC, and the rest. The former can be seen to be much the more important of the two; in 1983 it accounted for over 40 per cent of UK exports and 50 per cent of imports from all sources. The situation may be compared with that of the early 1960s when those proportions were half or less.

Within the Common Market, Germany is Britain's major market and supplier of imports (mainly machinery and manufactured goods including cars and chemicals). Next in importance are France (which sends Britain manufactures and food) and the Netherlands (dairy produce and other foodstuffs). Ireland is more important as a market for UK exports than as a supplier of imports. The shares of the other EEC member countries can be seen in Figs 9.7 and 9.8.

Countries outside the EEC together supplied only about a third of total UK imports from Europe. Of them, only Norway, Sweden and Switzerland were sufficiently important to be shown on the diagram.

North America

Trade with the USA and Canada rose in the early postwar years, but is now back to its prewar level, accounting for around 15 per cent of the total. The USA has been Britain's largest market, apart from two years in the late 1970s, when it was overtaken by Germany. The principal goods the USA sends to Britain are machinery and other manufactures, but she is also richly endowed with natural resources and exports some of them to Britain, especially cereals, tobacco, cotton, non-ferrous metals and ores. Canada's links with the United Kingdom were much greater when intra-Commonwealth trade was in its heyday, especially in the 1930s. She is still an important supplier of wood and pulp, metals and ores and foodstuffs, and ranks roughly equal in importance today with, say, Norway.

Rest of the 'developed' world

The four nations in this category, Japan, South Africa, Australia and New Zealand, may be said to have reached a state of economic development broadly comparable with that of North America and Western Europe; they are accordingly, if somewhat arbitrarily, placed in the same group. The trade of the four

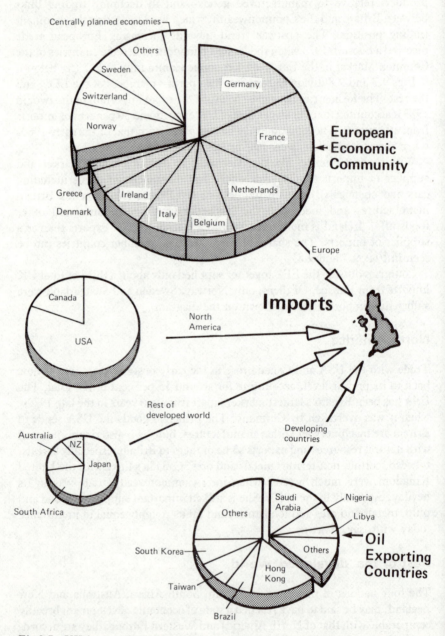

Fig 9.7 UK imports by origin 1983

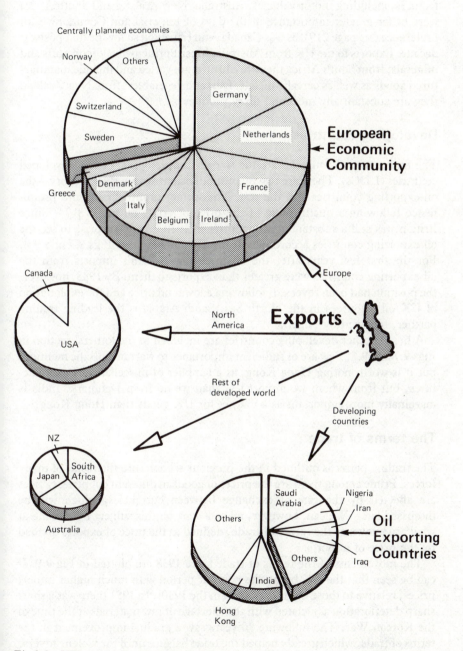

Fig 9.8 UK exports by destination 1983

together, however, is only about a third that of the United States and Canada. Japan heads the list of Britain's suppliers, with machinery and manufactures, including motor vehicles. Australia, New Zealand and South Africa were of far greater importance in the days of Imperial and Commonwealth preference (*see* page 219), as was Canada, and remained so for the first postwar decade. Exports to the UK from Australia consist principally of foodstuffs and minerals; from South Africa they are a little more varied and include manufactured goods as well as cereals, metals, fruit and vegetables; from New Zealand they are substantially meat and dairy produce.

Developing countries

The final group of countries are the so-called 'developing' or less developed countries (LDCs). There are two main subdivisions within this category—the oil-exporting countries and the rest. The former group sprang into prominence following a quadrupling of the price of crude oil in 1973–74. Since Britain was still a substantial oil importer in 1980 it is no surprise to see the oil-exporting countries accordingly featuring quite large in Figs 9.7 and 9.8. For the first few years after the oil price rise Britain's imports from the oil-exporting countries were greater than exports to them. By 1983, however, the position had been reversed, following a lower oil price and the exploitation of UK oil resources in the North Sea. Saudi Arabia is the leading trading partner, followed by Nigeria.

A host of other developing countries are included in the 'others' section in Figs 9.7 and 9.8. Few are of sufficient importance to warrant specific mention, but it is worth noting Hong Kong, as a supplier of miscellaneous manufactures, but from whom we import less than we do from Denmark. India is marginally more important as a market for UK goods than Hong Kong.

The terms of trade

The trading patterns outlined in the previous sections are the result of many forces. Prime among them are the prices of goods in different countries. Prices are affected by the rate of exchange between currencies, which will be discussed later. We can, however, make a start on this subject by looking at what are known as the **terms of trade**, defined as the price of exports divided by the price of imports.

The movements of the terms of trade since 1938 are plotted in Fig 9.9. It can be seen that the UK began the postwar period with much higher import prices, relative to those of exports, than in the 1930s. In 1951 there was a short sharp deterioration associated with the shortage of raw materials at the time of the Korean War. The following 20 years saw a gradual improvement in the terms of trade, which greatly helped the trade balance until the violent adverse shock of 1973–74, when the price of oil quadrupled following the action of the

OPEC countries and the prices of many other primary products also rose substantially. Between 1972 and 1974 the world price of copper, lead, tin and cotton approximately doubled; that of zinc, rubber and cocoa tripled; and that of sugar went up by a multiple of four. It is true that the prices of goods that Britain exports were also rising at the time, but not nearly so rapidly; in the last 10 years or so relative prices have moved only slightly, as can be seen from the graph.

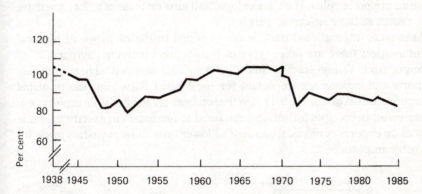

Fig 9.9 Terms of trade UK 1938 and 1945–84 quantity of imports obtainable for a fixed quantity of exports (an upward movement corresponds to an improvement in the UK's terms of trade)

The terms of trade give an impression only of the average prices of British imports and exports relative to each other. To ascertain the competitiveness of British goods requires a comparison of the prices of British exports relative to those of other countries with which she competes. Some idea of this can be gleaned from Fig 9.10, which shows the increase in the average export price of manufactures of various countries over the ten years between 1975 and 1984. It can be seen that the export prices of UK manufactures increased more than all other countries (with the exception of Italy) shown in the diagram. This record suggests one possible explanation for the UK's declining share of world trade in manufactures noted earlier (*see* Fig 9.2 page 197). No doubt there are also other non-price factors at work, such as quality, delivery dates and after-sales service.

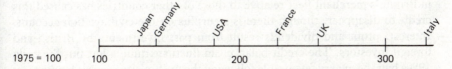

Fig 9.10 Prices of manufactures in 1984 as a percentage of 1975 (selected countries)

Invisible trade

The careful reader may have noticed that the value of the UK's imports in 1983 exceeded that of her exports (in Fig 9.4) by roughly £700 million. This is quite normal. In order to explain how it comes about it is first necessary to point out that there is no reason, in principle, why the value of exports and imports should be exactly equal in any particular year. So long as people in other countries are prepared to make loans (or even gifts) to us, Britain can always have an import surplus. If we make loans and gifts on balance to foreigners we can expect to have an export surplus.

However, international trade is not confined to the exchange of physical commodities; there are other types of transaction involving payments to or receipts from foreigners for 'invisible' services rendered. These invisible imports and exports are important for the United Kingdom; the principal categories are set out in Fig 9.11. On the top lines are the invisible exports (+). They result in receipts for services rendered to foreigners in exactly the same way as do exports of physical goods. The lower lines show payments made for invisible imports (−).

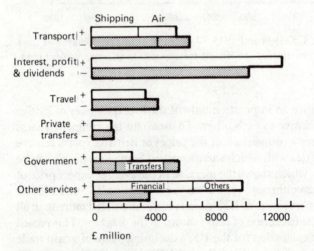

Fig 9.11 Invisible trade UK 1983

Transport is a large item and covers, in the main, freight charges for shipping. Traditionally this used to be a net credit for the UK but the decline in Britain's merchant fleet relative to those of other countries has caused this credit to disappear, though there is a surplus on the civil aviation account. Interest, profit and dividends result from past investments by British and foreign investors. The credit balance can fluctuate quite a lot; but the early 1980s have been very favourable following the upsurge in overseas lending (*see* page 212). Foreign travel payments and receipts cover spending by tourists and travelling businessmen. It was a net credit item in the 1970s, but the upward trend in holidays abroad has turned it into a net debit in the 1980s. The item called private transfers consists mainly of personal transactions, involving gifts and the transfer of assets by migrants. These fluctuate from year to year, but are usually a small net outflow for Britain. The major source of drain among invisibles is government expenditure, some of which is military, but also includes diplomatic expenses, grants made to developing countries in the form of aid and UK contributions to the EEC budget.

The one category of invisibles which traditionally shows a substantial credit balance for the UK is that labelled 'other services'. It covers several important items, including receipts by the City of London for banking, insurance and other financial services and royalties.

The balance of payments

The visible and invisible trade of the UK with the rest of the world is only part of the financial relations that this country has with those overseas. Payments are made, and received for purposes other than the purchase of goods and services.

A full statement of all transactions between the residents of a country and non-residents is contained in its **balance of payments**. Note, this must *not* be confused with a balance sheet, which states assets and liabilities at a particular moment of time (*see* pages 61–2). The balance of payments records the flow of all payments and receipts between residents and non-residents over a period of time, usually a year.

The balance of payments is usually divided into two main sections—the current account and the capital account (with what is called 'official financing', often included in the latter).

The current account

The current account comprises all payments and receipts involving imports and exports, both visible and invisible; i.e. those trading items we have already dealt with. The difference between the values of imports and exports in any year is known as the **visible trade balance**. The difference between the values of invisible exports and imports is known as the **invisible balance**; and the difference between the total values of imports and exports, visible and invisible, is referred to as the **current balance**.

Fig 9.12 shows the history of the current account balance of payments since 1971. The UK has traditionally recorded a surplus of receipts over payments on its current account as far back as the 19th century, if not earlier. This has usually been due to invisible earnings which have, in the past, been more than enough to offset the deficit on trade in goods. Apart from one or two years, the latter hardly ever showed a credit balance. The balance of visible trade went through a particularly adverse period in the 1960s and, although invisible transactions continued to show a surplus, the gap between the visibles and the invisibles narrowed. This was partly because British exports did not keep pace with expanding world trade, and partly because imports were maintained at a relatively high level. Then, in the late 1970s, and into the 1980s, the effects of the exploitation of North Sea oil came to the rescue. Exports of oil exceeded imports for the first time in 1980 and a record visible trading surplus followed in 1981. Thereafter, as can be seen from Fig 9.12, the current account of the balance of payments deteriorated, and by 1983, the UK was running a small deficit, despite the contribution of oil to exports, of which they accounted for more than 20 per cent of the total. This was no more than the continuation of the trend in trade in manufactures and semi-manufactures, with imports rising faster than exports.

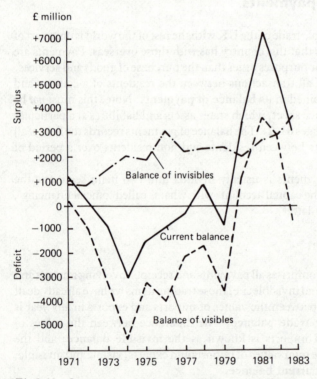

Fig 9.12 Current account balance of payments 1971–83

An important feature of the current balance record displayed in Fig 9.12 is its volatility. This is almost entirely due to swings in the balance of visible trade, sometimes reaching crisis proportions, outstandingly so in 1974. The experience of that year was almost entirely attributable to the quadrupling of the price of oil by the major oil-exporting countries belonging to the group known as OPEC. Other occasions on which the current account has been particularly unfavourable have tended to be associated with boom conditions. These lead to rising incomes and imports and at the same time provide less incentive to export, since the home market is buoyant. In so far as booms are worldwide, which they often are, they also have an effect similar to the oil price rise of 1973–74, i.e. they push up the price of raw material imports.

The capital account

While the current account records all payments and receipts for trading items, visible and invisible, the capital account of the balance of payments contains movements of capital funds between residents and non-residents, lending to, and borrowing from, the rest of the world, both on short and on long terms.

Long-term foreign investment can take one of two forms—**direct investment** and **portfolio investment**. Short-term investment, sometimes called monetary movements, includes transfers of funds between bank accounts, e.g. when an individual decides to hold dollars instead of sterling (or vice versa), to earn the top rate of interest on his or her money, or for any other reason.

Direct investment is when transfers are made between a domestic parent company and its overseas subsidiaries. Portfolio investment involves the purchase of foreign securities, or shares, in foreign owned companies. Both types of transaction appear in the capital account of the balance of payments, but it is exceedingly difficult to know, especially with portfolio investment, which are really long-term. Once a person, or a company, has bought shares in a foreign company they may be held indefinitely, perhaps resulting in the acquisition of a controlling interest. Alternatively, they may be sold the week after they are bought. Moreover, a great deal of international investment in the modern age is done by corporations known as multinationals. Companies such as General Motors (USA), Shell (Netherlands/UK), IBM (USA) and BP (UK) own subsidiaries throughout the world. The last of these has subsidiary companies in well over 50 countries. The multinationals engage in the switching of funds between their subsidiaries in different countries and the accounting practices they employ sometimes make it difficult to identify all the international investment that takes place.

These difficulties do not, of course, mean that we have no idea at all about how much long-term investment is taking place. Identifiable private long-term capital inflows and outflows are shown in Fig 9.13 for the period since 1971. There we can see the substantial rise in UK investment overseas in the late 1970s, which was aided by the government's decision to abolish all exchange controls on capital movements by UK residents, which had existed for half a century. The total value of overseas assets trebled in the four years ending in 1984, by which time *net* assets reached a figure of £70 000 million, equivalent to more than 20 per cent of Gross Domestic Product. This build-up

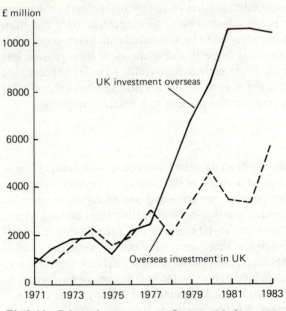

£ million

Fig 9.13 Private investment outflows and inflows 1971–83

was largely the result of the current account surpluses during that period, and it should produce higher receipts of interests, profits and dividends on the invisible trade account in the future (*see* page 208).

The balance of payments as a whole

As previously stated, the balance of payments is a record of all payments made by and to residents from non-residents. Since the sum of all credit items must be matched by an equivalent sum of debit items, it follows that the balance of payments must itself balance. This may be explained with reference to the balance of payments of the UK in 1983, which is shown in Table 9.1. The table is in summary form for ease of exposition, with capital transactions on both short and long-term being shown as a single net figure (and all figures rounded to the nearest £10 million).

The table shows that the UK had a current account surplus in 1983 of £2920 million. This represents an **inflow** of that amount, which was more than offset by an **outflow** due to net overseas lending of £3730 million. The difference between these two sums is £810 million, which is accounted for by what is called 'official financing'. This is the term used to cover transactions by the UK government, and which, in the year in question, consisted in running down the reserves of foreign exchange held by the Bank of England (to the extent of about £600 million) and official borrowing (of about £200 million).

Table 9.1 United Kingdom balance of payments 1983

£ *million*
Current account

Visible imports	61 340	Visible exports	60 630
Invisible imports	31 340	Invisible exports	34 970
Total payments for goods and services	92 680	Total receipts for goods and services	95 600
Surplus on current account	2 920		
	95 600		95 600

Capital account

Foreign lending by UK (net)	3 730	Balance on Current Account	2 920
		Official financing	810
	3 730		3 730

The balance of payments and the national income

When we were discussing the determinants of national income (in Chapter 2) and its composition (in Chapter 7), we drew attention to the relevance of overseas transactions. We are now able to elaborate a little on them. There are two important points to appreciate. The first is that the sum total of incomes accruing to the factors of production in a country includes those of exporters who sell their products to foreigners. The second is that expenditure on imports adds to incomes overseas.

The implications of the last statements are twofold. One is concerned with the relationship between the national income and the standard of living. We learnt earlier (*see* pages 145–6) that, although associated, these are not the same. We now have an additional reason for this conclusion. While an export surplus causes an increase in national income, it does not mean a parallel rise in the goods available to British consumers. Conversely, an import surplus can keep living standards up in the face of declining incomes. Of course, a country cannot indefinitely maintain an import surplus any more than it can maintain incomes by postponing renewal of capital, without in the long-run suffering a decline in national income.

There is another implication of the utmost importance arising from the relationship between national income and foreign trade. It is quite straightforward and explains why the booms and slumps of the trade cycle tend to spread from country to country. When a boom begins in one country it raises incomes there, and some part of the extra income finds its way into imports, which are no more than the exports of other countries. When foreigners experience rising exports this pushes up incomes in their countries too. So the boom spreads. The opposite follows in depressions. Falling imports have depressing consequences for exporters. A similar transmission process occurs with inflation. Rising prices of imports find their way into domestic costs, as they outstandingly did after the oil price rise in 1973 adding a twist, as the saying goes, to the inflationary spiral.

Government and the balance of payments

There are a number of economic forces at work which may help to maintain equilibrium in a country's balance of payments. As already explained, relative price movements may play a part. So, too, may income changes. A country whose exports are falling and showing a deficit on current account will find that the falling incomes of its exporters lead to falling imports in consequence.

However, market forces can work slowly and painfully and government intervention in the balance of payments is common. Moreover, enough has been said of the relationship between national income, the price level and the balance of payments, to make it clear that governments cannot pursue the major goals of economic policy in complete disregard of the international position. Attempts to raise the rate of economic growth, (*see* pages 248–50), by fiscal policy, can cause balance of payments crises and have done so in the past. Indeed, British government economic policy has at times been dubbed 'stop-go', mainly because of adverse movements in the balance of payments following 'go' policies which led to 'stops'.

Countries experiencing pressures on their balances of payments have a number of alternative policies open to them. Firstly they can use up some of their reserves of gold and foreign exchange to tide them over temporary difficulties. Secondly they can seek loans from other countries or international agencies. The UK has borrowed heavily from the International Monetary Fund (*see* pages 221–2) and from foreign central banks on several occasions in the past.

Borrowing and using reserves are inevitably of limited help. For longer-term problems the government has three other courses of action. First, it may try to slow down the rate of growth in the economy. Second it can try to change the foreign exchange rate. Third it can introduce restrictions on international trade and payments.

Slowing down the rate of growth may be attempted using monetary policy or fiscal and other policies (*see* pages 248–52). Falling incomes, and slowing down the rate of inflation can help reduce imports and stimulate exports, although it must be realised that all is not necessarily plain sailing, such a policy may, therefore, interfere with the attainment of other economic goals, such as full employment.

Alterations in the exchange rate

The level of trade in imports and exports depends to a significant extent on their relative prices. We saw earlier how the terms of trade are relevant to this matter. However, the prices paid by importers and received by exporters are affected, not only by those in their domestic currencies, but also by the rate of exchange between currencies. The reasons were explained in Chapter 2 (*see* pages 28–9). Briefly, importers in the USA, for example, are not interested in the *sterling* price of British exports so much as they are in their *dollar* price. They only have dollars to spend. Admittedly they have to buy sterling to pay British exporters, but the number of pounds they can obtain for, say, $100 depends on the dollar-sterling exchange rate.

We cannot devote space to explaining how exchange rates are determined. In the absence of intervention by governments they will be subject to the interplay of supply and demand for foreign exchange and settled, just like the prices of commodities, as outlined in Chapter 1. This means that there is a tendency for the exchange rate to alter to equate supply and demand for foreign exchange. It implies, too, that exchange rates can at times move to compensate for changes in domestic prices. A country with a persistently higher rate of inflation than others, for example, will tend to experience a fall in the value of it currency, i.e. its buying power in terms of other currencies declines. However, governments can set the exchange rate, and use it as a balance of payments policy instrument.

Fixed exchange rates have a long history. They operated through a system known as the **gold standard** in the 19th century, when the majority of countries tied their exchange rates to gold, so effectively fixing also the rates of exchange between their currencies. The gold standard broke down in the inter-war years, but something very like it was agreed upon internationally when the International Monetary Fund (IMF) was set up at the end of the Second World War (*see* pages 221–2). The UK became a member of the Fund and operated a fixed exchange rate system for more than a quarter of a century. This gave it the opportunity to change the rate by devaluation (or revaluation). Devaluation lowers the price of sterling to foreigners. It means, for example, that an American importer can obtain more pounds for every dollar. Hence, it provides some stimulus to exports, although whether enough to increase their value is another matter; it depends on how responsive demand is to price changes.

We should mention too that devaluation may also help to improve a balance of payments under pressure from the import side. Lowering the price of sterling raises the price of imports, and can reduce their volume and value if demand is sufficiently responsive to price changes.

It is important to realise, however, that devaluation is not necessarily an unmitigated benefit as far as the balance of payments is concerned. Insofar as higher prices of imports cause costs to rise and feed inflation, they destroy some of the advantage of devaluation. They can also lead to higher wage demands as the cost of living rises.

There are several problems with fixed exchange rates which have led countries to abandon them. One is that they insulate an economy to some extent from market forces. Another is that they can lead to excessive speculation in foreign exchange, especially if there is a lot of 'hot' money around, moving into and out of a currency on rumours of devaluation. The UK has been exceptionally vulnerable to this kind of situation because of the fact that sterling has been an international reserve asset for many countries; more so in the past than in the present. Fixed exchange rates were abandoned by Britain in 1972. Since then the rate of exchange has been allowed to rise and fall with changing conditions, subject to government intervention from time to time to even out excessive fluctuations in the rate, which might inhibit trade. When the government intervenes in this manner, the exchange rate cannot properly be described as freely floating, but is called a 'managed' or 'dirty' float.

Fig 9.14 shows the course of the US dollar-sterling rate since 1972. The diagram charts three phases of the recent history of sterling (*i*) its depreciation in the years up to 1977, when the current account of the balance of payments was in deficit; (*ii*) its strength up to 1981 due to a combination of internal and external influences—government policy, North Sea oil, weakness overseas and high domestic interest rates; (*iii*) its renewed depreciation after 1981, largely because of relatively high interest rates in the USA.

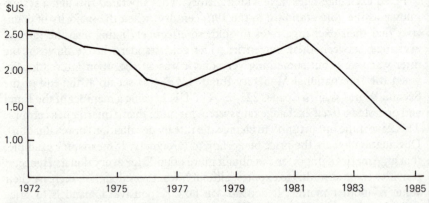

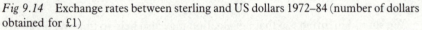

Fig 9.14   Exchange rates between sterling and US dollars 1972–84 (number of dollars obtained for £1)

These high rates of interest can be largely accounted for by the large budget deficit of the US government, and to growing demand as the American economy enjoyed boom conditions. Their effect was to attract large movements of capital into the USA, thereby weakening the exchange rate (from the point of view of sterling). The tremendous strength of the dollar, which almost touched parity with the pound (£1 = $1) in early 1985, was viewed with growing concern by European countries and interfered with the UK government's domestic policy (*see* page 253).

Restrictions on trade and payments

The last set of policies open to a government trying to influence the balance of payments are restrictions on trade and payments. There are four main types to be considered; tariffs, quotas, non-tariff barriers, and exchange controls.

Tariffs

Tariffs, or import duties, are taxes levied by a government on the import of commodities. They may be general or levied on specific products. Tariffs are either stated in percentage terms or fixed in money value. During the second part of the 19th century and up to the First World War Britain did not impose tariffs but followed a free trade policy. Some minor duties were introduced during and after the war, but a major departure from free trade occurred with the passage of the Import Duties Act of 1932, designed precisely to remedy the very unfavourable balance of payments position brought on by the Great Depression. Many reductions have since taken place in the level of tariffs. These are discussed below.

Quotas and subsidies

Quotas are a more certain method of restricting imports than tariffs. They do not rely on higher prices to choke off demand, but involve the direct quantitative restriction of imports, usually by the granting of licences. They were popular with many countries in the first few years following the Second World War, but have been largely eliminated as a result of international action, shortly to be considered.

The trade restrictions mentioned above relate to imports. Others can be used to stimulate exports, e.g. by means of subsidies, which are really negative tariffs. Overt subsidies to exporters are quite rare. Hidden subsidies (effected, for example, by exempting certain classes of goods likely to exported from domestic taxes on expenditure) are more common, although they are often likely to be in breach of international agreements.

Non-tariff barriers

Since the mid 1970s, world trade has been affected more by restrictions other than tariffs. The so-called 'New protectionism' involves the use of non-tariff barriers, which impede free trade. These include agreements between developing and developed countries stipulating actual quantities of exports and imports of clothing and textiles, voluntary export restraint (VER) agreements involving Japan in particular, and rules governing trade laid down by governments and governmental groups, such as the European Economic Community.

Exchange controls

Tariffs, quotas and export subsidies are mainly designed to affect visible trade. Exchange control, in contrast, aims to restrict the purchase and sale of foreign exchange for *all* purposes, including visible and invisible transactions and capital movements. The machinery for the operation of exchange control in the UK has been run by the Bank of England, to whom applications for foreign currency were made.

Exchange controls may be general, applying to all foreign currencies, or they may be discriminatory and affect only those currencies in particularly short supply ('hard' rather than 'soft' currencies, in the jargon). In the UK, exchange controls were imposed on the outbreak of war in 1939 to limit the use of currencies to essential purposes. They were progressively relaxed as the international situation settled down after the war, although they were relaxed more fully for non-residents than for residents. Complete abolition of exchange controls did not occur until 1980, since when it has no longer been necessary to obtain permission from the Bank of England to buy foreign exchange for overseas travel, import of goods, export of capital or any other purpose.

International co-operation

During the depression of the 1930s countries throughout the world resorted to trade restrictions and exchange controls to try to protect themselves from balance of payments deficits. As time went on and batteries of restrictions mounted they began to cancel each other out while world trade spiralled downwards.

It is all too easy for countries individually to impose trade restrictions. Removing them is more difficult. It is usually helpful if this is done by groups of nations on a reciprocal basis. Broadly speaking, there are two ways of approaching the issue of trade liberalisation. One is to seek agreement between a large number of countries, and to have rather limited objectives. The other is to look for a more ambitious programme among a smaller group of nations.

Regional co-operation

There have been many attempts at regional co-operation between trading partners, including those in Latin America and East Africa. The UK has been involved mainly in trading agreements with the countries of the Commonwealth and with western Europe.

Commonwealth preference

The origins of Imperial preference, as it was first known, go back to 1919 when the relatively few goods subject to import duties in the UK were reduced by one third if they came from countries in the Empire. The value of preferential treatment was greatly enhanced after the introduction of the British general tariff of 1932, when mutual agreement was reached at an historic conference of Commonwealth countries in Ottawa. The preferences were later extended to some outside countries, outstandingly Ireland and South Africa, and they covered approximately 50 per cent of UK-Empire trade.

Parallel to the reduction of trade barriers, exchange controls were also lifted for countries joining what was known as the sterling area. Membership overlapped greatly with the Commonwealth preference system. Countries in the sterling area had access to a pool of hard currencies and were subject to less severe operation of UK exchange controls. In return they agreed to hold minimum proportions of their foreign exchange reserves in sterling.

The last two paragraphs are in the past tense because they are, in fact, of little more than historical interest. Commonwealth preference and the sterling area were important in the 1930s and the early post-war years. The shift in UK trade away from the Commonwealth, (referred to earlier in the chapter) greatly diminished the significance of the agreements. Britain's entry into the EEC (*see* below) virtually eclipsed it. Likewise with the sterling area, reduced to a marginal matter after the adoption of a floating exchange rate for sterling in 1972, and becoming meaningless after the abolition of all exchange controls in 1980.

Western Europe

Economic co-operation in western Europe in modern times has its origins in the need for reconstruction after the disruption caused by the Second World War. American aid was instrumental in setting up the organisation now known as OECD (the Organisation for Economic Cooperation and Development). The most significant move towards integration, however, came a few years later with the birth of the 'Common Market', properly called the European Economic Community (EEC).

The EEC really began with an economic union between Belgium, Luxembourg and the Netherlands (Benelux) shortly after the end of the war. They then joined France, Germany and Italy in 1952 to form the European Coal and Steel Community aimed at creating a unified market in these products. Five years later the Six, as they were called, signed the Treaty of Rome establishing the EEC and outlining a programme for the elimination of tariffs, within the Community and a unified schedule of import duties for outsiders. There were other aims too, such as a Common Agricultural Policy (*see* page 241), the free movement of people and capital within the EEC and 'harmonisation' of a number of social and economic policies. The plans also included a degree of exchange rate stability through a European monetary unit (EMU), though the UK has not so far joined in this scheme (*see* page 222).

The UK was at first reluctant to join the EEC, partly on political grounds and partly because of her links with the Commonwealth. Instead, Britain made an agreement with Austria, Denmark, Norway, Portugal, Sweden and Switzerland (and subsequently Finland) to set up the European Free Trade Association (EFTA) in 1960. The aims of EFTA were more modest than those of the EEC. In one particular way they were attractive for Britain. Although tariffs were to be abolished within the Association, a common external tariff was *not* proposed. This allowed the UK to continue Commonwealth preferences.

Meanwhile the countries of the EEC were, in general, enjoying more prosperous conditions with regard to living standards, inflation and the balance of payments than the UK. At the same time Britain's trade with the Commonwealth was declining. The UK therefore decided to apply for membership of the EEC. The first application was turned down (effectively by the French) in 1962. The second was successful, although the negotiations about terms of entry were lengthy. Ireland and Denmark joined too, turning the Six into the Nine in 1973.

The decision to enter Europe was a highly controversial one. A national referendum was held in 1974 to determine whether to continue membership. Economic arguments were heard on both sides. Pro-Marketeers stressed principally three potential areas of gain: the advantages of large-scale production; of specialisation under free trade between members of the EEC; and the hope that high rates of economic growth would spill over to Britain. Anti-Marketeers were sceptical about the economies of scale argument. They were more concerned with the common external tariff which discriminates against imports from low cost producers outside the EEC. This was held to apply with force to primary products, including foodstuffs, under the Common Agricultural Policy. The heavy majority in favour of continued membership when the referendum was taken, may have been more influenced by political than economic considerations. Most independent observers believe the economic arguments to be evenly balanced.

It is difficult, even with hindsight, to know whether the right decision was taken. On the one hand, food prices are certainly higher than they were before (*see* pages 241–2) and the high growth rates of the first members have not been maintained. Moreover, an aspect which was not, perhaps, fully appreciated in the referendum days came to light in the shape of a heavy contribution to the Community budget from the UK in the late 1970s. On the other hand, it can be argued that despite these disadvantages, the performance of the British economy would have been worse if she had remained outside the EEC. No one will ever know for sure which set of arguments are correct. They are exceedingly difficult to test. At least the British experience has not completely deterred outsiders from trying to join the Community. Greece became the tenth country in the EEC in 1981, and Spain and Portugal are to join in 1986.

Global co-operation

International co-operation on a global scale has involved a number of agencies. Each tends to concern itself with one or other of three main areas; finance, general trade restrictions and economic development of the poorer countries of the world. We shall consider the most important institutions.

The International Monetary Fund (IMF)

This is an association of nearly 150 countries set up under the auspices of the United Nations Organisation at a conference at Bretton Woods, USA, in 1944. The origins of the Fund can be found in the collapse of the system of international payments in the 1930s. This was attributed in substantial measure to the abandonment of the gold standard and the rounds of retaliatory exchange rate devaluations that took place in 'beggar-my-neighbour' exercises.

The prime aim of the IMF was to provide a degree of stability between the exchange rates of the currencies of member countries. A secondary objective of importance was to add to the stock of internationally acceptable money and to provide short-term credit facilities to act as cushions for countries in temporary balance of payments difficulties. Gold was in short supply and needed supplementing as world trade expanded. It was not, however, until 1970 that a new class of reserve assets, known as special drawing rights (SDRs) was introduced. Outside the IMF action was also taken to increase international liquidity for particular occasions. For example, a group of 12 central bankers signed an agreement in 1968 in Basle which helped Britain over difficulties in that year (known as the 'Group of Twelve' not the 'Gnomes of Zurich'!). It should be realised that acceptance of foreign loans, from the IMF or from anywhere else, can at times carry with it vague or explicit 'strings', for instance, a commitment to try to lower the rate of inflation. These are controversial and essentially political matters which we shall not pursue.

The period of fixed exchange rates lasted for more than 20 years after the war, thanks to the IMF, although countries suffering 'fundamental' and lasting imbalance were permitted to devalue their currencies.

The strains on the system of fixed exchange rates proved too strong, despite an agreement at the Smithsonian Institute in Washington in 1971, which worked out a new set of international exchange rates. A major reason for the collapse of the IMF system was the fact that international currency reserves did not grow sufficiently fast to finance the expansion of world trade. Another contributing factor was the periodic crises which occurred from time to time, when large amounts of short-term capital moved out of currencies which were expected to be devalued. The current of world opinion swung towards floating exchange rates. The UK, as we have seen, abandoned the fixed parity for sterling in 1972, and most other countries did likewise at about the same time. It should, however, be appreciated that floating rates are, by and large, 'managed', by governments in the interests of maintaining some degree of day-to-day stability of their exchange rates. The European Monetary System, mentioned earlier, was set up in 1979 for this very purpose within the EEC, and was designed to keep the exchange rates of participating countries within $2\frac{1}{2}$ per cent of each other.

The International Bank for Reconstruction and Development (IBRD)

This is also known as the World Bank. It is a sister organisation to the IMF set up by the Bretton Woods agreement in 1944. The Bank makes loans for development programmes which are regarded as worthwhile but do not attract private investors. Its early activities were concentrated on post-war reconstruction. It then became involved in lending to developing countries (*see* below) and, most recently, with helping to solve the world debt problem, which we discuss at the end of this chapter.

GATT

GATT stands for the General Agreement on Tariffs and Trade. Its objectives are the reduction and removal of barriers on visible trade. The method by which GATT seeks to achieve its goals is to arrange for negotiations around a conference table. The first meeting took place in 1947 and has been followed by others, including a so-called 'Kennedy Round' 20 years later and a seventh 'Tokyo Round' in 1979. At such meetings the participating nations engage in reciprocal bargaining with each other for tariff and other trade concessions.

GATT was successful in eliminating quota restrictions on international trade in its early years. Progress with tariffs, however, has been slow. This is hardly surprising when it is realised that there are over 80 participating nations. The Tokyo Round, for example, took 4 years to complete. Tariffs have, however, been reduced, but recent years have seen the growth of what are called non-tariff barriers, such as health and safety standards and customs and other administrative procedures. These can be quite genuine, but there is evidence that they are often used with the intention of restricting imports.

Economic development

One outstanding characteristic of the international economy is the inequality of the distribution of income between countries. Fig 9.15 has been prepared to illustrate this. The diagram shows national income per head of the population in US dollars for a selected group of countries. Before discussing it a word or two of caution is in order.

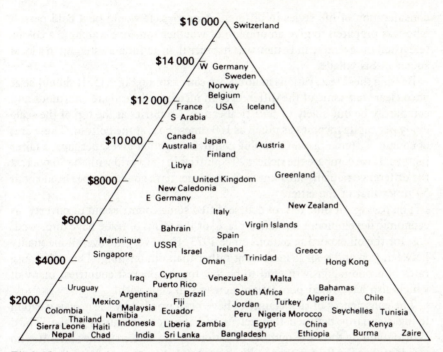

Fig 9.15 Average income per head of population, selected countries 1980 (GNP per capita in US dollars)

We learnt earlier that it is dangerous to assume that the national income of a country is always a good indicator of its standard of living (*see* pages 145–6). International comparisons of national income are subject to many qualifications discussed previously, but also to others equally serious. One is that income estimates vary greatly in quality from country to country. A second is that such estimates are initially recorded in local currencies and have to be converted to a common standard for the purpose of making international comparisons. Exchange rates are often used for the conversions. However, they can fluctuate widely and are not necessarily respresentative of the purchasing power of individual currencies at a particular time. Moreover, for technical reasons they tend to understate the real incomes of poor countries.

It must also be remembered that the basis of national income calculations are the goods and services *bought and sold in markets*. In subsistence economies in poorer parts of the world, however, families tend to be more self-sufficient than in advanced countries, and to meet fewer needs by trading outside the family. In such circumstances, conventional methods of estimating the national income tend to omit relatively more output of poorer countries and, therefore, to underestimate their living standards.

Finally, we must be careful not to equate national income per head with 'happiness'. This is a subject beyond the boundaries of economics and involves consideration of life styles in different countries. It would be a bold person who was prepared to give an opinion of whether someone watching a colour television programme in Britain was happier than an Indian listening to a local singer in his village.

Bearing these reservations in mind, we can examine Fig 9.15. It should be at once clear that some of the differences in income per head are enormous and can hardly be due solely to statistical errors. Countries at the top of the scale enjoy per capita incomes as much as 100 times those at the bottom. These are, of course, extreme cases. Grouping countries together gives, perhaps, a fairer picture. If we compare the richest 20 countries in the world with the 20 poorest the difference remains substantial. The former have an income per head about 50 times that of the latter.

The passage of time has, of course, lifted some countries out of poverty, as economic development has taken place, or the terms of trade have improved, e.g. for the oil exporting nations since 1973. However, the overall inequality between rich and poor is increasing rather than diminishing. This is because rates of economic growth tend to be low for the poorest countries, many of which also have rapid population increases to cope with.

The consciences of rich countries have been pricked by the growing gap in living standards between themselves and the poor countries of the 'Third World', and by the large number of nations at the bottom of the scale. It is no accident that Fig 9.15 is shaped like a pyramid. As one goes down the income scale the numbers tend to rise.

Action to help the less developed countries of the world has not been on the massive scale that would be necessary to make a substantial impact on international income inequality. The United Nations Organisation set a target of 0.75 per cent of GNP for developed nations to try to provide aid to their poorer neighbours, but few countries have consistently achieved this. Official government aid of the wealthier nations was running at a rate of about 0.5 per cent of national income in the early 1960s, but by the late 1970s and early 1980s this had fallen to below 0.4 per cent. However, the 'new-rich' Arab oil-producing states, especially Saudi Arabia, joined the ranks of the big donors after the mid-seventies, making substantial contributions to the economies of LDCs (less developed countries).

There are a number of international agencies specifically concerned with economic development. They include the World Bank mentioned earlier (*see* page 222). The Bank makes loans for economic development and provides expert field service teams to assist with projects. The funds for loans are in the main derived by borrowing in the capital markets of member countries. Accordingly interest is charged to borrowers. Moreover, the charter of the World Bank requires its loans to be guaranteed by governments in borrowing countries. These are not always easy to obtain for private businesses. An affiliate but independent organisation, the International Finance Corporation (IFC), was set up in 1956 to help overcome this problem. A second affiliate of the World Bank is the International Development Association (IDA). This was established in 1960 to make 'soft' loans to less developed countries on generous terms, usually without interest charges. The International Bank and its affiliates have made loans totalling many billions of dollars since their inception; a substantial sum, though small in comparison with the total of aid from all sources.

An alternative method of assisting the poorer countries in the world is by 'trade not aid'. The prime international organisation concerned with the promotion of trade is UNCTAD (The United Nations Conference on Trade and Development) established in 1964 under the auspices of the United Nations Organisation. High sounding resolutions have been passed at UNCTAD conferences and a so-called 'north-south dialogue' has attempted to integrate the economies of some Third World countries more closely with those of the developed nations, especially in Europe. One of UNCTAD's more recent policies was the introduction in 1971 of a general system of preferences (GSP), the object of which is to give the exports of manufactured goods from less developed countries preferential access to markets in developed nations. Success with GSP has, however, been less than the poorer nations had hoped for because of qualifications and limitations placed on it in many advanced countries. UNCTAD did, however, mark up an achievement in 1978 when it was agreed by a number of developed countries, including the UK, that some of the poorest nations should be relieved of at least part of their outstanding debts. GATT is another international organisation which is involved in measures to assist developing countries. Several were included in the Tokyo Round (*see* page 222) when, for example, tropical products were given priority treatment.

The world debt problem

The problems of developing countries discussed in the previous section, took on a new aspect in recent years, which have seen the appearance of a major problem of international indebtedness, and which reached a quite massive scale by the early 1980s.

The origins of the current problem are usually traced to the 'oil price shock' of 1973–74, when the OPEC countries quadrupled the price of oil (*see* page 210–11) which severely hit non-oil-producing developing countries, raising their import prices and reducing their export markets. Anxious to maintain their growth rates, these developing countries needed to borrow to finance the deficits in the current accounts of their balances of payments. Private commercial banks were glad to oblige, partly by recycling the large credit balances of the oil exporters, because investment prospects in the industrialised countries had, at the same time, taken a turn for the worse.

The situation was already dangerous. It became disastrous after 1980. There were two main reasons for this. The first was that there was a second oil price shock. The price of oil more than doubled between 1979 and 1980. In the second place, counter-inflationary policies became widespread in most industrialised countries in the early 1980s. These, in turn, had the effects of further reducing imports from developing countries, and of raising interest rates, thereby increasing the burden of debt servicing. To make matters worse, the bulk of the external debt of developing countries was fixed in terms of US dollars which were appreciating.

All these served to aggravate the problems of non-oil producing debtor nations, the total of whose indebtedness rose from less than $200 billion in 1973 to close to £700 billion in 1983. Moreover, even some oil exporters appeared in adverse circumstances in 1982 when the price of oil weakened— one of the first countries to be on the verge of default being Mexico.

Neither creditors nor debtors usually benefit from the latters' bankruptcy. Hence negotiations between the parties were entered into with a view to 'rescheduling' the debts, by which is meant extension of the period of loan. Some private rescheduling arrangements were made, but the problem had reached such proportions that intervention by an international agency was highly desirable and the IMF involved itself as mediator.

IMF officials were well placed to act in this capacity, having the authority to recommend politically unattractive economic policies of restraint, and having access to funds of their own—IMF quotas were raised by almost 50 per cent in 1983. The help from the IMF was, moreover, reinforced by the World Bank (*see* page 222).

The World Bank was originally intended to play a distinctive role of providing long-term finance for economic development, while the IMF concentrated on relatively short-run balance of payments problems. The distinction between short- and long-run needs was never too well defined nor, perhaps, even sensible. What is clear is that the new situation brought the two institutions into closer contact than before. It also led the World Bank into collaboration with commercial banks in joint ventures. So far, catastrophe has been averted, but the scale of the problem of international indebtedness is such that one can expect it to be with us for quite a long time to come.

Exercises

For key to symbols indicating sources *see* pages xii–xiii.

1 For the latest year available find out (*a*) the value of imports in pounds sterling and (*b*) the population of the following countries:

Australia	South Africa
Belgium	Switzerland
Canada	United Kingdom
Germany	United States
Greece	

Where necessary convert from local currency to pounds sterling using the exchange rates in the *Times* or *The Financial Times*.
Calculate the value of imports per head of the population in each case. (*WA*).
2 Calculate the percentage increase in the value of total exports between 2 recent years from each of the following countries. Place them in rank order of growth. (*WA*)

Australia	Italy
Denmark	Japan
France	Sweden
Germany	United States

3 Calculate the percentage of the total value of United Kingdom imports accounted for by each of the following groups of commodities in the most recent year for which you have statistics:

Food, beverages and tobacco	Mineral fuels, lubricants, etc.
Crude materials	Manufactured goods

Compare your results with Fig 9.4. (*AS, MDS, F*)
4 Calculate the percentage of the total value of United Kingdom exports of manufactured goods accounted for by the following items in the most recent year for which statistics are available. (*AS, MDS*)

Chemicals	Iron and steel
Transport equipment	Textile yarns and fabrics
Electrical machinery	

5 Prepare a graph on the lines of Fig 9.9 showing the quarterly movements in the UK terms of trade for the past 3 years. (*MDS*)
6 Prepare 2 historical graphs for as many of the last 5 years as you can obtain statistics showing:

a the value and volume of UK imports
b the value and volume of UK exports
c the sterling-dollar exchange rate

Can you suggest reasons why the value and volume figures in *a* and *b* may or may not have moved in parallel? (*MDS, AS, F*)
7 Following exercise **6**, prepare another graph showing again the value of exports and imports of the UK for the same period and the gross domestic product. Which series have moved in closest association? (*MDS, AS, F*)
8 Make a list of the countries of origin of all things bought by your family this week which came from abroad. What proportion came from Commonwealth and from EEC countries?
9 Make up a table showing the total value of the official reserves (of gold, convertible currencies and special drawing rights) held by the UK for each of the last 5 years. Use

these figures to prepare a new column in the table showing the changes in reserves for each period. What proportion is the average level of reserves to the average value of imports? Is it the same in the first and in the last of your years? (*AS* or *MDS*)

10 Prepare a table showing details of the balance of payments of the UK last year, including the following items. Compare your results with the table on page 213. (*MDS, FS, AS, F*)

Value of imports	Balance on current account
Value of exports	Balance of investment and other
Balance of visible trade	capital flows
Balance of invisible trade	Changes in official reserves.

10 Government

This chapter describes certain of the major activities of the government. It makes no attempt to deal with them all. They are too many and varied, and several have already been discussed in their particular contexts in the course of this book. For example, we described the organisation of the nationalised industries (Chapter 4), regional and competition policy (Chapter 5), industrial relations policy (Chapter 6), monetary policy (Chapter 8) and balance of payments policy (Chapter 9).

The examples given in the previous paragraph serve to illustrate the diversity and range of governmental activities. The purpose of this chapter is not to bring all such activities together. It is twofold; first to outline the income and expenditure patterns of central and local government bodies, and second to examine the role of the state in the pursuit of the major goals of economic policy. The government is not like a fairy godmother blessed with a magic wand which can conjure things like armies, schools and hospitals out of thin air. These have to be paid for, and it is our immediate concern to examine the principal goods and services which the state provides and the ways in which it finances them.

Government revenue and expenditure

Fig 10.1 sets out the main sources (and proportions) of government revenue for the UK, for the financial year 1984–85.

Changes in the government's income and expenditure are quite common. Although they may be made at any time, changes concerned with taxation are usually made when the Chancellor of the Exchequer presents the annual budget statement to parliament in March. (In 1982 the government announced that the Chancellor would make a regular budget statement in the autumn as well.)

Government income

By far the most important source of government income comes from taxation, as Fig 10.1 shows. Taxes are best considered as belonging to one of two types—taxes on income, and taxes on expenditure.

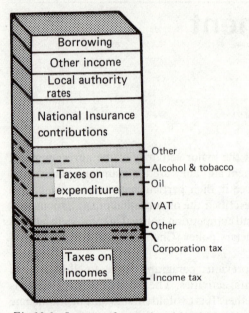

Borrowing

Other income

Local authority rates

National Insurance contributions

Taxes on expenditure

- Other
- Alcohol & tobacco
- Oil
- VAT
- Other
- Corporation tax

Taxes on incomes

- Income tax

Fig 10.1 Income of central and local government, 1984–5

Taxes on incomes

Taken together, taxes on incomes of individuals and businesses account for nearly 40 per cent of the revenue of the central government. Easily the most important is the **income tax**. This is levied on a person's income, although not all of it is liable to tax. A number of allowances are made, which are deducted from gross income to give a figure of **taxable income** on which the tax due is calculated. The chief of these allowances are in respect of a man's wife, children and other dependants, but there are other deductions, such as mortgage interest on loans made to individuals for house purchase, which single persons may also enjoy. Some people with very low incomes are not liable to tax at all.

The real value of allowances would, if unchanged, vary with the rate of inflation. Since 1977 they have been indexed, although not necessarily to compensate fully for changes in the price level. In 1985–86, the allowances were £2205 for a single person and £3455 for a married couple.

The basic rate charged on taxable income was 30 per cent in 1985–86. Higher rates running from 40 up to 60 per cent are charged as taxable income rises above fixed points starting around £16 000 for the 40 per cent rate and £40 000 for the top 60 per cent rate. These rates apply to income from all sources. Prior to 1984, an additional tax was charged on income derived from investments (so-called 'unearned income') as distinct from 'earned income' from employment or self-employment. This investment income surcharge was levied at a rate of 15 per cent on unearned incomes in excess of a threshold of about £6000. The combination of rising tax rates and the fact that a portion of everyone's income is exempt from tax, means that the *percentage of income* paid in tax rises with income. Such a tax is described as **progressive**, in contrast to a **regressive** tax, where the proportion of income paid in tax falls with income.

In addition to the taxes on income as conventionally defined, taxes have also been levied since 1962 on *increases* in the value of the capital assets owned by an individual. The real part of these increases is equivalent to income, since a person can, if he wishes, spend any gain due to a rise in the real value of his assets between the beginning and the end of a year, without leaving himself any worse off from the point of view of his accumulated wealth. This **capital gains tax** is levied at a flat rate of 30 per cent on net realised money gains, after the deduction of any realised losses from the sale of other assets. There are exemptions for certain classes of asset, such as one private house, chattels, and the first £5900 of gain for individuals and married couples in 1985–86. Since 1984, this exemption has been indexed, i.e. increased to allow for rises in the general price level.

Taxes are levied on the income of companies as well as of persons. This arises as a result of treating joint stock companies as separate legal entities from their shareholders. Companies are assessed for **corporation tax** on their profits (and capital gains, *see* below). The base on which tax is calculated for companies is their **taxable profits**, a notion similar in some ways to that of taxable income for private individuals.

Companies do not, of course, qualify for personal allowances but they are permitted to deduct all expenses properly incurred in the earning of profits and, additionally, to offset sums to help provide for the depreciation that occurs in the value of their capital. Standard depreciation allowances are given and deductions are permitted for investment allowances for industries and regions where the provision of such help is part of the policy of the government. From 1976–84 an important allowable deduction was for the increase in the value of stock held by businesses in excess of 15 per cent of their gross trading profits. This very substantially reduced the corporation tax burden on many companies.

The rate of corporation tax is fixed in the budget. It was 52 per cent in 1983–84, when the Chancellor of the Exchequer announced a phased reduction to a level of 35 per cent for 1986–87. There is a reduced rate of 30 per cent for small companies. There is no difference in the rate of tax whether profits are distributed to shareholders or retained in the firm. This may be contrasted with an earlier system which ended in 1975, whereby distributed profits were taxed more heavily. That practice (intentionally) discriminated in favour of profit retention and was introduced to encourage investment. However, it was recognised that it tended at the same time to create difficulties for new and growing companies to attract outside capital—hence the policy change.

Other taxes on income have been levied in the past and may always be introduced. For example, between 1976 and 1985 a **development land tax** was charged on the difference between the proceeds of the sale of land and its cost; and proposals for a local income tax by local authorities have been mooted.

Capital taxes

Taxes on capital, as distinct from those on capital gains (*see* above), yield very little revenue for the state. This does not mean, however, that they are of little significance.

The oldest capital taxes are **estate duties** which were levied until 1975 at a person's death on the property left behind. The tax was progressive (*see* page 230), the rates on large estates being very high (80 per cent) although there was an exemption limit below which no tax was payable. Estate duties were not as effective as they might have been, notably because of the existence of various perfectly legal devices by which the liability to tax could be substantially reduced.

In 1974 **capital transfer tax** (**CTT**) replaced estate duty. When introduced, CTT rates stretched from 5 per cent to 75 per cent on a wide band of transfers from £5000 to just over £2 million, at which the top rate was levied. The nature of the tax has, however, been radically altered in recent years. The exemption limit has been significantly raised (and indexed); the band of chargeable rates has been narrowed; and the size of transfer at which the top rate is levied has been substantially reduced. In 1985–86, the lowest rate, of 30 per cent, is applied to transfers at death over £67 000, while the top rate, of 60 per cent, comes into force at a figure of about £300 000. Since 1984, also, the rates on lifetime gifts have been half the rates on death.

It is worth mentioning one other capital tax although it has never been levied in Britain. This is an **annual wealth tax** assessed on the total value of all the assets owned by an individual. Such a tax has been included in the proposals of past governments but has not been proceeded with. If it is ever introduced it will almost certainly be levied at low rates. Those suggested in 1974, for example, were of the order of 1 per cent on property worth £100000 and between $2\frac{1}{2}$ and 5 per cent on that worth over £5 million.

Taxes on expenditure

The difference between taxes on income and capital dealt with so far, and those on expenditure is that the latter are related to the goods and services bought by individuals. It may be possible, in theory, for someone to avoid paying such taxes by refraining from buying taxed goods, but as the range and number of goods covered by such taxes is very wide this is not a seriously practicable proposition. A more important observation is that some expenditure taxes tend to be **regressive**, the opposite of progressive, insofar as they may take a higher proportion of the income of the poor than of the rich.

Taxes on expenditure bring in about 15 per cent more revenue for the government than do taxes on income. The chief earners for many years have been duties on alcohol, tobacco and oil. The last of these recently assumed increased importance with the imposition of a **petroleum revenue tax** on the profits of North Sea oil (technically this should be regarded as a tax on income) and royalties from state owned oil companies.

There are many other goods and services subject to tax, e.g. betting, entertainment and television advertising. Licences must be bought to operate a television set and to run a car, and there are many legal documents, such as those transferring ownership of property, which require the affixing of a special tax stamp.

In addition to the taxes on specific commodities mentioned in the previous paragraph, the government also levies a much more general expenditure tax. It was introduced in 1973 at the time when the UK was starting to bring her taxes into line with those of other members of the EEC (*see* pages 219–20). These countries operate a **value added tax** (**VAT**). VAT is levied on firms on the amount they add to the value of the goods they produce, i.e. on the difference between their sales revenue and their costs of purchasing (intermediate) goods and services from other firms. These goods and services, of course, will already have been subject to VAT by firms operating at earlier stages in production.

VAT is essentially a tax on consumer spending, and is levied, in instalments, at each stage in the production process. For example, the manufacturer of a starter motor for a car pays tax on his value added; when he sells the motor to a car manufacturer, the price he charges reflects the tax he has already paid. The firm producing the car is then permitted to deduct the cost of this VAT (and VAT for other items bought) from its revenue from sale of cars when calculating its liability for VAT.

VAT was levied first at a flat rate of 10 per cent on all goods and services other than certain 'essentials' (such as food, children's clothing, books and buildings) on which the rate was zero. Certain other intermediate goods, including education, health and insurance, are classified as 'exempt' from the tax, which means that traders do not have to charge it to their customers but are not entitled (as they are with zero rated goods) to reclaim tax paid by suppliers earlier in the production process. For a few years, between 1975 and 1979, there were two VAT rates; a basic 10 per cent and a higher 25 per cent on goods classed as 'luxuries', such as furs and cameras. In 1979 both were amalgamated into a new standard rate of 15 per cent on all goods chargeable to VAT.

The tax has become an important source of revenue for the government, with a yield greatly in excess of that of any other single tax on expenditure, as can be seen from Fig 10.1.

VAT replaced two taxes previously operating in Britain. One was the **purchase tax** which was a special tax on expenditure on certain luxuries and semi-luxuries; the other was the **selective employment tax** (SET).

SET was introduced in 1966 as a tax on all employers of labour. To that extent, it may be regarded as one of a family of so-called **payroll taxes**. However, the particular form of the tax adopted in the UK was selective. One of its intentions was to favour manufacturing businesses and thereby to promote economic growth. Eligible firms in the manufacturing sector of the economy were, therefore, able to obtain refunds of SET. In addition, the SET system was used to help manufacturers in declining areas of the country by granting them a regional employment premium (REP) based on the numbers on their payrolls, as well as a refund of SET.

Unlike direct taxes, the majority of expenditure taxes are collected by the Board of Customs and Excise. **Customs duties** are imposed on articles imported from overseas. The remainder are known as **excise duties** and are by far the more important revenue earners of the two. All taxes on expenditure, but especially those fixed in money terms, such as the duty on alcohol and tobacco, are liable to be changed at any time.

Local authority rates

Over half of the revenue of local authorities comes from central government by way of grants and loans. They are based on estimates of regional needs and some are 'tied' to particular types of expenditure, e.g. on roads and the police. However, a substantial income is derived from **rates**.

In much the same way that the central government collects taxes, so local authorities levy what are called rates on the owners of land and buildings, the only major exceptions being those buildings used for agricultural purposes. Property is assessed from time to time by the Inland Revenue and a value placed on it. It is on this basis that the rate is calculated. The rate is usually expressed as *poundage*, i.e. pence per pound of rateable property.

The importance of rates as a source of revenue varies considerably from district to district. The larger the amount of valuable property there is in a region, the more important is the income from rates. This is offset partly by rate support grants from central government, which are larger for authorities where there is relatively little valuable property but which have heavy needs for services, e.g. education, because of the relatively large number of children in the community.

Rates have been regarded as a means of giving independence to local authorities from the central government. However, this independence was threatened in the 1980s as the Treasury put pressure on local authorities to keep their spending down to support the government's drive to control the rate of inflation. The 1984, so-called 'rate capping', legislation gave the central government the power to cut its rate support grants to local authorities which did not comply with requests to reduce their spending. The issue became highly controversial, not only because of the reduced autonomy of local governments, but also because those local authorities threatened by the Treasury with rate capping happened, like the Greater London Council, to be Labour-controlled.

National insurance contributions

There is one major source of government revenue which has not yet been described—national insurance contributions. These are levied on employers and employees. They provide a very substantial source of income to the State—close on half of that from all taxes on incomes.

The revenue from these contributions goes into the National Insurance Fund and, augmented by a subsidy, is used to provide social security benefits, such as unemployment, sickness and retirement benefits related to contributions. Non-contributory benefits, such as supplementary benefit and family income supplements are financed from general taxation.

National Insurance contribution rates in 1985–86 were 9 per cent for employees and 10.45 per cent for employers. Lower rates were introduced at that time to encourage the employment of young persons. These ran from 5 per cent between the threshold of £35.50 per week and £90 for employees and £130 for employers.

Other income

The category described in Fig 10.1 as other income of the government includes trading surpluses, royalties from North Sea oil, and interest and dividend receipts from state-owned property.

Government expenditure

The principal categories of total government expenditure, i.e. both central and local, are shown in Fig 10.2. There are several ways of classifying them; the method used here is based on specific programmes, i.e. for defence, social security, etc.

The social services are by far the largest category if the term is used to include health, education, housing and social security benefits provided out of

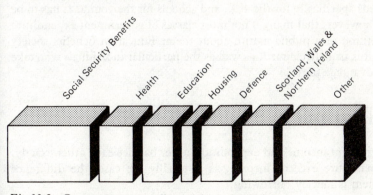

Fig 10.2   Government expenditure (planned) 1985–6

national insurance contributions and taxation. Much of the expenditure on education and housing is paid for by local authorities. Defence is an important category, taking about 14 per cent of the government budget according to plans for 1985–86. The other items of expenditure are of a varied kind. About a tenth of the total is used to provide services in Scotland, Wales and Northern Ireland. The rest is used for such things as law and order, the construction and maintenance of roads, overseas aid, support for industry and agriculture (including both private sector and nationalised industries) and interest on the national debt (see below) which varies both with the amount outstanding and the rate of interest payable on it.

As previously stated, the method used for classifying items of government expenditure for Fig 10.2 is not the only method possible. We could alternatively distinguish between **current expenditure**, such as retirement pensions and drugs for use in hospitals, and **capital expenditure**, such as the provision of new schools or prisons. The former are concerned with immediate effects on the distribution of income or resources. Capital items, on the other hand, have lasting effects.

A third alternative classification has different and important implications. It is based on a distinction between what are known as transfer payments as distinct from exhaustive expenditures. The former we have already met (see page 150), and know to include personal grants, such as pensions and family income supplements. **Exhaustive expenditures** are those on goods and services, such as roads and hospitals, where the state decides directly how the money should be spent. In contrast **transfer payments** permit individual recipients to allocate the proceeds as they wish. It is important to note that transfer payments have grown relative to exhaustive expenditures in recent years.

A fourth and final classification is between goods and services which benefit the community generally, as distinct from those that are provided for individuals. The former are referred to as **public goods** and include roads, courts of law and environmental services. The latter comprise all transfers, as well as hospital beds specifically for the sick, and schools for the young. It has to be admitted, however, that many if not most classes of government expenditure have something of a public nature about them. Education benefits society generally, it is usually claimed, as well as the particular individuals who take personal advantage of it.

The national debt

Total government income and expenditure never balance each other exactly. When expenditure exceeds income, as is usually the case, the difference between them is met by borrowing.

Government borrowing in past years has, at times, been on a very large scale, e.g. to finance wars and to pay compensation to industries taken into public ownership. The total outstanding balance is known as the **national debt**. In 1950, after the Second World War and the large nationalisation programme of the Labour government, the debt stood at a figure of about £25 000 million. Compared with the size of the national income, this was an all-time high— approximately 250 per cent. Although by 1984 the total outstanding national debt had risen to more than £100 000 million, this figure was only half the size of the annual national income. Moreover, something like a sixth of the total consisted of government securities held by government departments. The net *change* in public sector debt can be understood as a measure of the government's need to borrow to finance an excess of expenditure over income in any year. It is known as the **public sector borrowing requirement (PSBR)**.

The size of the public sector

The description, in the preceding pages, of the revenue and expenditure of the government, suggests something of its impact on the economy of the country. It is, however, important to be clear that there is no single unambiguous measure of the size of the public sector in the economy. A great deal depends on what exactly is included in the total, and how it is measured. For example, the public sector appears relatively larger if the nationalised industries are included than if they are not. However, the output of the nationalised industries is sold to consumers, whereas other services, like education and defence, are provided out of public funds derived, in large part, from taxation. These are properly regarded as different in nature from commercially marketed goods and services. Moreover, the public sector appears larger if transfer payments are considered as part of the total than if they are excluded; but transfers, as we know, are different from exhaustive expenditures.

We cannot devote space in this book to inspecting all the conceivable measures of the size of the public sector. (The size of the nationalised sector was referred to in Chapter 4, *see* page 72, though it must be remembered that this has been changing in the 1980s as a result of the privatisation programme of Conservative governments.) One wide measure, worthy of mention, is the proportion of gross national product that passes through the hands of the state. This proportion was running at around 45 per cent in the 1980s. If transfer expenditures are excluded from the total the percentage drops to about 30 per cent. This is a measure of the amount of goods and services pre-empted, as it were, by government for public provision of schools, doctors, armies, high court judges and all the other goods and services provided directly by the state.

It is important to add that the size of the public sector underwent a long-term increase for many years. Part of the reason for this can be traced to events of a special kind, such as the Second World War, during which a big upsurge in government activity naturally occurred. After the end of the war public expenditure did not drop back to its previous level. The post-war years saw instead a substantial expansion in social services, sometimes referred to as the **welfare state**.

There is, however, a more general reason why the public sector tends to grow relative to the rest of the economy. It is known as the **relative price effect**. Put simply, the reason is that productivity in government services rises more slowly than in manufacturing industry because of the reduced scope for mechanisation and, therefore, for economies of large-scale production. The prices of government services tend to rise in consequence *relative* to those of the rest of the economy. (This is why it is called the *relative* price effect.) Since the output of the public and private sectors is valued by reference to their prices (or costs), the size of the former has a natural tendency to increase relative to that of the latter. This is not, of course, an iron law. Governments can exercise control over the total expenditure from the public purse, if they are really determined to do so, as the Conservative governments of Margaret Thatcher declared their intention.

As we have seen, the bulk of government expenditure is financed out of taxation of one sort or another. The size of the public sector measured by the ratio of taxes to GNP, therefore, is not basically different from that of public expenditure to GNP. This is equally true with regard to past trends. There is, however, another aspect of government revenue of importance to take note of. This is the extent to which the UK is highly taxed compared to other countries. The facts in this case, as in the previous one, depend on how exactly the measurements are made as well as the precise countries with which comparisons are required.

International tax burdens

Fig 10.3 shows taxes and social security contributions as percentages of gross national product for a number of countries in 1982, where it can be seen that, contrary to popular belief, the UK is not one of the most heavily taxed nations in the world. Norway, Sweden, the Netherlands, Belgium, France and Western Germany are all ahead of Britain in the 'league table'.

In interpreting Fig 10.3 it is important to remember that the lengths of the bars in the diagram indicate total taxes *and* social security contributions as proportions of national income. Countries differ greatly as to the relative importance of these components of revenue, as can be seen. Some, such as Italy and the Netherlands, derive approximately two-fifths of total government income from social security contributions, while others, including the UK, take less than half this proportion. Countries also vary in their choice of methods used to achieve given objectives, and these can result in the figures being misleading. For example, help can be given to people through the tax system, e.g. by giving tax deductions for families, or via the expenditure side of the account, e.g. through a system of family allowances. Lastly, it must be

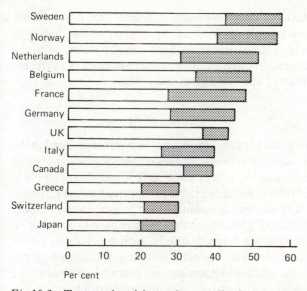

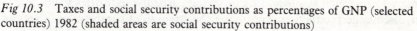

Fig 10.3 Taxes and social security contributions as percentages of GNP (selected countries) 1982 (shaded areas are social security contributions)

borne in mind that similar overall average tax burdens can conceal quite different tax treatments for particular groups.

The role of the state in the national economy

The subjects dealt with in this chapter have so far been concerned with government spending out of its income from taxation on specific categories of expenditure. However, it is useful to consider the role of the state in the national economy as having certain general aims or goals.

The goals of economic policy

It is convenient to distinguish two sets of goals of economic policy. The dividing line between them is not hard and fast. It corresponds to the distinction between the division between microeconomics and macroeconomics, which comprised the subject matter of Chapters 1 and 2, respectively, in this book.

Microeconomic goals are concerned with the allocation of resources. There are two of them, **efficiency** and **equity**. Resource allocation is said to be efficient if the collection of goods and services are produced at minimum cost, and best satisfy the needs of the community. When resource allocation is said to be equitable, it means that it is regarded as fair and just.

Macroeconomic goals are concerned with the performance of the economy as a whole. There are three primary macroeconomic goals, related to the achievement of a high rate of economic growth, a relatively stable price level, and a low and stable level of unemployment. A fourth goal is sometimes mentioned, related to the balance of payments. It is, however, secondary in nature, insofar as there is no direct advantage for a country arising from the balance of payments position, though an unsatisfactory balance of payments may inhibit the attainment of one or more of the primary goals.

Efficiency

Chapter 1 explained how a market economy works, and we commented at the time that there are a number of reasons why its efficiency is sometimes in doubt. The reasons for the market system sometimes falling short of what is desirable were explained then as being related to matters such as the existence of monopolies, insufficient information available for proper decision-taking by consumers and the failure of profit-motivated businesses to provide for all social needs and to avoid unsatisfactory side effects, such as pollution, associated with certain kinds of production. The actions of the government trying to correct inadequacies of the market mechanism and promote efficiency take many forms, such as subsidising or taxing particular industries to encourage or discourage production, improving the strength of competition in sectors where monopoly power is significant, and providing goods and services where the private sector is regarded as inappropriate (e.g. education, health, postal services).

We have encountered many such policies in this book. No more can be said of them now, except to point out that the reasons for state intervention are sometimes to be found in equity, as much as in efficiency—the National Health Service for example. One industry which has been the subject of government intervention for a long time, agriculture, falls into this category. It is somewhat of a special case and, since we have not so far discussed it, we do so now.

Government and agriculture

In the decades before the outbreak of the Second World War the farming community had, on balance, a fairly difficult time. It is true that every year was not equally bad, but competition from foreign food producers was intense, and even the best years were less prosperous in agriculture than in many other industries. By the beginning of the 1930s the situation had become so serious that the government began to adopt a number of piecemeal measures to improve the lot of the farmer.

After the war the major political parties agreed that every effort should be made to prevent agriculture from returning to its depressed state. Over the years a variety of measures were therefore enacted, including grants for land improvement, support for farm amalgamations, sponsorship of agricultural research and the provision of a farm advisory service. However, the principal element of UK agricultural policy, which lasted for a quarter of a century after the end of the war, took the form of subsidies for British farmers. The system was based on the free import of foodstuffs into Britain while subsidising domestic farmers by means of so-called **deficiency payments**, representing the shortfall in the price they received from the sale of their produce on the open market, and **guaranteed prices** for individual products. These guaranteed prices, as well as standard quantities to which they would apply, were set at annual price reviews after meetings between the government and representatives of British farmers.

All this changed radically as a result of Britain's entry into the European Economic Community (*see* pages 219–20). The objectives of the EEC policy, including those of stabilising farm incomes at 'reasonable' levels and promoting agricultural efficiency, are broadly similar to those of the UK which it replaced, but the methods of application have certain important basic differences. The most important is that the **common agricultural policy** (**CAP**) operates through a system of minimum prices which apply in all member states. These prices are maintained both by intervention buying by a Common Market agency and by import levies on products entering the EEC from outside.

It is beyond the scope of this book to describe the complexities of the CAP, which include grants for farm modernisation and a system of artificial exchange rates used to determine minimum support prices in local currencies— the value of the so-called 'green pound' in the case of the UK. However, it must be made clear that there is tremendous scope for disagreement between member countries on the level of support for individual products and on the means of financing them, not least because of differences in productivity. It is well-known that the levels have sometimes been so high as to generate enormous surpluses of some commodities—'mountains' of butter and sugar and 'lakes' of wine, as they have been called.

One of the most controversial aspects of the CAP is related less to its effect on farmers than to its effect on consumers and the balance of payments. Compared with the previous British system of deficiency payments, based on low-price imports and farm subsidies, the CAP has kept domestic prices above—usually well above—world prices. This has caused problems for certain countries in the rest of the world which, though low-cost producers, have had to face high import duties on their exports to the EEC, e.g. New Zealand meat and dairy farmers and West Indian sugar producers. It has also removed a source of cheap food supplies from the UK consumer.

It is no easy task to estimate the increased import bill nor the higher food cost to the British consumer of the CAP, especially as it has not even been constant over the years. The cost of farm support itself has to be borne by someone. In the previous UK system, subsidies came from the general tax-payer. Under the CAP they are derived partly from the proceeds of import levies, with consequent rising food bills, and partly from contributions made to the EEC pool by individual countries. Britain is thought by many commentators to have had to carry a heavy share of this burden at times, and much political bargaining has taken place at a high level on this matter.

Equity

When the state takes action on account of the equity attaching to the allocation of resources, this means that it is trying to make the distribution fairer. Economists have no special rights to pronounce on what is fair or unfair any more than other citizens. But they are interested in the policies used for this purpose, and in their effects.

Many methods of redistributing income are available, several of which have been referred to in this book. For example, agricultural policy can raise the incomes of farmers, and regional policy can help those living in less prosperous areas. Government intervention in wage settlements can have redistributive effects, as can the Sex Discrimination Act of 1975, and the Equal Pay Act of 1976. The former forbade discrimination in employment between the sexes, while the latter stipulated that men and women doing identical work should receive the same pay for doing it.

There is little doubt that the Equal Pay Act has had some equalising effect. In the first place, agreed minimum wage rates in negotiations between employees and employers became identical within a year. In the second place, average *hourly* earnings of women rose from 64 per cent to over 70 per cent of those of men by the end of the decade, where they appear to have settled. However, the *weekly* earnings sex differential fell much less and female unemployment rates rose more rapidly than male rates. The main reasons why women are paid less than men are those pointed out in Chapter 6 pages 123-4. They relate to the concentration of women in certain industries and occupational groups, their lower trade union membership and the fact that they work fewer hours, as well as such matters as job commitment and expenditure on training. These are far harder to legislate away.

Budgetary redistribution

One more direct way of bringing about a redistribution of income between rich and poor, is to use the government's budget, i.e. taxes and subsidies.

The most obvious, though quantitatively not the most important, policy tool, is taxation. Certain taxes are designed expressly to bear more heavily on higher income groups than on lower ones. Of outstanding significance in this connection is the income tax, which we described earlier as being progressive (*see* page 231). Fig 10.4 shows how progressive income tax was in 1985-6 by expressing the total tax burden as a proportion of total income for different income classes. It is important to emphasise that the diagram shows the situation only for a married couple without children whose entire income comes from the husband's employment, and who enjoy the minimum allowances of £3455 in 1985–86. A different diagram could be drawn for any individual or family with different circumstances. For example, the tax burden would be higher for a single individual, or lower for a blind person or for someone buying a house on a mortgage because of the tax allowances to which they would be entitled.

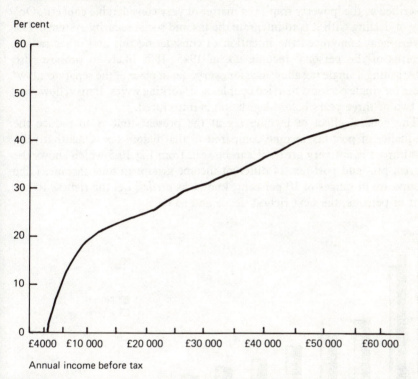

Fig 10.4   Income tax for a married couple 1985–86 (tax as a percentage of gross income)

The picture which emerges from Fig 10.4 is, nevertheless, reasonably representative of the progressiveness of income tax in Britain. It can be seen that the proportion of income paid in tax rises with income. It is zero until all allowances have been used, but rises to a figure of 40 per cent at an income of about £45 000 per annum. The progressiveness is due to the existence of the exemption limit, below which no tax is paid, and to the fact that the *marginal* rate of tax rises from the basic 30 per cent to 60 per cent on taxable incomes in excess of approximately £40 000.

We should note, however, that the British tax system can involve a rather curious and highly regressive element, in that some individuals with low incomes may find themselves faced with a very steeply rising marginal tax rate. This arises from the fact that certain personal subsidies, such as family income supplement, are income-related. When the income of a person drawing such benefits rises above certain thresholds of eligibility, they may both lose the benefit and find themselves paying income tax for the first time at the standard rate. The combined effect of withdrawal of benefit and liability to tax can mean that a low paid worker faces a very high effective tax rate on a marginal increase in income, sometimes even exceeding 100 per cent. This situation, sometimes described as the 'poverty trap', is a matter of very considerable concern. One way of dealing with it is to integrate the tax and social security systems. The government announced the intention of considering this and other radical reforms of the personal income tax in 1985. It is likely to propose also substituting a single tax allowance for everyone, in place of the separate allowances for single persons, married couples and working wives. It may, however, be two or three years before legislation is introduced.

The general effect of income tax at the present time is to reduce the inequality of post-tax income compared to that before tax. Quantitatively, this impact is not very great, as can be seen from Fig 10.5 which shows the shares, pre- and post-tax, of different income groups in total income. (The groups are in ranges of 10 per cent, known as *deciles*; i.e. the richest 10 per cent of persons, the next richest decile and so on.)

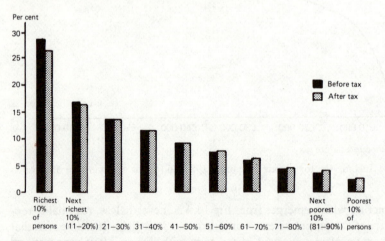

Fig 10.5 Distribution of income before and after income tax (decile shares), 1981–82

The shares of the richest 20 per cent of the population are less when measured after income tax is deducted; those of the lower income groups are larger post-income tax than before tax. However, only in the case of the very top decile (the richest 10 per cent) is the difference significant. Their share declines from 28.3 to 25.6 per cent of the total. The share of the poorest decile rises only from 2.0 to 2.4 per cent. If we represent the data in the form of Lorenz curves (*see* pages 151–2) we find the curve for post-tax income lies slightly nearer the diagonal representing complete equality, *see* Fig 10.6.

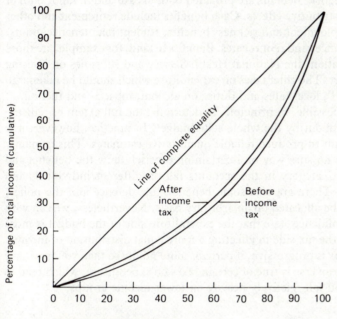

Fig 10.6 Income distribution (Lorenz curves before and after income tax 1981–2)

There are two reasons why income tax is not a very powerful redistributive tool. The first is that its progressiveness arises largely from the deductible allowances rather than from rising tax rates. The allowances do not vary with income, though they do mean that the *average* tax paid rises as income rises. The thresholds at which higher rates of tax begin to operate come into play only at relatively high incomes, affecting less than 5 per cent of all taxpayers. In 1985–86 the thresholds were about £16 000 taxable income for the 40 per cent rate and £40 000 taxable income for the top 60 per cent rate. Consequently, the vast majority of taxpayers pay at the same standard rate of 30 per cent, though, of course, for the very rich the rate is much higher. If you were one of the relatively few thousands of people whose annual income exceeds £100 000, the proportion of your total income paid in tax would be close to the maximum tax rate of 60 per cent.

The second reason for the relative ineffectiveness of income tax as a redistributive tool, is that there are substantial numbers of individuals too poor to be liable to any income tax at all. Their incomes are, by definition, the same both pre- and post-tax.

Even a neutral tax (which is neither progressive nor regressive) can be used to finance *spending* in a way that involves redistribution. There are a good many items on the expenditure side of the account of the UK government that fall into this category. Benefits are provided both in cash and in kind, both of which have redistributive effects. **Cash benefits** include retirement and other pensions, unemployment and sickness benefits, student maintenance grants, maternity allowances and rent rebates. **Benefits in kind**, for example, are those from state education, the National Health Service and subsidies on housing and rail transport. The chief taxes on expenditure which should be taken into account are VAT, local rates and duties on alcohol, tobacco and fuel oil.

It should be possible, in principle, to determine the full extent of redistribution brought about by the whole state budget. In practice, however, it is extremely difficult to produce reliable quantitative estimates. This is mainly because there is no sure way of ascertaining precisely how the benefits and burdens of each category in the accounts fall on different individuals and income groups. There are also some benefits, like defence and the police, which can only be allocated on an arbitrary basis. Nevertheless, we can with considerable confidence state that the expenditure side of the budget is more important than the tax side in effecting a more equal distribution of income. While income tax is progressive, if perhaps more mildly so than you may have suspected, the converse is true of certain taxes on expenditure, which tend to be regressive and fall relatively heavily on lower income groups.

Economic growth, price stability and full employment

We come, finally, to consider the role of the state in pursuit of the macro-economic goals of economic growth, price stability and full employment, which we first met in Chapter 2. The policies that are used to try to achieve these goals are fiscal policy, monetary policy, and prices and incomes policies; collectively all three are known as stabilisation policies.

The reason why recourse is had to such policies is that the historical experience in the UK and other industrialised countries, shows that the rate of growth of national income, the level of unemployment and the general price level have exhibited cyclical patterns.

The trade cycle

It may be recalled from the discussion of economic growth in Chapter 7 (*see* pages 159–60) that Britain achieved a long-term growth rate of about 2 per cent per annum from the beginning of the present century. This figure is, however, an average taken over all years, of which some were better than others. Variations were considerable. In the best years, rates approaching 10 per cent were reached while, in the worst, output declined almost as much. What is more, a regular pattern is observable. Prosperity and depression have tended to follow each other in a fairly systematic way; this is the trade cycle, which can be traced back well into the 19th century. Cycles have varied in length and severity, but they all exhibit four phases: a boom period, when output expands; a crisis or upper turning point; a slump when output falls and/or stagnates; and a recovery period, which marks the bottom of the depression leading to a new boom and prosperity.

Fig 10.7 shows the course of real national output since 1970. An upswing of the cycle can be observed at the start of the decade, an upper turning point in 1973, followed by a downswing that bottomed in 1975. Later in the period, 1979–80 saw the start of another depression that was reversed in 1981 when a new, though slow, upswing ensued. It is important to add that the cyclical behaviour of the British economy since the Second World War has generally been milder than that of some earlier times. The inter-war years, for example, witnessed serious and prolonged periods of depression, so much so that the 1930s earned the title of 'the Great Depression' because of the great decline in output that took place at that time.

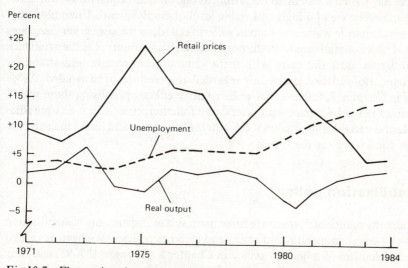

Fig 10.7 Fluctuations in output, prices and unemployment UK 1970–84 (percentage unemployment and year to year changes per cent in prices and output)

Depressions are accompanied by low output and also by high unemployment, while booms are periods of high output and low unemployment. As far as the price level is concerned, the pattern used to be one of inflation accompanying booms, while depressions were periods of stable, or sometimes falling, prices. However, an extremely important change began to appear after the end of the Second World War, which was for the price level to rise continuously throughout the cycle. In the 1950s and 1960s, the inflation rate was low by modern standards—3 to 5 per cent per annum. In the 1970s the rate began to accelerate. Between 1971 and 1982, the price level rose substantially every year. The lowest inflation rate was $8\frac{1}{2}$ per cent and the highest 24 per cent (1974–75), while the average rate was over 12 per cent per annum. Moreover, the rate of increase in the general level of prices, as noted above, no longer followed its traditional pattern of falling off during recessions. For the first time high unemployment and high rates of inflation existed simultaneously, giving rise to a new phenomenon which has come to be called **stagflation**.

In the light of the experience of the trade cycle described in the previous paragraphs, the state takes upon itself the task of trying to avoid worst excesses. This is not the place to elaborate the reasons why a high rate of economic growth, price stability and full employment are generally regarded as desirable goals. Briefly, economic growth is the main mechanism of rising living standards. The UK's decline vis-à-vis several other industrial countries, charted earlier (*see* page 160) is largely attributable to its relatively slow growth rate of national income. Unemployment is so obviously undesirable, that little needs to be said about it. Indeed, as long ago as 1944 the coalition government of the day issued a statement declaring, as one of their primary post-war aims, 'the maintenance of a high and stable level of employment'. Unemployment causes economic waste and human suffering, and, as we saw earlier (*see* pages 131–4) does not fall evenly on the population. Price stability, i.e. the avoidance of inflation, does not carry with it the same urgent sense of undesirability, perhaps. But inflation is certainly regarded as something to be avoided. As we saw in Chapter 7, inflation has redistributive effects, penalising those whose incomes fail to keep pace with prices; and inflation, especially at an unpredictable and variable rate, makes it difficult for businesses and individuals to plan with confidence for the future.

Stabilisation policy

As already mentioned, there are three main sets of instruments of stabilisation policy—fiscal, monetary, and prices and incomes policies. We have described the mechanism of monetary policy in Chapter 8 (*see* pages 189–92) and only brief reference will be made to it here. Let us, therefore, consider the other two.

Fiscal policy

Fiscal policy (sometimes referred to as budgetary policy, or as demand management) describes attempts by the government to influence the level of total spending in the economy. In particular, fiscal policy tries to control private sector demand, and to offset changes in it by changing the level of public sector demand through the government's budget.

This approach to stabilisation policy is associated with the name of John

Maynard Keynes (later Lord Keynes), the English economist writing in the 1930s, whose ideas formed the basis of what are nowadays described as Keynesian policies. It was Keynes who drew attention to the importance of the level of total demand for goods and services by emphasising the association between this and the level of unemployment in the trade cycle. Demand deficient unemployment (*see* pages 127–8), was also identified as a result of Keynes's work.

Stabilisation of economic activity through the use of fiscal policy is designed to work by stimulating demand for goods and services when output is running ahead of demand, and to inhibit it when demand is pushing ahead faster than capacity to produce.

Fiscal policy can be used in a variety of ways. In the first place the Chancellor of the Exchequer can use the range of taxes and subsidies in the Budget to stimulate or discourage spending by businesses and/or the general public, both on investment and on consumption. Raising taxes (or lowering subsidies) tends normally to discourage spending and is the suggested policy in times of excessive boom. Lowering taxes (or increasing subsidies) tends to stimulate expenditure and is, therefore, more appropriate when the level of economic activity is on the low side. The government can make changes in the Budget and, for speed and flexibility, it also has the power to vary tax rates on customs and excise duties by up to 10 per cent in either direction without the prior approval of Parliament. This provision is known as the **regulator**. It has not often been used in recent years, but can be invoked when required.

The second means of influencing total spending relates not to the private sector but to the government itself; for there is no very good reason why the state has to balance its own budget—raising in taxation exactly the same amount as it spends. In times of boom, when it wants to reduce the pressure of demand, it can run a **budget surplus**. Conversely, in periods of depression, when extra stimulus is called for, the state can run a **budget deficit**. Deficits tend to stimulate the economy because the government is putting more into it by way of spending than it is taking out in taxes. Surpluses tend to depress the economy (which might be a good thing if there is an overly strong boom) because they do the reverse. The extent to which the government and the nationalised industries borrow to finance an excess of expenditure over receipts is known as the public sector borrowing requirement (PSBR).

There is a third method by which the state can affect total spending. It is particularly relevant in periods when the government is trying to reduce total demand. At times it is easier for the central government to issue instructions for the reduction of public spending than actually to reduce it, simply because programmes for spending are in many cases long-term and difficult to cut. **Cash limits** were introduced in 1976 for particular categories of expenditure by government departments, local authorities and the nationalised industries, putting limits on the amount that they can spend in a year. This method relates to the PSBR.

Fiscal policy enjoyed widespread support among economists in many countries for more than three decades after its first use in the 1930s, but is less widely accepted today. There are several reasons for this.

In the first place, there is evidence that the use of fiscal policy sometimes worked in the post-war conditions to *de*stabilise, rather than to stabilise the economy. This is largely attributable to the practical difficulties of putting the policy into effect. In order to offset private sector expenditure changes, a government must have up-to-date and reliable information on what private spending will be over the near future, and it must quickly adjust its own spending plans in the opposite direction. Unfortunately, accurate advance information is not always easy to come by, and, for political and administrative reasons in particular, government spending is not as flexible as is sometimes needed.

A second major reason for growing disenchantment with fiscal policy is to be found in the changed economic conditions in the post-war compared to the pre-war world, and especially of the appearance of the new phenomenon of stagflation, mentioned earlier (*see* pages 33–4). The 1930s was a period when the prime economic goal was to reduce the level of unemployment and raise the level of output. There was no worry about inflation. But throughout the period since the end of World War II, and increasingly towards the present day, inflation has been a second problem that stabilisation has tried to face. Unfortunately, it seems that fiscal policy is a less efficient instrument for the control of inflation, than it is for reducing the level of unemployment. Hence it has been less to the fore in recent years.

Monetary policy

The second set of policy instruments available to the state for controlling the level of economic activity is described as monetary policy. The mechanism of monetary policy, which seeks to influence the amount of lending undertaken by banks and other financial institutions was described in Chapter 8 (pages 189–92). The policy is operated by the Bank of England, on behalf of the government, which acts on the quantity of money and/or interest rates to affect spending. There is little more that needs to be said about monetary policy itself, other than to emphasise that it, like fiscal policy, attempts to influence spending and to stabilise it in accordance with the needs of the time.

Monetary policy in the UK was generally regarded as subordinate to fiscal policy until the mid to late 1970s. Reservations on the effectiveness of fiscal policy in dealing with stagflation, however, raised monetary policy to prominence, and it found favour with the school of thought known as monetarism, then gathering strength under the leadership of Professor Milton Friedman of Chicago.

At this time, inflation was accelerating into double figures, with the result that politicians were beginning to think more of inflation than of unemployment as the major enemy. People were also attracted by the idea of monetary policy being easier to implement than fiscal policy. The latter had been shown to involve *active* decision-taking while the former was alleged to involve the more *passive* setting of targets for the growth of the money supply, it having been established that a close statistical association exists between the quantity of money and the price level. Some monetarists argued at one time for the government to decide on the proper target rate of growth of the money supply to achieve its goals, but to do no more about stabilisation. Such a process could be described as automatic, rather than discretionary, stabilisation, as is needed with changing budgetary decisions in fiscal policy. Most economists today, however, believe that monetary policy also calls for some discretionary decision-taking, as circumstances change.

Both fiscal and monetary policies have been used for most of the post-war period, hence it is difficult to disentangle their separate influences.

Fig 10.8 shows the course of inflation, as measured by the retail price index, the money supply (sterling M3), unemployment and interest rates (MLR) since 1970. There is no doubt that inflation and the money supply were closely correlated. The size of the public sector borrowing requirement has been deliberately omitted from the diagram on grounds of clarity, but if it had been included further positive associations between the PSBR and both inflation and the money supply would have been apparent.

Too much should not, however, be read into the historical record in Fig 10.8. The fact that the money supply and the price level moved closely

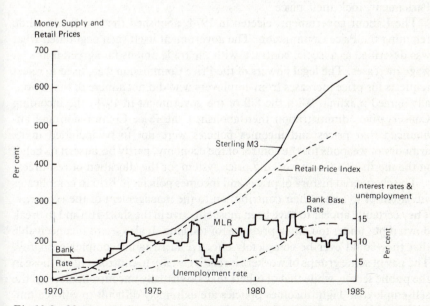

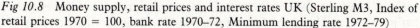

Fig 10.8 Money supply, retail prices and interest rates UK (Sterling M3, Index of retail prices 1970 = 100, bank rate 1970–72, Minimum lending rate 1972–79)

together, cannot be taken to mean that one *causes* the other. Most economists have no difficulty in accepting the existence of the statistical correlation, but the causal forces behind them are quite differently interpreted.

Equally to the point is that, as we know from Chapter 8, there are several ways in which the money supply may be defined and measured. Fig 10.8 records the history of only one of them—sterling M3. This was the monetary target chosen by the 1980 government as its 'prime control variable'. More recently it has focused on the narrow MO (*see* page 192 for definition) as well as £M3, in its declared 'medium-term economic strategy', which does not pretend to try and avoid very short term fluctuations in the economy.

Prices and incomes policies

The third line of approach for the government, designed for the control of inflation in particular, goes under the name of prices and incomes policies. Such policies have a fairly long history and can be traced back to the late 1940s when the Labour Party was in office and the trade unions were asked to accept a 'wage freeze'. Subsequent governments varied in the extent to which they favoured this approach. The first independent body set up to give advice on these matters was a Council on Prices, Productivity and Incomes, in 1957. A National Incomes Commission and a National Board for Prices and Incomes came and went in the 1960s, but as the pace of inflation accelerated in the 1970s a Price Commission and a Pay Board, operating a pay code approved by Parliament, took their place.

The Labour government, elected in 1974, abolished the Pay Board while retaining the Price Commission. The government itself then negotiated what was described as a 'social contract' with the trade unions for agreed limits on wage increases. The legal powers of the Price Commission were used to reject requests for price increases from employers who did not adhere to the nationally agreed maxima. With the fall of the government in 1979, the incoming Conservative administration then abolished the Price Commission and announced that prices and incomes policies were not to be included in its armoury of weapons for the control of the economy, partly because of its belief in the merits of a freely working price system for the allocation of resources.

The chequered history of prices and incomes policies in Britain complicates any attempt to assess their contribution to the management of the economy. They certainly appear to have been most effective in the short-run and to break down if put under too much pressure for too long. It also seems inconceivable that they could ever be completely effective in Britain's complex economy. The pay of some groups of workers is relatively easy to control, e.g. of those in the public sector, while that of others may be virtually uncontrollable, e.g. the self-employed. Tight incomes policies are extremely difficult to enforce universally. Much the same can be said of total price controls. The black economy (*see* page 146) and black markets for goods tend to flourish when pressures are applied with great rigour. It may also be said that trade union support is likely to be critical for the success of incomes policies, but the faith of that movement in the principle of free collective bargaining is traditionally strong and may be difficult to change.

Balance of payments policy

When we described the goals of economic policy earlier in the chapter, we referred to a number of primary goals—growth, price stability, etc and a single goal which we called secondary. This was the balance of payments.

The balance of payments was stated to be a secondary rather than a primary policy goal because there is no inherent reason for wanting the balance of payments to be satisfactory in itself. However, the balance of payments cannot be ignored. Its condition inevitably affects the domestic economy of a country.

We explained earlier how the trade cycle can spread from country to country, and how the internal objectives of fiscal (and monetary) policy can be frustrated by balance of payments effects. Witness the 'stop-go' attempts by past British governments to stimulate economic growth, which had to be abandoned when rising domestic incomes partly spilled over to imports (*see* Chapter 9, page 214).

Of course, governments need not sit idly by and watch what is happening to their balances of payments. In the short run they can make use of their foreign exchange reserves or seek loans from foreign governments and international institutions. They also have a number of ways of influencing the balance of payments. These are changing the exchange rate, imposing restrictions on trade and payments, and changing the level of aggregate demand. The mechanisms of these policy instruments were described in Chapter 9, in outline. A full explanation of the complications that arise when domestic and international policies interact, as they virtually always do, is complex and beyond the scope of this book. This is, in one sense, a pity. But, in another sense, it may have some merit if it prompts you to carry your study of economics further. I hope you do. It can be very rewarding.

Exercises

For key to symbols indicating sources *see* pages xii–xiii.

1 Prepare a graph for the last 10 years showing the proportion of total public revenue of central and local government derived from taxes on incomes and taxes on expenditure. Have the proportions changed? (*AS, F*)

2 Find out the size of each of the main items of central government expenditure in a recent year and 10 years ago. Calculate the percentage of the total for each item and pick out any significant changes which may have taken place. (*AS, F*)

3 Prepare a table showing the amount spent on the various kinds of national insurance benefits as a proportion of the total for the most recent financial year for which statistics are available. (*AS*)

4 The current rate charged by your local authority is given as so much in the pound. Find this and the rateable value of the house in which you live and calculate the rate bill for the year. How is this sum distributed among the various expenditure items?

5 Calculate how much direct tax each of the following has to pay in the current year. (*WA*)

a a single man earning £9000

b a married man with two children, earning £15 000

c a married man with no children, earning £42 000, with mortgage interest payments of £3000

d a single woman earning £10 000 in a job and £5000 dividends on shares

6 What is the maximum sum that your parents could give you without incurring capital transfer tax next year? (Assume they are wealthy enough and survive.) If they gave you the same sum by a legacy how much tax would it attract? (*WA*)

7 Prepare a chart on the lines of Fig 10.5 showing the number of incomes of different sizes before and after tax for the latest year available. Calculate also the proportions of total income taken in tax for all persons for the different groups. (*AS, F*)

8 What was the target public sector borrowing requirement set by the government 2 years ago? How did it compare with the outcome? (Refer to the Budget day issues of *The Times* or *The Financial Times* in your local library.)

9 Draw a graph on the lines of Fig 10.8 for the decades of the 1930s and the 1960s. How do they compare with the years in Fig 10.8 and with each other? (*KS*)

10 Collect figures of the percentage rate of unemployment and of the rate of inflation in Britain for the last 12 months. Plot the two series on a graph. Do they appear to be related in any way? (*MDS*)

11 Find out for France, Germany, Italy, Japan and the USA (*a*) how much prices have risen (*b*) how much industrial production has grown over the last 5 and 10 years. Calculate (*c*) the average unemployment rate for each country for the two periods. Which has the best record and how does the UK compare on each count? (*N*)

Index